EYEWITNESS COMPANIONS

Cats

DR BRUCE FOGLE
Additional contributor
Candida Frith-Macdonald

"WHO CAN BELIEVE THAT THERE IS NO

SOUL BEHIND THOSE LUMINOUS EYES!"

Théophile Gautier, writer, 1811–1872

LONDON, NEW YORK,
MUNICH, MELBOURNE, DELHI

Project Art Editor   Maxine Lea
Project Editor   Rob Houston
Editorial Assistant   Miezan van Zyl

Managing Editors   Sarah Larter, Liz Wheeler
Managing Art Editor   Philip Ormerod

Publisher   Jonathan Metcalf
Art Director   Bryn Walls

DTP Designer   Laragh Kedwell
Production Controller   Louise Minihane

First published in 2006 by
Dorling Kindersley Limited
80 Strand, London WC2R 0RL
Penguin Group

Produced for Dorling Kindersley by

studio cactus ltd ⓒ

13 SOUTHGATE STREET WINCHESTER HAMPSHIRE SO23 9DZ UK
TEL 00 44 1962 878600 EMAIL MAIL@STUDIOCACTUS.CO.UK WEBSITE WWW.STUDIOCACTUS.CO.UK

Senior Editor   Aaron Brown
Senior Designer   Dawn Terrey
Project Editor   Jo Weeks
Project Designers   Sharon Rudd, Claire Moore
Editorial Assistants   Jennifer Close, Robert Walker
Design Assistants   Steve Wade, Laura Watson,
  Sharon Cluett

Creative Director   Amanda Lunn
Editorial Director   Damien Moore

2 4 6 8 10 9 7 5 3 1

A CIP catalogue record for this book
is available from the British Library

ISBN-10: 1-4053-1557-1
ISBN-13: 978-1-4053-1557-9

Colour reproduction by Colourscan, Singapore
Printed and bound in China by Leo Paper Products Ltd.

Discover more at
www.dk.com

CONTENTS

THE DOMESTIC CAT IS A MODERN-DAY SUCCESS STORY. SMALL, CLEAN, SELF-SUFFICIENT, AND SELF-ASSURED, IT HAS QUIETLY DISPLACED THE DOG AS OUR MOST POPULAR ANIMAL COMPANION – AND FOR GOOD REASON: A COMPANION CAT UNIQUELY SATISFIES OUR DEEP-SEATED NEED TO BE AN INTEGRAL PART OF THE NATURAL WORLD.

RECENT EVOLUTION

In evolutionary terms, the domestic cat is a relative newcomer, and a recent convert to the benefits of human society. It is only 5,000 years since the African wildcat evolved into the domestic cat, choosing to cohabit with us in return for our protection from larger predators and for a reliable source of food. It is only 1,000 years since, with our help, it made its way across Asia to Japan, and only 300 years since it spread to the Americas, Australia, and New Zealand, in fact to every major island in the world. Today, it is estimated that there are perhaps 400 million domestic cats living throughout the world, half of them by their wits, the other half in our homes. Over the last 100 years, the role the cat plays in our lives has changed significantly, from practical mouser to comforting companion. As we embraced the cat as a family member, its inherent genetic plasticity allowed for this smooth evolutionary change.

Relative values
The African savannah-dwelling serval uses its agility, hunting skills, and camouflaged coat to survive. The domestic cat retains the basic traits essential to its wild, distant relatives.

Choosing a cat can be a difficult task, because of the sheer range of breeds and types available. Through our intervention in selective breeding, we have enhanced certain feline characteristics, not just coat length and colour, but also aspects of behaviour and temperament, such as sociability and vocalizing. Ultimately, deciding which cat is for you is very much a personal decision.

ADAPTABLE BEHAVIOUR

The reasons behind the cat's dramatic success at wending its way into our homes and our hearts are many. On the surface, however, it is an unlikely combination of species: humans and cats have widely dissimilar lifestyles. While dogs are as naturally sociable as we are, cats have an inherent independence of spirit; they march to their own drumbeat. Cats are very comfortable with themselves, less so,

PERSIAN

SIAMESE

Breed extremes
Every cat remains close in form and size to its small wildcat ancestors. However, selective breeding has produced a variety of physiques, face shapes, and coat types.

in general, with the company of other cats or different species. There is, however, a fascinating window of opportunity early in their lives for cats to become accustomed to other species and to other lifestyles. Whatever new experiences kittens under seven weeks are exposed to – being picked up by people, being licked by dogs, living with other, unrelated cats, even living with natural prey animals such as mice and rats – become accepted as a normal part of that cat's culture. The young cat's wonderfully accommodating mind is the reason it has become so successful at modifying its own lifestyle to cohabit harmoniously with us. It is no bad thing that in our eyes, the tactile, elegant, and independent cat is an incredibly attractive species. Quiet, fastidiously self-cleaning, self-contained, but prepared to bestow affection on a trusted owner, it is no wonder that the cat is a companion ideally suited to modern human lifestyles.

Independent spirits
In nature, the cat is a solitary hunter and supremely self-sufficient individual. The domestic cat relishes outlets for its independence, curiosity, and desire to explore.

CARING FOR YOUR CAT
Owning a cat means being rewarded with friendship, constancy, entertainment, and most importantly, a front-row seat from which to view the natural world. At the heart of every cat lurks the superb small predator of its ancient ancestry, and it is an enduring joy to watch its grace, balance, fine judgement, and quick instincts at work. As self-sufficient as they may be, however, domestic cats depend upon us for nourishment, security, and maintaining good health.

Mutual respect
It is easy to see why the cat gained such a secure place at the centre of our homes. While demanding little, it gives unstintingly of companionship, entertainment, and pure, purring affection.

For example, with unique dietary needs, cats will die if they don't eat meat. Threats to domestic cats are relatively few, but if they do become ill or are affected by injury, their natural behaviour is to withdraw and hide. This book will teach you how to care for your cat and how to cat-proof your home, making it an ideal environment in which to raise your feline friend. You will be rewarded with many years of satisfaction.

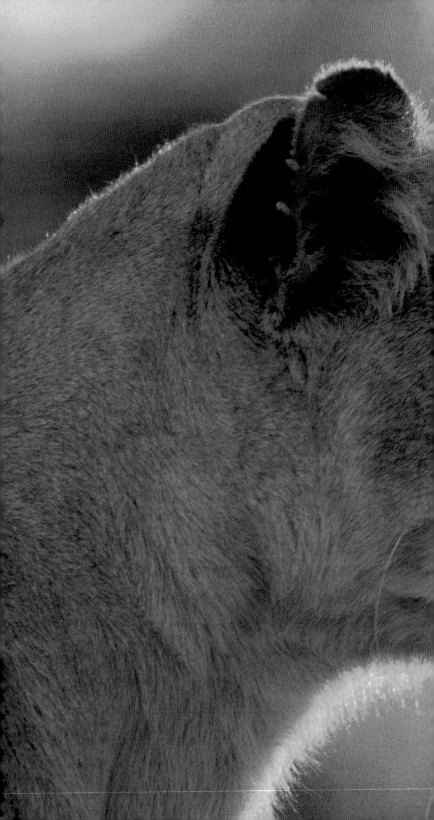

THE STORY OF THE CAT

Wild thing
It may look fierce, but this Scottish wildcat is actually one of the closest relations of the domestic cat.

CAT EVOLUTION

It is only recently in the evolutionary timescale that the domestic cat has become a human companion, a constant presence in our homes and in our hearts. From its origins in a family of African wildcats, the domestic cat evolved and rapidly colonized all corners of the globe. Today, it outnumbers the dog as the world's number one pet.

THE STORY OF MODERN CATS

All cats, be they wild or domestic, belong to the same family of animals called Felidae. Between 8 and 12 million years ago, cats had evolved into two groups that scientists call Old World and New World species, based on where they are found today. Big cats that roared were further classified as *Panthera*, while small cats that did not roar were classified as *Felis*. It was from this genus of smaller-sized felines that wildcats – looking very similar to our modern household companions – evolved. One of these lines was the African wildcat (*Felis silvestris lybica*), which around 5,000 years ago chose to live in close proximity to humans in Egypt. It is from this

One of the family
Big cats share their origins with their smaller relations. However, the future of large wild cats like this leopard, found from Africa through to the Far East, is not so certain.

wildcat that the domestic cat (*Felis silvestris catus*) is thought principally to be descended. From Egypt, Phoenician traders took cats into Italy, and within 2,000 years the domestic cat had spread throughout Europe and western Asia. It wasn't until the 19th century, however, that cats inhabited every continent and major island of the world except Antarctica.

Today, the classification of cats has diverged once again. The numbers of housebound cats now vie with those of latchkey cats – owned individuals given the freedom to roam outdoors at will. And there are now more feral, or unowned cats, than owned individuals. Luckily, there is an abundance of cat lovers and cat charities offering care and protection to these cats in need.

The feral factor
Ferals are cats born and raised away from humans. They survive in the wild by their wits. People can take them on as pets, however, helping to limit feral numbers.

Meet the ancestors

The cat's ancestors, the early mammals, developed two crucial evolutionary traits: fur and skin glands. With insulating fur, temperature-control from sweating, and the ability to suckle their young, mammals thrived. Primitive cats continued to evolve over tens of millions of years.

THE ORIGIN OF THE SPECIES

Cats, like all modern carnivorous mammal species, evolved from a family of early mammals that thrived in the post-dinosaur age around 60 million years ago: the miacids. It is thought that a bigger brain, bringing the flexibility to adapt to change, enabled the miacids to survive while other carnivores declined. The miacids were long-bodied, short-legged mammals, from which evolved the variety of modern families of carnivores we know today. From these early mammals the first "cat" developed – *Proailurus*, a half-cat, half-civet carnivore. About 20 million years ago, *Proailurus* gave way to *Pseudaelurus*, the first feline digitigrade, which walked on the tips of its toes and had stabbing canine teeth. These species are considered the first members of the modern cat family, Felidae. Genetic studies show eight major lineages within the modern feline family. Panthers were

SABRE-TOOTH SPECIALIZATIONS

Evolution is seldom a straightforward progression: successful mutations may occur, be lost, then reoccur as environmental conditions change. The cat's family tree has many "dead-end" branches, such as the sabre-toothed Smilodon (below), an offshoot of the pseudaelurids that survived until less than a million years ago. Sabre-toothed species evolved independently on at least four occasions. With their long, yet fragile teeth, probably designed to subdue and kill prey after bringing it down, sabre tooths evolved to hunt large grazing mammals. When prey numbers fell, the over-specialized sabre tooths were too selectively adapted to hunt other species, and died out.

SMILODON SKELETON

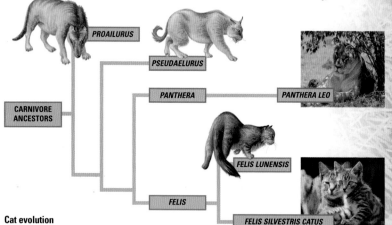

PROAILURUS

PSEUDAELURUS

PANTHERA

PANTHERA LEO

CARNIVORE ANCESTORS

FELIS LUNENSIS

FELIS

FELIS SILVESTRIS CATUS

Cat evolution

Experts disagree on the exact details of feline evolution, but fossil evidence suggests that there is a direct relationship between ancient "cat-like", forest-dwelling carnivores and later "cat-like" species such as *Proailurus* and *Pseudaelurus*. The *Panthera* evolutionary line, leading to present-day lions and panthers, evolved around 10.8 million years ago, while animals in the cat's own genus, *Felis*, emerged 6.2 million years ago.

King of the beasts
The Panthera genus includes *Panthera leo*, the African lion. Lions live in "prides" of related females, a characteristic also found in the domestic cat.

in the first line to emerge, while later lines produced smaller cats such as the bay cat, ocelot, and, in European forests 6.2 million years ago, the domestic cat's immediate ancestor, *Felis lunensis*. This extinct species is the ancestor of all the small wildcats that today inhabit Europe, Africa, and Asia.

THE SPREAD OF THE CAT
Early big cats spread around the world, with lions emerging out of Africa through Europe, Southeast Asia, as far west as parts of America, and as far north as Siberia. Leopards and jaguars dispersed through large areas of Europe, Asia, Africa, and the Americas, while the oldest tiger fossils are found in China. However, some parts of the world were felid-free until man imported the domestic cat along trade routes. In Australia, separated from the rest of the world around 85 million years before the evolution of the cat, a marsupial carnivore called the tiger cat, *Dasyurus maculatus*, fulfilled the small predator role. North America was free from small cats, with the predator's niche being filled by the mustelid family, including the mink and skunk.

Beauty spot
The jaguar is the only big cat found in the Americas. Unlike other members of the *Panthera* genus, such as lions and tigers, the jaguar does not roar.

Cats in the Americas

Millions of years ago, continental drift broke up supercontinents into land masses, and emerging cat populations became separated by oceans. In the Americas, the rich diversity of climate and topography led to a wide variety of species in the genus *Felis* developing there.

Lynx *Felis canadensis*
The only member of the cat family that lives on both sides of the Atlantic, the lynx is widespread throughout its native habitat. Often growing no bigger than domestic cats, a reliance on snowshoe hare is detrimental to the species: fluctuations in hare populations directly affect lynx numbers.

Puma *Felis concolor*
Ranging from southern Canada to Patagonia in South America, the puma is also known as cougar, panther, and mountain lion. The largest member of the genus *Felis*, its prey ranges from rodents to deer.

Bobcat *Felis rufus* (left)
Probably a subspecies of the lynx, the bobcat, or red lynx, inhabits vast areas of North America from Nova Scotia down into Mexico. Slightly larger than the lynx, with a longer tail, the bobcat has large ears, but less dramatic ear tufts than its relation.

PRIME CAT TERRITORY
Although the Americas have only one native large cat, the jaguar, they support a variety of smaller cats, ranging in size from the puma, largest of the *Felis* genus, to the kodkod, up to 3kg (7lb) in weight. Most of the smaller cats are concentrated in South America, but scientists believe many developed in North America and migrated south when continental drift brought the two Americas together.

Ocelot *Felis pardalis* (left) Once widely distributed, the ocelot has suffered the misfortune of having a handsome orange-yellow coat, black-striped and spotted, for which it has been hunted to extinction in parts of North America. A superb climber, it hunts in trees and sleeps during the day.

The American cats are probably all closely related, but without genetic testing this cannot be verified. The tiger cat, kodkod, ocelot, margay, and Geoffroy's cat may be variants of a single species, and the North American lynx and bobcat may be similarly related. Time is running out for the study of many cats, because wild populations are at threat. Regrettably, the fur trade has experienced a resurgence in recent times, and while trade in exotic animals has decreased, many formerly hunted species are still critically endangered. Furthermore, the habitats of these animals continue to be eradicated by cultivation and urbanization, leaving many on the verge of extinction.

Margay *Felis wiedii* (right) The margay, sometimes called the long-tailed spotted cat, looks much like a mini ocelot. Although a close relative, it is considerably smaller – about the size of a large domestic cat. Its habitat extends from Mexico to Argentina, although it has become extinct in vast areas of the Americas.

Pampas cat *Felis colocolo*
Also called the "gato pajero" or grass cat because of its favoured habitat, the pampas cat ranges from Ecuador to northern Chile and Argentina. It is a nocturnal predator, and preys on ground-nesting birds and small mammals. The size of a domestic cat, the pampas cat arches its back dramatically and its fur stands on end when it is excited or aggressive.

Mountain cat *Felis jacobita*
This rare cat inhabits the high areas of the Andes. It is the same size as the average domestic cat, although males can be slightly larger. Its silver-grey coat, spotted or striped with brown or orange, is dense, and makes it well adapted for the bitter weather of its high-altitude habitat. It has been seen at altitudes of up to 5,000m (16,000ft) above sea level.

Tiger cat *Felis tigrinus*
Also known as the little spotted cat, ocelot cat, and oncilla, the tiger cat is often mistaken for its close relative, the margay. Its range extends from Costa Rica to northern Argentina, but it is rare, because it is hunted for its coat, which varies in colour from cream to rich ochre. Although a forest dweller, it does not live in trees to a great extent. It preys on birds, mammals, lizards, and insects.

Jaguarundi *Felis yagouarundi*
(right) Sometimes called the ottercat or weaselcat, this feline inhabits dense undergrowth from Arizona to Argentina. Because its fur has never been popular, it has escaped the hunters, but little is known about its behaviour. Most active in the morning, jaguarundis eat rodents and rabbits but also frogs and birds. South American Indian stories tell of taming jaguarundis for use in rodent control.

Kodkod *Felis guigna*
The smallest of the American cats, the male kodkod, or guiña, is never more than 3kg (7lb) in weight and 52cm (21in) long. This spotted, grey-brown tree-dweller is found mostly in central and southern Chile, but there are also populations in western Argentina. Very little is known about its social behaviour or hunting habits, although farmers claim that it attacks poultry.

Geoffroy's cat *Felis geoffroyi*
(right) Sometimes called Geoffroy's ocelot, this tiny cat is closely related to the kodkod and the much larger margay. An excellent climber and swimmer, it preys on small mammals and birds. Its habitat extends from Brazil and Bolivia south into Argentina. The colour of the coat varies from shades of ochre to silver, but spotted grey is the most common.

Feeding time
Found from southern Canada to northern Mexico, bobcats thrive in habitats with dense vegetation and a variety of prey. Fresh from the hunt, this cat leaps with a horned lark in its mouth.

Cats in Africa and Eurasia

The small and medium-sized cats of Eurasia and Africa share many traits with the domestic cat. However, while many have been observed displaying habits similar to those of pet cats, few carry the potential for domestication in their natural form.

WILD CAT SURVIVAL

The key factor in determining the individual anatomical and behavioural characteristics of each species of wild cat has always been the availability of food sources. Evolutionary adaptation has resulted in some species, such as the fishing cat, becoming aquatic hunters and catching fish, snakes, or rodents by grabbing their prey with their paws or by diving beneath the water's surface. Others, such as the Chinese desert cat, have adapted to life in an arid climate, and more typically prey upon small mammals.

Camouflage is key to the cat's survival: all cats have developed coat colours and markings that conceal them from their prey in their particular environments. In general, cats with spotted coats live in forests, while less vividly patterned cats live and hunt in tall grass or open territory. Regardless of their habitat, however, all of the domestic cat's close relations share common characteristics. In the wild, most cats are solitary and keep to their own territories, which they mark with scent.

SMALL CAT HYBRIDS

Small cats can successfully interbreed, although cross-species matings are very much the result of human intervention. Just as a lion mated to a tiger produces a "liger" or "tigon", hybrid small cats are born. With the correct cross-species alliance, the resulting kittens are fertile and thus able to perpetuate the new hybrid – something their big-cat relations cannot do. Some species have been bred with the domestic cat, creating handsome hybrids. However, the resulting hybrids are often intractable, especially in early generations. Tractability, fostered through continued breeding, is quickly diminished by mating with species that have not undergone the biofeedback or hormonal changes associated with tameness (*see* p.207).

Sand cat *Felis margarita*
This cat's territory stretches from Saharan Africa to the deserts of Baluchistan in Asia. Thick hair between the pads of its feet prevent it sinking into sand, and it is able to survive with very little water.

Caracal *Felis caracal*
(above) A member of the lynx family that has adapted to the heat of the tropics, the caracal has distinctive ear tufts. Its habitat ranges from Africa to the Arabian Peninsula and India.

African golden cat *Felis aurata*
This rare cat inhabits the forests of Africa, although it is not a tree-dweller. Its prey includes rodents and birds, which it hunts by night and day. Its coat varies from brown to grey.

Serval *Felis serval*
(above) A native of the African savannahs, the serval's coat is tawny with black spots. It can leap twice its own length to bring down birds.

Black-footed cat *Felis nigripes*
The smallest of the African cats, this spotted cat is found in the savannahs of southern Africa, where it preys on lizards and small rodents.

Chinese desert cat *Felis bieti*
Inhabiting the steppes and mountains of western China and southern Mongolia, this domestic cat-sized species has a dense coat, and thick hair on the soles of its feet. Its yellow-brown coat offers camouflage in its dry habitat.

Eurasian lynx *Felis lynx*
The largest of the European cats, the lynx can be up to five times heavier than the domestic cat. Ranging from Scandinavia to Siberia, it is largely extinct in western Europe, although its relative, the Iberian lynx, survives in Spain.

Asian leopard cat
Felis bengalensis (above)
Similar in size to the domestic cat, the leopard cat inhabits an area from northern China to the islands of Indonesia – where its success is aided by its ability to swim and catch fish. It has been bred with the domestic cat to produce the Bengal (*see* p.120).

Asian golden cat *Felis temmincki* Also known as Temminck's golden cat, this close relation of the African golden cat lives in rocky terrain from Nepal and southern China to Sumatra.

Iriomote cat *Felis iriomotensis* Discovered in 1967 on the Japanese island of Iriomote, probably fewer than 100 of these cats survive, each hunting in its own territory.

Jungle cat *Felis chaus*
This cat is misnamed, for it prefers open country, reedy marshes, and woodland, and is also known as the reed cat, swamp cat, and marsh cat.

Marbled cat
Felis marmorata
Named for the distinctive marbled patterning of its coat, the marbled cat is found from the eastern Himalayas to Borneo. It is now protected in India and Thailand.

Rusty spotted cat *Felis rubiginosus*
(right) The smallest of the Asian cats, this tiny feline inhabits the scrub and grassland of southern India and the humid mountain forest of Sri Lanka. This cat is nocturnal and hunts small mammals, birds, and insects.

Fishing cat *Felis viverrinus*
(above) With slightly webbed toes and less retractile claws than other cats, this cat lives in the mangrove swamps of India, Sri Lanka, China, and Myanmar.

Pallas's cat *Felis manul*
From Iran to western China, Pallas's cat inhabits mountainous terrain. It has evolved with small ears and a very dense coat to survive subfreezing temperatures.

Closest relations

Having agreed that the domestic cat is most closely related to the wildcats of Africa, Europe, and China, geneticists now believe that pet cats are virtually identical to the African wildcat, and that these two varieties are appreciably different from their Asian and European relatives.

VISUALLY SIMILAR, GENETICALLY DIFFERENT

So similar in appearance are the wildcats that make up the species *Felis silvestris* that experts have long been unable to determine exactly whether each is a distinct species or simply a regional race or subspecies adapted for its environment. What makes the task even more difficult is that all of these cats – including the domestic cat – can be interbred, producing fertile offspring. And until recently, taxonomists have failed to agree on the significance of their differences. Subtle visual differences between varieties of these small, lone hunters do exist, with coat colour and texture varying according to habitat, and there are also differences in temperament between the wildcats of Africa and those of Europe. In Somalia, for example, African wildcats have displayed signs of tameness by living in close proximity to human settlements, while in Britain, Scottish wildcats are seldom seen, remaining reclusive animals. Recent studies may explain these disparities, with the results indicating that there are distinct genetic differences between the European wildcat and the African wildcat.

DISTINCT DESCENDANT

The domestic cat may well be an emigrant from Africa, but sufficient subtle differences remain between the genes of African wildcats and domestic cats to identify an individual as one or the other, even when populations are mixed. However, experts have disagreed whether the African wildcats and Scottish wildcats are full-blooded wildcats or wildcat–domestic hybrids: genetic testing may reveal the answer to this question.

Scottish wildcat *Felis silvestris grampia* (below) Once prevalent throughout Britain, wildcats had disappeared from England by the 1800s, retreating to Scotland, where they survive north of a line drawn from Glasgow to Edinburgh. With protection, their numbers have begun to recover. The Scottish wildcat has a broader head and shorter tail than the domestic cat.

Spanish wildcat *Felis silvestris iberia* (left) Looking similar to heavily built domestic tabbies, the wildcats of Iberia are a remnant of the wildcats that once lived throughout Europe. Hunted for their pelts and persecuted because they are believed to prey on livestock, they survive today only in isolated regions.

European wildcat
Felis silvestris europeus
(left) After declining
almost to extinction, the
populations of European
wildcats are now stable in
many countries. Intractable
and virtually untamable,
this indigenous wildcat is
now a protected species in
many countries, including
Germany, the Czech
Republic, and Slovakia.

HYBRIDIZATION OF THE WILDCAT

Wildcats in Europe, such as this European wildcat
(below), have been threatened by human persecution
and the spread of agriculture. Less obviously, they may
also have been endangered by hybridization with the
domestic cat. It is likely that male wildcats have fathered
kittens with female domestic cats. At adolescence, these
hybrid kittens exhibit the father's wild ways and move
away from human settlements. As a result, wildcats are
unlikely to play a role in the development of the domestic
cat, but it was once thought domestic cats could play a
role in the future evolution of the wildcat. Interestingly,
genetic testing shows that the Sardinian wildcat (*Felis
silvestris silvestris*) remains genetically distinct and is
not threatened with dilution through hybridization.

Indian desert cat
Felis silvestris ornata (right)
Also called the Indian desert
wildcat, the habitat of this cat ranges
south from Russia down to central
India. It is smaller than its African
and European relations, and its coat
is spotted rather than striped.

African wildcat
Felis silvestris lybica (right)
The African wildcat, like its European
relatives, has a larger brain than the
domestic cat, which is probably due to
the demands of survival. Unlike European
wildcats, the African wildcat can be
relatively tame if raised in captivity.
Genetic investigations indicate that this
is the true ancestor of the domestic cat.

Taming the cat

Of all the species that have become domesticated, the cat is, uniquely, the only one that was, and still is, a solitary hunter. Historically, it competed with humans for birds and small mammals for survival before taking its first tentative steps towards domestication.

MOUSE CONTROL

Between 9000 and 5000 BC, the development of agriculture created a new biological niche for countless species, and the cat was to be a major beneficiary. However, judging from the number of mouse skeletons found in the archaeological excavations of ancient Egyptian dwellings from around 4000 BC, the aboriginal mouse was one of the first species to take advantage of these changes. Attracted to permanent human settlements, which housed grain stores and silos, in turn these concentrations of rodents would have provided rich

A new form of pest control
The role of the newly domesticated cat was not as pet, but instead it found an ecological niche as a rodent-exterminating operative.

pickings for local wildcats. Only certain lines of wildcats succeeded in moving into human settlements, however – those that were the most successful in controlling their "fight-or-flight" response. An animal has two options when faced with danger: it can either face the threat ("fight"), or it can avoid the threat (by taking "flight"). The African wildcat (*Felis silvestris lybica*) was brave enough to embrace this human proximity, and it would have taken only a short time, relatively speaking, for natural selection to make this form of self-control

Cats in early civilization
The first tamed cats were used for pest control in ancient Egypt. This detail, from a wall painting (created *c.*1550 BC) in the tomb of Nakht in the ancient Egyptian capital of Thebes, depicts a cat being rewarded with a fish.

DOMESTICATION ELSEWHERE?

The history of the cat is best documented in ancient Egypt, but Egypt was not necessarily its first domestic home. Dating back over 5,000 years, archaeological evidence from Pakistan and India points to what appear to be domesticated cats. Bones were discovered in the Indus Valley and other regions, and genetic tests will reveal whether these remains originate from locally domesticated cats or whether they are the skeletons of individuals accompanying traders along the commercial routes that connected ancient Egypt with Persia, Mesopotamia, Afghanistan, and the Indian subcontinent.

a prominent characteristic within the local wildcat population. The result was that cats began to live a symbiotic existence with people; these felines were welcome to their new-found food source because of their usefulness as pest controllers.

EARLY DOMESTICATION

In the wild, female African wildcats have been seen to care for the young of their sisters or mothers. This ability to live so closely to other wildcats is another factor in the taming of the species and its eventual evolution into the domestic cat. Those individuals willing to share their new habitat within human settlements with other cats were most likely to breed and pass this trait on to their young. These kittens were then hand-reared or fed by people. In time, those cats that perpetuated dependent, kitten-like behaviour into adulthood were the most likely to survive and breed. The cat's behaviour was now being determined both by natural selection and by human intervention. These influences led to physical and physiological modifications. As it was no longer necessary to patrol an extensive terrain, regions of the brain needed for mapping a large territory became smaller. In fact, this more sedentary lifestyle resulted in the size of the cat's brain being reduced by almost 25 per

Domestic appliance
Although the domesticated house cat hasn't changed its habits much from its wild brethren over the millennia, we still willingly welcome these aloof and independent hunters into our homes.

cent. Similarly, as the fight-or-flight response was no longer as vital for survival, the size of the cat's adrenal and pituitary glands decreased. And because camouflage was no longer essential, even those cats with recessive, single-coloured coat colours were able to survive and multiply. As a consequence of these behavioural and biological adaptations, by around 3000 BC, the African wildcat had been successfully domesticated.

EVIDENCE IN ART

Early Egyptian art illustrates in detail the swift evolution of the cat from cautiously welcomed vermin-killer to deified household companion. Around 3,000 years ago, the cat's role in art had progressed from a minor presence on the periphery of Egyptian culture to becoming associated with the Egyptian sun-god, Ra, and the fertility goddess Bastet. The cat soon became the most popular animal in Egyptian religion and ideology. This association with Egyptian deities, together with the cat's natural vermin-killing abilities, increased its value as a commodity and helped to ensure its expansion out of Egypt, south in Africa, north to Europe, east to Asia, and eventually throughout the world.

Out of Africa

Phoenician traders were the first to transport domesticated felines out of Africa *en masse*. Cats appeared in what is now Israel and Palestine over 3,700 years ago, and in Greece a few hundred years later. By 3,000 years ago, they had spread throughout the Mediterranean region.

ANCIENT TRAVELLERS

Curiously, despite the domestic cats' exodus from Africa four millennia ago, African wildcats were first transported out of the continent some 6,000 years earlier. The recent discovery on Cyprus of a cat buried in a Neolithic grave dates back 9,500 years. Cyprus has never had any indigenous wildcats, so the theory is that wildcats arrived on the island soon after humans and mice did, and were probably intentionally introduced there as rodent-catchers. It was not until thousands of years after their introduction to Cyprus, however, when the cat had become domesticated, that large numbers of felines accompanied ships around the world as companions, good luck charms, and as commodities of trade – keenly valued items to barter with.

TRADE AND CONQUEST

Cats were considered nothing more than a novelty at the time of the founding of Rome in the 8th century BC, but around 700 years later, the cat was regarded as a highly prized pet. While Phoenicians trading in tin may have brought cats to Cornwall in Britain up to 3,000 years ago, the Romans certainly introduced

In human company
Cats spread from Africa and eventually inhabited virtually all parts of the world by accompanying men on trade, conquest, and emigration routes. In the earliest phase, they joined traders moving throughout the Mediterranean basin. Over the next millennium, they travelled further away, across Asia, and finally, in their most recent migration, they accompanied ships to all regions of the New World.

● ● ● ● ● **PHASE 1: 9000 BC–200 BC**

➤ **PHASE 2: 200 BC–AD 1400**

➤ **PHASE 3: AD 1400–PRESENT**

● **EARLY ARCHAEOLOGICAL SITES**

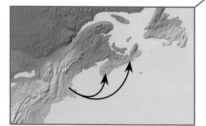

"Digitally enhanced" cats
Among the first cats to arrive in Boston, US, from across the Atlantic were polydactyls – cats with extra toes. These cats quickly spread east along the coast to Nova Scotia.

them to Britain when they invaded 1,000 years later. During the ensuing centuries, the cat travelled north, eventually reaching southern Russia and northern Europe around AD 100. Cats also accompanied traders on the silk routes to the East, as well as joining Christians, Moslems, and Buddhists as these faiths were exported around the world. As European nations colonized North and South America, southern Africa, Australia, and New Zealand, cats travelled on ships, duly establishing themselves wherever there were people. By the 1700s, cats appeared in the New World in appreciable numbers, and by the 1800s, cats inhabited all continents and major islands of the world except Antarctica.

YOUR PET CAT'S TRUE ORIGINS REVEALED

Biologists have long questioned whether the domestic cat (*Felis silvestris catus*) descends wholly from the African wildcat (*Felis silvestris libyca*) or whether the European wildcat (*Felis silvestris europeus*) played a role in its ancestry. Recent DNA studies in Italy of all three types of cats showed that although the date of divergence from its African ancestors cannot be calculated accurately, the domestic cat descends wholly from the African wildcat.

DOMESTIC CAT

Phase 1
Found only in Egypt and the Middle East, cats made the transition from semi-wild residents of human settlements to fully domesticated animals. Some cats arrived in Rome via trading ships.

Phase 2
Cats spread through Europe and Asia with the expansion of the Roman Empire, the silk trade, and various religious movements. By the end of this period, domestic cats could be found from Ireland to Japan.

ROME, ITALY

SHILLOUROKAMBOS, CYPRUS

EGYPT, NORTH AFRICA

Phase 3
Cats travelled on ships as mousers. By the 15th and 16th centuries, they began to cross the seas. Colonization by European countries brought cats to other continents. By 1850, cats could be found almost anywhere there were people.

Cats in Europe

For centuries, Europe has provided an ideal habitat and breeding ground for cats. Ever since tame tabbies from Egypt were first introduced there, populations of cats have thrived thanks to the continent's moderate climate and hospitable geography.

NORTHERN MIGRANTS

While it was easy for cats from Africa to adjust to the balmy Mediterranean regions of Europe, colder, more northerly locales proved a greater challenge. In high altitudes and at northerly latitudes, only individuals with superior insulation could survive the harshest winters. A single gene is responsible for coat length, and those cats born with dense, thick, downy hair and longer guard hairs were better protected from the elements than their less-hirsute relatives. From the forests and mountains of Norway to the northern wastes of Russia, emigrant cats soon developed the richer, more luxurious coats that the conditions of their new homelands necessitated. It was not until the 20th century that these regional varieties of cat were recognized by breed registries as indigenous local breeds, such as the European and Asian examples of Norwegian Forest Cat, Turkish Van, Turkish Angora, and Siberian.

A model of warmth and efficiency
Long before they were recognized as a breed, cats with dense insulating coats, such as this Norwegian Forest Cat, were best equipped to survive the harsh winters of Europe.

COAT COLOURS

In addition to coat length, elsewhere in Europe it was coat colour that varied from one region to another. In France, for example, the slate blue-coloured Chartreux, possibly originating in Syria, was once common in the Chartres region. Today, non-agouti coat colours (*see* pp.74–77, *Coat colours and patterns*) are more prevalent along Europe's inland river trade routes, such as the Rhône. The further away from Africa, where agouti colouring is most common, the higher the incidence of non-agouti individuals. There may be two reasons for this. First, it is possible that there is a relationship between coat colour and fearful behaviour. (There is certainly such a correlation in the fox, where silver foxes are less fearful than red foxes.) The cats most likely to continue north along trade routes were the most amenable to handling, and some experts think that non-agouti coloured cats are less fearful than agouti-coloured individuals. The other reason is human whim. We are fascinated by the unusual, and our ancestors may

BREEDING IN ISOLATION

Over 30 years ago, population-genetics experts observed that cats with coat-colour combinations of orange and dominant-white are rare throughout Europe, except on the northern and western coasts of Scotland, in rural Iceland, and on the Faroe Islands. Cats in these regions descend from the first felines taken there by the Vikings who, in turn, acquired them from their Black Sea contacts: the orange and dominant-white coat colour combination is common only in the Van region of eastern Turkey. Through genetic isolation in these remote outposts of European civilization, the founder effect of these first cats is perpetuated in their present-day coat colours.

TURKISH VAN CAT

well have selected the most strikingly different colours for onward trade. Whatever the reason, incidences of non-agouti colouring increase as the distance from Africa increases, reaching their highest concentration in Britain.

THE EUROPEAN FELINE FAMILY

There are well over 80 million companion cats in the continent of Europe. For each of these pampered pets, however, there exists a feral cat (see pp.36–37), individuals that breed, feed, and survive on their own in the cities, towns, and rural regions of Europe. Their numbers vary according to the availability of food. In regions such as the Hebridean islands of Scotland, for example, there are commonly around three feral cats per square kilometre, while in Mediterranean fishing ports there may be 300 unowned cats in the square kilometre surrounding a fish processing plant. From the Baltic states down through Poland and the Ukraine to Hungary and the Balkans, feral farm cats thrive where traditional farming methods continue. It is in temperate Mediterranean Europe, however, where food, shelter, and mates all are readily available, that feral cats have achieved their greatest success, with ferals outnumbering owned cats.

Feline congregations
These related cats, waiting in a Mediterranean fishing port, willingly live together in large numbers to benefit from any scraps of nourishment that come their way.

CAT OWNERSHIP IN EUROPE

Cat ownership is increasing in virtually all European countries, but especially in countries such as the United Kingdom, France, and Germany, where numbers of dogs owned have recently fallen. These figures are for "owned cats" only. If they are summed, together with rough estimates in countries where accurate counts are unavailable, they total 84 million cats in the whole of Europe. In many countries, including Spain in particular, the "unowned" or feral cat population is much larger than the owned pool of cats.

1	France	9.2 million
2	UK	8.3 million
3	Germany	7.8 million
4	Italy	6.6 million
5	Poland	5 million
6	Netherlands	2.4 million
7	Spain	2.3 million
8	Hungary	2 million
9	Czech Republic and Slovakia	1.6 million
10	Belgium	1.5 million
=11	Austria	1.4 million
=11	Switzerland	1.4 million
=11	Baltics	1.4 million
12	Sweden	1.3 million
13	Portugal	1.1 million
14	Denmark	850,000
15	Greece	800,000
16	Norway	750,000
17	Finland	650,000
18	Ireland	450,000

Estimates:

Slovenia, Croatia, Bosnia, Serbia and Montenegro, Macedonia	3.5 million
Romania, Bulgaria, Ukraine, Belarus, Russia in Europe	24 million

Cats in Asia

Cats spread rapidly through the Levant, north into Anatolia, then east to the Indian subcontinent. Some accompanied travellers on the silk routes to China and Japan while others journeyed south to Burma and Siam. These cats evolved into the breeds now classified as "foreigns".

MIGRATION TO THE EAST

It was in Anatolia, the Caucasus, and Persia – what are now Turkey, parts of the Russian Federation, and Iran – that the mutation for long hair was first perpetuated intentionally. So-called "Persian" cats first arrived in Europe around 400 years ago. In the mountainous regions of eastern Turkey, an isolated cat population perpetuated the founder characteristic of a coat-colour combination of orange and dominant-white, a feature that is emblematic of what is now the Turkish Van cat.

There is historical evidence that, through trade, cats had reached the Indus Valley of present-day Pakistan by 4,000 years ago. It is believed that these cats, together with those that followed from their original home in the Mediterranean's eastern basin, formed the founding stock for all Asian cats today. At least one geneticist, however, suggests that cats were domesticated independently in what is now Pakistan, and that this population interbred with the new arrivals, creating the stock of cats seen today. From coastal ports, but also from the great cultural centres of the Indus Valley and the Ganges, cats were traded further east along the silk and evangelical Buddhist routes to China and southeast into Asia, arriving in Siam (now Thailand) where they became highly valued and were awarded legendary status. The dates of the cat's arrival in China and Southeast Asia are tentatively put at between 2000 BC and AD 400.

Hitching a ride
An elderly man carries his cat on his shoulder as he cycles along a street in Chengdu in the Sichuan province of China. In some Far East countries, keeping cats or dogs as pets is regarded as a sign of Westernization.

A REPRIEVE OR A CURSE?

The treatment of cats in Asia has always been a contentious issue. To some nations they are prized possessions, to others a source of food. This caged cat (right) in Xin Yuan market in the southern Chinese city of Guangzhou is being fattened up for the table. Attitudes in the Far East towards cats may be changing though, but not on compassionate grounds. The outbreak of potentially fatal viruses such as bird flu, which spread from Southeast Asia, is forcing cat-eating nations to reassess their standpoint on these animals. As well as consuming birds, cats can infect each other with this virus, and there is concern that it may combine with a human strain to produce a mutation that is more dangerous and difficult to combat.

HUNTER AND HUNTED

As well as being valued in the Far East for their grace and beauty, cats were also employed in their more familiar role of vermin- and snake-killers. Unfortunately, they had one other, less glamorous part to play in Far Eastern culture: that of food. Just as in the case of dogs, cats were regularly consumed by humans during times of hardship and starvation. This multipurpose role – of pet, hunter, and hunted – in Southeast Asia at this time may in part explain the region's culturally ambivalent attitude towards felines today. While many cats are treasured as family companions and others are respected for their predatory prowess in catching all things rodent, in southern China, Korea, Vietnam, and the Philippines millions are slaughtered annually and eaten. In Korea, while the prevalence of dog consumption is decreasing slightly, demand for soup made from boiled cat – said to act as a tonic for elderly women – is increasing as the population of older women continues to rise.

ARRIVAL IN JAPAN

The first cats arrived in Japan in AD 999. Cats were the prized pets of the nobility, and because eating any mammal was forbidden in Japan, cat and dog were never consumed there. However, this close association with the upper classes meant that felines were often distrusted by society's lower social ranks. Among the first arrivals were cats with shortened tails. The founder effect of this family of cats is still evident in the variety of short, stubby, or tailless cats in Japan today, a genetic vestige comparable to what happened on the Isle of Man in the UK (*see* p.90). There, some of the first feline arrivals carried a slightly different genetic predisposition for either short or no tails. Cats on Russia's Kurile Islands, Japanese-owned until 1945, are also commonly short-tailed.

The modern *Maneki-neko* (*see* p.50), the Japanese good luck cat, is often portrayed with a half-length tail, a common variation of the Japanese bobtail. For centuries, artificial male sex organs were kept on shelves for good luck in Japanese homes, but when this tradition was abandoned in the 1870s, the phallic symbols were replaced by the beckoning *Maneki-neko*, its raised paw a coded invitation to sexual mischief.

Art and craft
This porcelain snuff bottle from Asia, decorated with a black-and-white moggy pouncing on a group of feasting grey rats, shows the cat employed in its role as hunter.

Crossing the oceans

Through Europe's colonial empires, the cat spread to southern Africa, the Americas, Australia, New Zealand, and eventually to every inhabited island in the world. The routes of this modern migration can be traced by studying the coat colours and patterns of these emigrant cats.

FELLOW TRAVELLERS

Cats conquered the world by hitchhiking on human transport. They were ferried intentionally to the New World as cargo, efficient rodent-killers destined for new colonies. A good example of cats that have made this transition successfully can be found in the US, where the genetic profile of modern city cats mirrors their European origins. Although the cities of New York and Boston are geographically very close, cats from New York are more similar to cats from Amsterdam in the Netherlands than they are to cats from Boston. North of Boston, in Canada's Halifax, the cats originated in southern England and still share coat colours with their English relatives. A curious additional trait of modern New England cats that originated from southern England is the high frequency of polydactyl cats – individuals with extra toes. This mutation from the genetic "norm" took hold in New England because when these cats were first taken there, they represented a large

POLYDACTYL CAT

Two extra toes on each forepaw

percentage of a small gene pool. These founding cats had a potent influence on the new population, known as the "founder effect" (*see* p.73). While the characteristic of having extra toes is a rare phenomenon elsewhere in the world, in coastal towns from

SHIPWRECKED CATS

The devastation caused by shipwrecks often affords little chance of human survival, but cases have been recorded of cats managing to reach isolated, uninhabited islands. Daniel Defoe's fictional story *Robinson Crusoe* was based on the true experiences of the Scottish sailor Alexander Selkirk. When, in the early 1700s, Selkirk found himself marooned on the island of Juan Fernandez, 400 miles off the coat of Chile, although he had no human acquaintances, he enjoyed the companionship of island cats (and parrots) that had survived previous shipwrecks. They became his friends during his four-and-a-half-year stay on the island, helping him to stay sane in the face of such stark isolation and the ever-present threat of cannibals. This illustration (right), by the American artist Elenore Plaisted Abbott, was first published in the mid-1930s.

Massachusetts north to Nova Scotia, it is a common occurrence, affecting approximately one in ten cats.

THE SIGNIFICANCE OF COAT COLOUR

The colour of a cat's coat reflects its country of origin. For example, Brazilian cats share colours with their ancestors in Portugal, Mexican cats with their Spanish relatives, and Tahitian cats with their French antecedents. Population geneticists are particularly grateful to the old British Empire because, using feline coat colours, it has provided them with an especially fruitful opportunity to trace human migration patterns. One example of coat-colour exportation is the blotched tabby pattern, which emerged in Britain in low numbers more than 400 years ago and has been increasing ever since. Over the centuries, and for reasons unknown, the blotched tabby gradually displaced the native wildcat striped (or mackerel) tabby pattern. So great was this displacement that today, eight out of ten tabbies born in the south of England have the blotched pattern. Blotched tabbies arrived in the US city of Boston

Prevalent pattern
The broad bands, whorls, and spirals of dark colour on a pale background in this blotched, or classic, tabby pattern have gradually displaced the vertical fishbone-like patterns seen in the mackerel tabby.

around 1650 – some 50 years after their emergence in Britain – and today's incidence of 20 per cent of blotched tabbies in Boston reflects the level of this new pattern in southern England at that time. In Brisbane, Australia, where they arrived around 1850, blotched tabbies account for just under 50 per cent of the tabby population, similar to the level of frequency they had achieved in southern England at that time.

A MIXED RECEPTION

Regardless of their colour, the arrival of cats where there were previously no equivalent land-based predators has been welcomed and rejected in equal measure. In regions of Australia and New Zealand, cats were released intentionally to control local populations of rabbits, rats, and mice, but some of these cats have themselves become an environmental nuisance. This is a particular problem in New Zealand, where there are few natural predators and the native wildlife possesses poor behavioural mechanisms with which to defend itself from cats. On smaller, uninhabited islands, there is evidence of cats decimating native species. For example, the remarkably small cats that evolved on Macquarie Island in the frigid Southern Ocean ravaged the ground-nesting bird population and as a result, the cats have been eradicated from the island. Similar eradication programmes have been necessary on other isolated islands to ensure the survival of indigenous species.

Feral cats

Cats that survive and breed on their own, called feral cats, make up around half of the world's domestic cat population – around 200 million individuals. Feral cat populations appear to be self-sustaining, but owned cats probably play a minor role in maintaining feral numbers.

FERAL OR WILD?

There is often confusion in understanding the difference between feral cats and wildcats. Feral cats (*Felis silvestris catus*) are domesticated African wildcats (*Felis silvestris lybica*) that survive and breed on their own. They exist in plentiful numbers throughout the world. African wildcats are relatively rare, preferring to stay clear of people. So too do other wildcats of Europe, found in countries such as Scotland (*Felis silvestris grampia*), Spain (*Felis silvestris iberia*), and central Europe (*Felis silvestris europeus*), that occupy a range of habitats, including forest, grassland, and mountainous regions.

Feral cats living in sparsely populated countryside are the most independent of all felines. These cats can have two litters, in spring and early summer, averaging

Countryside cats
Rural ferals are often found in the vicinity of farms, where they perform a useful role in controlling rodents – a trait their antecedents displayed thousands of years earlier.

four kittens a litter. Few survive to become adults, but those that do are weaned at eight weeks and become sexually mature relatively late, at around ten months. Rural ferals are mainly nocturnal and require a constant supply of fresh animal protein to survive and reproduce. Ideally, they prefer live animal food, although carrion and waste will suffice. Their major diet is small mammals, but they also eat birds,

Eating on the go
Fending for yourself as a feral cat is a capricious business. Grabbing food as and when you can comes with the territory. Here, a fisherman's tasty catch proves too much of a temptation for this famished feline.

lizards, and insects. In Australia, these voracious hunters depend on rats, mice, and rabbits as major food sources.

Urban feral cats lead modified lives. Because they are habituated to humans and human activity from kittenhood, they are less fearful in our presence and more dependent on us for nourishment, living off both our handouts and our surplus food waste. Litter survival is greater as a constant supply of food is more readily at hand. The availability of resting and nesting sites, rather than just the availability of food, limits their ability to reproduce.

POPULATION DENSITIES

Where food is scarce, cats range over a large territory, perhaps two cats in an area of 1 sq km ($^2/_5$ sq mile). When food is abundant, however, their social behaviour is plastic enough to permit intense concentrations of animals to live in relative proximity. Around fish processing plants in Japan, for example, there can be up to 1,000 cats per sq km ($^2/_5$ sq mile). This still allows more space per cat than is available to a pair of felines sharing a typical human home. At first glance, these groupings of up to 1,000 cats look like one massive colony. In actual fact, the population amounts to a cluster of smaller groups, each of which is an independent, stable feral cat colony.

Survival of the fittest among ferals includes developing immunity to feline viruses transmitted by close contact. Studies of Australian feral cats have shown that there is widespread immunity to feline parvovirus, an infection that pet cats are inoculated against. Due to demarcation disputes among feral cats, ferals are, however, a common source of feline leukaemia virus (FeLV), which is spread through saliva.

Aloft and aloof
Although urban feral cats may rely on humans for handouts, they are not tame and will avoid human company, preferring the security of inaccessible roosts in daylight hours.

A MATRIARCHAL SOCIETY

The social structure of feral cats is matriarchal – mothers, aunts, sisters, and kittens. Italian observational studies in the 1970s revealed how sisters may actually suckle kittens while the biological mother is off hunting. The matriarchal group jointly protects and disciplines the young and, as the play activity of male kittens becomes more robust, the response of the females becomes more vigorous until, at between six and twelve months of age, the young males are driven away from the group. Female kitten activity is markedly less physical and, although occasionally a female may be treated as a pariah or driven from the group, in general several generations of females remain together as an elastic but curiously cohesive unit.

THE BROTHERHOOD

Male feral kittens ostracized from the matriarchal group may either become independent operators or join a kind of "brotherhood". Within this band of tom cats, there is a distinct hierarchy that determines who has first option on mating with females. Once this hierarchy has been determined through fighting, the gang of males then benignly live, eat, and sleep as a group. This social behaviour may arise through cats living in enforced proximity due to their dependency on food supplies not found elsewhere.

TERRITORY MARKING

Cats use urine and faeces as visual and olfactory markers to stake out their hunting territory. Being naturally tidy animals, the vast majority of cats bury their faeces immediately after passing it. Dominant feral cats don't. They leave their droppings unburied, as visible claims to ownership of their turf. If you find unburied cat faeces in your garden, don't be too quick to apportion blame: it is more likely to have been left by a feral cat than by a pet cat belonging to a neighbour.

Latchkey cats

Latchkey cats are owned individuals, given the freedom to roam outdoors at will. Unlike in communities of feral cats, there is very little organized structure among free-roaming owned cats. When they wander, they often find themselves on territory governed by a local feral cat.

CULTURAL INFLUENCES

Our attitude towards permitting our cats to roam freely outdoors is influenced both by cultural pressures and legal requirements. In most of Europe, for example, the prevailing cultural outlook is to allow pet cats the freedom to roam, although that freedom is curtailed in some countries by laws restricting the distance a cat may stray from home. This is the case in Denmark and Germany, where cats are legally protected within approximately 150m (490ft) of their homes, but beyond that distance, they may be killed if they

Standing guard
Pet cats often use their owner's territory markers – fences – to delineate their own patch. An elevated position also provides this cat with a perfect vantage point.

A demarcation dispute
Latchkey cats often encounter other cats while outdoors. Most of these confrontations are resolved without fighting when one cat, in this case the cat on the left, quietly withdraws.

rather than to eliminate hunger. If it shares its indoor home with another cat, it is likely they will also share the outdoor territory. This example of safety in numbers is strengthened further by a curious advantage that latchkey cats enjoy: their owners often help their pets defend the back garden against intrusion by other cats!

are deemed to be causing a nuisance. In the US, on the other hand, the general view, certainly among many breeders of purebreds, is that the outdoors is too dangerous and cats should remain indoors. In Australia and New Zealand, there is intense social pressure on cat owners to keep their pets indoors, not simply for the cat's protection, but also to protect indigenous wildlife from feline predation.

DEFINING A TERRITORY
Latchkey cats often use our territory markers to define their parameters. When a pet cat goes through its cat-flap into its outdoor terrain, it may initially visit its regular marking and resting sites. These locations are usually man-made and elevated – on fences, for example – from where the cat views its territory.

Studies of urban latchkey cats in London, UK, showed that the size of a territory depends upon the sex of the cat and whether or not it has been neutered. While in southern Europe owned cats are not routinely neutered, in northern Europe approximately 80 per cent of latchkey cats are spayed or castrated. The London studies revealed that while an unneutered female typically patrolled an outdoor territory defined by three terraced-house back gardens, after she was neutered, she was happy to patrol a single back garden. Unneutered males typically patrolled an average area of seven back gardens, but after neutering, they reduced their wandering and marking to just three.

The latchkey cat's territory is chosen for resting and hunting, although it hunts primarily for the pleasure of the chase

DANGEROUS DISPUTES
While neutering is a socially responsible practice, it is something of a handicap to latchkey cats in their meetings and disputes with local, unneutered feral cats. Resident ferals look upon owned cats as threats to their territory, food sources, social structure, and sexual status, and it is common for owned cats to be attacked by ferals. In some instances a chase ensues, not just back to the cat-flap but through it, into your home. To prevent this, cat-flap manufacturers created magnetically controlled flaps that open only for your own cat. While latchkey cats *are* capable of forming relationships with other outdoors cats, these are usually informal affairs, without social structure.

CAT STUCK UP TREE
You read it in the local paper every so often – the obligatory cat-stuck-up-tree story. Far from being a design fault, this behaviour is simply a consequence of cats being adapted from birth to jump, leap, and climb. It's not unusual for a latchkey cat, through either curiosity or fear, to climb a tree, but getting down is another matter. While feral cats learn through gradual experience how to back down from great heights, some latchkey cats only discover this ability after they find themselves stranded. Few, however, will deign to do so while a crowd of people looks on.

Access to the outdoors
A cat-flap gives latchkey cats the freedom to come and go as they please. The best cat-flaps allow owners to set them to prevent any feline intruders entering the house.

The housebound cat

Confining cats to an indoor lifestyle guarantees their safety, but it also means a lack of natural outlets for natural activities, such as territory marking. As a result, "behavioural problems" are more common in housebound than in latchkey or feral cats.

LIFESTYLE RESTRICTIONS

The life expectancy of cats has increased enormously in the last 20 years, and this is most attributable to the huge reduction in risks taken by living permanently indoors. In densely populated urban areas, the life expectancy of unneutered outdoor cats can be very short – as little as two years. The most common cause of early death is road traffic accidents. Indoor cats, on the other hand, have a median life expectancy of 15 years. It is not uncommon, however, for indoor cats to survive into their early twenties simply because the risks from fighting, injury, and infection are so greatly diminished. Not all cats are agreeable to living indoors though. It can be difficult for an indoor cat to fulfil its biological need to explore, to hunt, to mark its territory – in short, to behave like a cat. This is why play is so important to cats (see pp.254–55).

COMMON INDOOR CAT BEHAVIOURS

Indoor cats retain many of the natural behaviours of their outdoor relatives. They are most active at dusk and again at dawn, often waking their sleeping owners with demands for food or play. These cats carry out routine rodent

Up the stimulation stakes
If you provide your cat with enough stimulation, it will not miss being outdoors. Indeed, many cats will not attempt to go outside, even when given the chance.

patrols, often swatting at flies and moths in their absence. However, while they are content to share a small territory with us because we are sufficiently un-catlike, they are rarely willing to share this small space with a new, unknown cat, which will almost invariably be seen as a threat.

Indoor cats are adaptive and innovative at finding ways to fulfil their biological needs to mark out their territory, to hide, to hunt, to climb, to investigate, to explore, and to create mental activity. With nothing else to chase, some cats will stalk their owner's ankles, pounce, "kill", and depart. Others are creative in marking their territory with visible signs that they are the owners and occupiers. Scratching

Stalking indoors
A cat needs to do what a cat needs to do. Despite being restricted to a conservatory, this cat intently stalks potential prey. Moths and flies are favourites of indoor cats.

the arms of sofas is a particularly good example because these markers are intentionally left to be highly visible. Scaling curtains or sitting atop the fridge are your cat's equivalent of tree-climbing.

NO NEED TO DISCIPLINE

Hunting, clawing, and climbing are perfectly natural feline activities. We erroneously call them behaviour problems because we don't like aspects of our housebound cats' natural behaviour. In some countries, the US in particular, people dislike indoor cats behaving in this way so much that they routinely and unthinkingly amputate their pets' claws so that they don't damage household possessions. Compassionate owners understand that it is perfectly reasonable to keep a cat indoors for its entire life as long as we are willing to compromise and allow these individuals certain freedoms to behave as their evolution and biology dictates. Instead of disciplining your cat, learn how to tackle these so-called behaviour problems instead (*see* pp.284–87).

BRINGING THE OUTDOORS INDOORS

Many owners recognize the restrictions placed upon their cats by indoor living. Cat owners and manufacturers of cat products in the US and Australia in particular have created a variety of ways by which cats can experience satisfying aspects of outdoor life while at the same time remaining safe and conforming to local laws and regulations. The most successful solution is to create a securely enclosed outdoor space where a cat is free to roam. This should be escape-proof, but allow for climbing, sunning, "roosting", and hiding. Prefabricated enclosures are available, and nylon mesh walkways are also options so that cats can walk safely to secure outdoor areas.

Happy in-house
Cats kept indoors from kittenhood rarely want to venture out, despite the occasional window or door being left open. A cat that has lived indoors for its entire life knows no other existence: it is domesticated in the full sense of the word.

The cat's friends

Cat welfare and rescue organizations have existed throughout the world for well over 100 years. Wherever there are stray or feral cats, there are individuals who take it as their responsibility to provide food, shelter, and, when necessary, veterinary care for local cats.

THE CAT SHELTER

The local cat shelter is at the heart of cat welfare. The mission of these organizations is to assist stray and unwanted cats by providing foster care, complete medical care, and adoptions to carefully chosen homes. The best and most efficient shelters are often non-profit organizations, staffed by volunteers, and run on a dispassionately commercial basis. They are generally funded by donations and adoptions; cats are not given away, because shelter directors understand that something that is "free" does not appear to have any value. All donations are used to purchase food and supplies and to pay for veterinary expenses. Additional donations of food and supplies may be solicited from pet food suppliers, local businesses, and private individuals. Businesslike shelters have their homeless cats microchipped for identification purposes, examined by a vet, treated for medical conditions, sterilized, and analysed for possible behaviour problems before they are offered, at a reasonable price, to people looking for healthy feline companions.

Often, these organizations have a no-kill policy, and a cat in their care is only euthanized as a last resort when it is so sick or injured that the vet feels euthanasia is the only humane option. The cat shelter is at the interface between feral cats and owned cats and is the logical focus for people who want to be involved pragmatically in cat welfare.

DEDICATED CAT LOVERS

While some ailurophiles devote their time to managing efficient shelters, other fans of cats take their love to greater extremes, sometimes devoting their lives and their incomes to feline friends. "Feeders" are people who provide food for feral or stray cats, often making daily deliveries to where these cats live. "Rescuers" trap feral cats, usually in well-designed trap-cages, take the trapped cats to a vet where they are sterilized, inoculated, and treated for internal and external parasites, before having a nick placed on an ear so they can be identified easily in the future. The cats are then returned to where they were trapped and are promptly released. Alternatively, rescuers may try to find homes for their rescued cats.

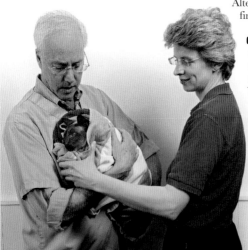

OBSESSIVE FRIENDS

Cat collectors, also known as cat hoarders, present a somewhat problematic scenario. Well-intentioned "animal lovers", they feel compelled to collect cats and get to a point where they just can't cope. Animal collecting is a universal phenomenon which has been studied in countries throughout the world. The

Taking strays to the vets
Rescued cats such as this stray should be taken to the vets where they can be checked for microchip identification as well as injuries or disease.

Many mouths to feed
Feral cats colonies, such as this one in Italy, survive on food provided by self-appointed "feeders". It is vital that cats within such a colony are routinely neutered, to ensure numbers do not exceed the capacity of the territory.

practice is not confined to cats; incidents of dogs and other animals being hoarded are often reported in the news. Recent research in the United States suggests that in many cases, offenders are not in control of their actions and could be suffering from an obsessive disorder.

In the case of cats, psychologists say collectors identify with "abandoned" or "neglected" animals. A typical collector is female, unmarried, with no children, and her collection averages 35 cats. Although these animals are often well cared for, the owner frequently neglects her own nutrition and health. In terms of the cats' well-being, overcrowded and filthy conditions, combined with a lack of basic veterinary care, are the most pressing concerns. The cats are commonly stockpiled, often until disease occurs or neighbours complain about the noise or smell, and by then, the damage has been done: huge numbers of animals either die of disease or have to be destroyed. Tackling the problem is not easy, because prosecuting the owners does not get to the root of the problem, and imposing heavy fines or taking away the animals are not ways to solve a psychological condition.

RAISING THE PROFILE OF CATS

Some of the century's biggest celebrities and most eminent politicians have been proud owners of cats. In the early 1990s, Humphrey, a longhaired black-and-white cat, was employed as resident mouser at 10 Downing Street in London, while Socks, a black-and-white shorthair, occupied the White House in Washington under the presidency of Bill Clinton. The entertainment industry has also always held a place in its heart for all things feline. In the picture below, the year is 1961, the concept of pet passports is decades away, but actress Elizabeth Taylor and husband Eddie Fisher show just how to pamper a puss by jet-setting across the world with their Persian–Siamese, Ali-Kahn.

CATS IN CULTURE

Throughout history, humans have reacted to the cat with strong, often contrasting attitudes. In some eras, cats have been venerated. More often, they have been vilified. In the 20th century, as cats became an integral and welcomed part of both Western and Eastern cultures, we integrated them into our arts and entertainment.

A CHANGING CLIMATE

The cat's cryptic and enigmatic behaviour is no doubt why this animal has always been the subject of myth and folklore in many cultures. Cats were deified in Egypt; their export from the country was banned – an act that only increased their curiosity value elsewhere – and hundreds of thousands of them were mummified. Across the Mediterranean, Venus, the Roman goddess of love, was depicted with a kitten, and as cats spread to northern Europe they were quickly accorded legendary status. In Nordic myth, for example, the fertility goddess Freya arrived in a chariot drawn by cats, the felines symbolizing ferocity and fecundity.

Within the monotheistic religions that developed in the Middle East, the cultural position of the cat was more problematic. In Judaism there is no mention of the cat, but in Islamic regions cats were permitted to enter mosques. Crusaders returning to Christian Europe associated the cat with Islam, and this is one reason why the Catholic Church was so successful in equating cats with heresy, and later with witchcraft and the devil.

An Egyptian veneration
This sphinx – an iconic image of a recumbent lion with a human head – dates back to AD 380–362.

Throughout Europe in the Middle Ages, cats were persecuted for being demonic. It wasn't until the 19th century that the cat was accepted positively once more, as reflected at the time in European and American art, folklore, and fairytales. By the 20th century, the cat was a familiar cultural character, a family friend and confidant in children's stories and cartoons, and favoured by ad agencies the world over to represent attractive qualities of warmth, sensuality, and elegance.

A work of feline art
This delightful 1890s' illustration showcases the charm of the cat.

A familiar favourite
The cat's enduring appeal is on a global scale. Here, painted wood statues of cats are for sale in a shop in Bali, Indonesia.

Cats and religion

Most emerging cultures have worshipped animals at some time. Worldwide, cats have been venerated as symbols of protection and fertility, while the feline's nocturnal habits have made it an object of awe and ambivalence.

EARLY CAT CULTS

The domestic cat probably evolved in North Africa, and ancient Egypt saw the first recorded cult based on the worship of the domestic cat. The popularity of the cat-headed goddess Bastet is suggested by the temple of Bast at Beni Hasan, Egypt, where over 300,000 mummified cats were discovered in the late 19th century. Ritual mourning followed the death of a cat, and bodies were preserved after death as offerings to the gods. So venerated was the animal, that killing a cat was punishable by death.

The Roman goddess of love, Venus, was often portrayed with a cat, denoting her role as compassionate, yet savagely protective mother. In pre-Christian Europe, many religions also associated

Cat-powered chariot
Freya, the goddess of love and fecundity, travels in a chariot pulled by two cats. This pairing could comprise the mythological antecedents of the Norwegian Forest Cat.

the cat with both fecundity and fierce guardianship. The Norse fertility goddess, Freya, travelled in a chariot pulled by cats, while the Welsh pagan goddess Cerridwen, linked to a fertility cult, took the form of a cat. Elsewhere, the idea of protection was paramount. In the Americas, the puma, cougar, and jaguar were all part of native civilizations'

Feline offerings
Scantily clad Egyptian girls paint statuettes of cats in *The Gods and their Makers*, created in 1878 by British painter Edwin Long.

mythologies. The cougar became the *amigo del christiano*, or Christian's friend, after supposedly saving the life of a young Spanish girl. The puma has been worshipped in Peru from 600 BC, while South American medicine men were believed to turn into jaguars after dying.

SACRED CATS

In Islam, the cat became an important animal through its association with the prophet Mohammed, who was saved from a snake bite by the intervention of a cat. In general, Eastern religions have a tolerant attitude to the cat: Hindus have a duty to care for cats, whilst the Parsees consider it a serious crime to kill one. In Chinese Buddhism, the cat's self-containment is associated with meditation, while, in a Japanese Buddhist temple, offering a likeness of a cat after its death ensures good fortune to the family.

Christianity has historically shared a more ambivalent relationship with the cat. Jewish roots bequeathed a benign attitude, and the Christian Church took on some of the veneration and superstitions associated with cats from pagan religions. Early saints were sometimes depicted with cats, and one tradition has a cat giving birth in the stable alongside the Virgin

The supreme goddess
In Hinduism, the mother goddess Durga is depicted as a woman with multiple hands carrying weapons and assuming mudras, or symbolic hand gestures, whilst riding a tiger.

Mary. However, from the 600s BC onwards, cats started to be associated with heresy, and the devil was often portrayed as a black cat. Centuries of suspicion and persecution followed, with cats blamed for evils such as the spread of the plague and destroyed in their multitudes. It was not until the abolition of witchcraft laws in the 18th century that hostility towards cats waned.

A witch-hunt against cats
With widespread hysteria over witchcraft in the 15th century, cats were demonized as witches' familiars. Their poorly understood nocturnal habits were taken as signs of the devil, and cats became part of the iconography of witchcraft.

Monastical moggies
Buddhism and cats make for a holy relationship. These monks at Nga Phe Chaung monastery by Lake Inle, Myanmar (formerly Burma), stroke and play with their feline friends at the temple door.

The origins of myths

The cat's wide, reflecting eyes, secretive demeanour, and nocturnal habits have always imbued it with mystique. From associations with prosperity and benign magic, it has been a lamentably small step to suspicions of ill-omen and dark powers, and systematic persecution of the cat.

AGENTS OF FORTUNE

With the cult of Bastet, the cat was prized as a symbol of fertility and the cycle of life. Beginning in Egypt around 950 BC, and reaching a peak some 600 years later in the Ptolemaic period (332–30 BC), the cat played a central role in festivities and sacrifices to ensure good harvests. In later centuries, around the world, cats were buried with the new crops, or ritually "threshed" to death to mimic the corn harvest, in order to encourage fecundity of the soil. While Christianity denied their divinity, cats still played a part in rituals: in pagan-influenced Halloween and Easter celebrations, they were sacrificed in fires symbolizing purity and fertility.

In many cultures, cats are regarded as an omen: but as a harbinger of ill or good depends on the time and country. In Japan, the cat is seen as particularly felicitous. Legend has it that the first cat in the country was a gift to the emperor Ichijo from a Chinese mandarin in year 999, and her first litter of kittens was an augury for the prosperity of cats in

Lucky charm
The *Maneki-neko*, or Beckoning Cat, has become a symbol of prosperity and luck throughout Japan, and commonly seen images of a cat with right paw raised are talismans for success.

Japan. Another legend tells of a beckoning cat guiding samurai through a storm to the shelter of a shrine. The shrine became a place of veneration of the animal, and people brought cats to bury and to pray for their souls, asking for good fortune in their own lives. *Maneki-neko* talismans of beckoning cats commemorate the myth. Equally, the Japanese Bobtail is regarded as lucky, as its naturally short tale recalls the royal emblem of the chrysanthemum. Believed to ward off storms at sea, the breed is particularly popular with sailors.

BLACK CATS

Black cats in particular have very varied superstitions associated with them. In Britain, a black cat crossing your path is lucky, possibly a remnant of an old

NINE LIVES

The cat's remarkable ability to survive falls from great heights and other potential disasters may be behind the widespread belief that cats have nine lives. The idea probably originated in ancient Egypt, where the number nine had magical properties, but in the 17th century, it was incorporated into superstitions about cats and witchcraft. It was thought that a witch could transform herself into a cat nine times: thus the cat would be reincarnated on nine occasions. Several hypotheses for the cat's perceived durability and knack of laughing in the face of death have been suggested, but it seems likely it owes its resilience to finely-honed instincts and fearless acrobatics.

Surviving against all odds
A cat on the Indonesian island of Nias surveys the damage caused by an earthquake in April 2005 that claimed 1,000 lives. Some people believe cats can predict such events.

Magic cats of China
An instance of felines seen in a favourable light, these magical spirit-cats perform the vital function of keeping away the rats which would otherwise devour the silkworms.

superstition of evil passing by without harm. But in North America, a black cat is seen as an evil spirit, bringing danger. The contrast of black fur and reflective eyes in cats has long given rise to ideas of witchcraft, and from medieval times they have been associated with the devil and witches, and suspected of dark powers.

MAGICAL POWERS

As well as dark magic, cats are associated with more benign sorcery. There is a long tradition that cats can affect the weather, and in Cambodia a cat is carried round the villages and

Cat weather vane
Many superstitions from a host of different cultures associate the cat with the weather. The validity of sayings such as "If a cat washes her face o'er her ear, 'tis a sign the weather will be fine and clear" remains uncertain though.

sprinkled with water as an intercession to the god Indra to send rain for crops. Superstition that cats can predict the weather may have some basis in fact: it is thought that cats may be able to sense changes in atmospheric pressure that herald a storm. Cats have also been associated with divination: in the early Church, some horrific rituals to see the future involved the killing of cats. More harmlessly, it was believed that a way to acquire second sight was to live from early childhood with a tortoiseshell cat.

ANCIENT BURIAL RITUALS

Throughout Europe, mummified remains of cats testify to the prevalence of another superstition: a cat built into the walls or foundations of a building will protect the house from rodents. In Thailand, however, cats were walled up for different reasons. The soul of the deceased enters the cat and escapes to heaven as the cat emerges via a built-in escape route.

This Thai ceremony, like all the other rituals mentioned here, no longer takes place. However, it seems that cat-based superstitions are still a large part of many cultures, and such seasoned prejudices, especially against the black cat, die hard. If truth be told, cats are harmless animals – unless you happen to be a mouse.

Cats in Asian art

The artists of the East have long held a special regard for the cat. From Persia and India and on to China, big cats were used as images of power and leadership. As the domestic cat spread eastwards, it emerged from the shadows of its larger relations, finding its own niche in art.

PERSIAN ART

Muslims hold the cat in high regard because it was the chosen pet of Mohammed (*see* p.46), but images of cats from the Middle East – where cats were plentiful and longhaired cats evolved – are very rare because Islam does not embrace the concept of representational art. It is in the works of visiting Western painters that we first see cats curled asleep on the laps of Arab scribes or being fussed over by Arab women. However, paintings of narrative scenes of national folk-tales and stories from the Bible by anonymous Ottoman artists in the 14th century do often include domestic cats in incidental roles in their tableaux. Bicolours and

Cat crockery
There's no doubting who the central character is in the design of this ornamental Persian pottery dish – the wild cat's flowing mane and lithe physique obscure the man's face in the background.

tortie-and-white cats are by far the most commonly portrayed felines in Eastern art, suggesting that those patterns were preferred by the travellers who took the cat to the East, or by the people who lived there.

INDIAN AND FAR-EASTERN ART

In India, cats signify high status and wealth, as frequently portrayed in painted scenes. Most early interpretations of cats are found in carved or painted religious images; for example, a goddess of fertility may be seen riding a cat. House cats in Indian paintings often resemble the exclusive pets in court portraits, implying that there may have been little or no effort to create pedigree-type breeds.

Farther east, in Thailand, people showed great reverence for cats, painting beautiful scenes on papyrus to illustrate the wide variety of feline coat colours and postures. The many manuscript copies of the *Cat Book Poems*, written around the 16th century, depict pointed cats (ancestors of the Siamese), copper-brown "Sopalak" cats, and silver-tipped blue "Si-Sawat" cats, as well as tabbies, bicolours, and a multitude of patterns that would baffle even the most well-informed of today's geneticists and breeders.

It was during the Song Dynasty (960–1279) that cats first made a significant impression on Chinese art. As in India, they appeared in many court portraits, strongly suggesting that cats symbolized social prestige. Most Chinese artistic renditions of the cat are expressively natural. *Spring Play in a Tang Garden,*

Primitive Persian puss
This 17th century painting shows a cat listening intently to the teachings of Avicenna (980–1037), one of the greatest Persian physicians. It was during the 17th century that longhaired cats were brought from Persia into Italy.

attributed to the Chinese Emperor Xuan Zong, who reigned from 1426 to 1435, depicts kittens frolicking among flowers. By the 1500s, the cat was a popular subject for *cloisonné* figures and, because of its superb nocturnal vision, for porcelain lamp designs.

JAPANESE ART

The cat achieved lasting fame in Japanese art. Most paintings and woodblock prints show cats in the typical tortie-and-white Mi-ké patterning, seen in the Japanese Bobtail today, but in earlier works the cats tend to have longer tails. Through the 18th and 19th centuries, bobtails and predominantly white cats appear more and more often in illustration.

Utamaro (1753–1806) included cats as the companions of beautiful women, while Ando Hiroshige (1797–1858) portrayed cats in vividly realistic detail. But it was Utagawa Kuniyoshi (1797–1861), more than any other Japanese artist, who depicted cats with supreme

> ### BREEDS OF CAT FOR ARTISTIC INSPIRATION
>
> The concept of feline breeds is a wholly Western tradition, begun in Great Britain in the late 1800s. Cats with their origins in Asia were designated as specific breeds by Western breed associations, and their Western names were then exported back to Asian countries where these new "breed" names are now used. Asian artists were influenced by the lean, lithe cats that surrounded them. In Japan, artists portrayed tortie-and-white cats, a common colour combination in that country, as well as the ubiquitous bobtail. In Thailand, artists painted local cats that would one day be recognized as the Siamese, Burmese, and Korat breeds.

accuracy and acute observation. Perhaps Kuniyoshi's most famous work is the triptych woodblock print of the *Fifty-three Stations of the Tokaido Road*, with each station represented by a cat. Most of the cats are short-tailed and bicoloured, but there are also striped tabbies, as well as the double-tailed witch cat of Okabe.

Catnapping companion
Japanese artist Utagawa Kuniyoshi's woodblock print from 1852 beautifully depicts a woman – aided by her slumbering cat – reading a fortune-telling book to pick a suitable date for her wedding.

Cats in European art

Despite the domestic cat's popularity in Egyptian and Asian art, Greek and Roman artists preferred lions and tigers. Frequently stigmatized by the Catholic Church from the Middle Ages onwards, it was not until the 18th century that the cat began to take centre stage in European art.

SYMBOL AND ALLEGORY

Perhaps because of the Christian Church's disapproval of the cat, there are few feline representations in medieval art. Cats do appear in the illuminations for the Lindisfarne Gospels, the Book of Kells, various privately commissioned psalters, and in some carvings in Celtic churches, but these may indicate pagan roots. When the cat appeared in mainstream Christian art, it was often used symbolically, as a cipher for deceit and sin. Early Italian artists such as Domenico Ghirlandaio (1449–1494) and Jacopo Tintoretto (1518–1594) placed a cat at Judas's feet in portrayals of the Last Supper, to suggest his intended betrayal. The *Adam and Eve* woodcut by German artist and engraver Albrecht Dürer (1471–1528) linked a cat to Eve, suggesting

both lasciviousness and evil, while the Netherlandish painter Hieronymus Bosch (c.1450–1516) included cat-like demons in many of his fantastical works, such as *The Temptations of Saint Anthony*.

DOMESTIC SETTINGS

By the 18th century, the cat's association with the devil in European art was starting to wane. Painters portrayed other aspects of its character: the still lifes of Jean-Baptiste Chardin (1699–1779), including *The Thief in Luck*, concentrated on the cat's opportunistic greed. At the same time, William Hogarth's series "The Stages of Cruelty" showed human abuse

Advertising gambit
A mischievous puss looks on in this poster, for the French Chocolate & Tea Company, created by the famous cat artist Théophile Steinlen at the turn of the 19th century.

of cats, while the French painters Antoine Watteau (1684–1721) and Jean Fragonard (1732–1806), and the Italian Giovanni Tiepolo (1696–1770), drew on feline sensuousness, relaxation, and frivolity. And although Leonardo da Vinci (1452–1519) had pioneered the realistic portrayal of cats in his delightful cat sketches, it was not until the popularity of the famous French painter and naturalist Jean-Baptiste Oudry (1686–1755) that realism became an important factor in feline art.

Cats in early European art
This 17th-century painting by Dutch artist Judith Leyster is entitled *Laughing Children with a Cat*. Felines featured prominently in several of Leyster's works.

CAT PORTRAITURE

The 19th century saw an interest in feline portraiture, with Dutch-born Henrietta Ronner (1821–1909) and Swiss-born Gottfried Mind (1798–1814) producing studies of cat behaviour. Fellow Swiss artist Théophile Steinlen (1859–1923) produced thousands of humorous cats sketches, intended as comic strips, and highly prized for their take on feline behaviour. Elsewhere, the cat's sensuality was exploited thematically by French Impressionists Pierre-Auguste Renoir (1841–1919) and Edouard Manet (1832–1883), whose provocative portrait of a prostitute, *Olympia*, included a sensual depiction of a cat.

MODERN ART

Since the 20th century, the popularity of the cat in art has flourished and become unassailable, with artists such as Gwen Jones (1876–1939) praising cats in their art. German Expressionists like Franz Marc (1880–1916) exaggerated and stylized aspects of cat behaviour, while in the hands of Cubist Pablo Picasso (1881–1973) the feral qualities of the cat showed through. Surrealists such as British-born Leonora Carrington prized the cat's mystique. Marc Chagall (1887–1985) combined his native Russian folk art with the influence of his adoptive Paris to create a highly individual style. And probably the most famous cat in art of modern times is the eponymous white cat in *Mr and Mrs Clark and Percy*, a well-loved work by British artist David Hockney (1937–).

Cubist cat
Spanish artist Pablo Picasso was the inventor of Cubism, overturning ways of perceiving form. This piece, *A Cat Devouring a Bird*, was painted in 1939.

Cats in American art

The cat was only a peripheral character in early American art, with feline characters featuring occasionally in folk paintings. The lead-up to the 20th century marked a new epoch, however, as American artists chose to include – and even highlight – the feline form in their work.

FOLK MEMORY

By the end of the 19th century, the centre of American art was in Paris. Until this time, it was mainly the self-taught folk artists native to the "land of the free" who had put forward their interpretations of cats in American art. No longer associated with paganism and the devil, the cat had become a modern symbol of beauty and peaceful civilization. In the portraits painted by American travelling limners, cats make a frequent appearance accompanying children. Cats were also often painted on their own. One

The cat sat on the mat
An example of how varied American folk art can be, this hooked rug is made from wool and features a cat design. The art of rug hooking continues to be popular to this day.

THE INFLUENCE OF EUROPEAN ART

Europe opened the eyes of America's emigrant artists to the realms of what art had to offer, and soon these apprentices were producing their own competent works with understated savoir-faire. This was the era of paint and portraiture, of oil on canvas: the idea of producing cartoon or illustrated cats such as *Felix* or *Garfield* was several decades away.

Beaux's black cat
American painter Cecilia Beaux created this piece, *Sita and Sarita*, in 1896. Sarita is a nickname for Beaux's mother; Sita the name of the barely-there cat.

such example is *Tinkle, A Cat*, painted in 1883 by an unknown American artist. Tinkle is a blindingly white shorthaired cat who sits upon a velvet hassock adorned with black and gold braid. Unequivocally a much-treasured pet, Tinkle wears a collar on which hang two golden bells.

Perhaps the most famous piece of American folk-art portraying felines is *Cat and Kittens* by an anonymous artist, painted *c.*1872–1883. It features a domestic scene of what is presumably a mother cat with her young, a somewhat plaintive and serious expression on her face as her piercing eyes gaze out at the observer while her kittens are preoccupied with unravelling a ball of wool.

A NEW DAWN

The seeming communion between artists and cats was never more obvious than in America at the start of the twentieth century, as this intimate bond was fondly translated via the creations of a diverse range of artists. Although cats are not the central theme of the paintings by the American artist Will Barnet (1911–), Madame Butterfly, the beloved family cat, is often included in his family portraits.

While the major achievement of Judy Chicago (1939–) is *The Dinner Party*, a work regarded as a major statement of feminist art, she is also a prolific cat sketcher. *Little Veronica* and *Poppy* are featured in her *Autobiography of a Year* from 1993, while in 2005 she published *Kitty City: A Feline Book of Hours*, which is a celebration of life with her cats.

Frank Romero (1941–), a California native lauded for his artistry and role in galvanizing Hispanic artists, produces richly coloured canvases, painted sculptures, and neon-enhanced art, and often includes his studio cat Scamp in his work. His 2003 acrylic on canvas works *Cat in a corner* and *Green teapot* feature his perennial black and white feline companion.

Joan Brown (1939–1990) was the youngest member of the Bay Area Figurative Movement of San Francisco and attempted to merge figuration with abstraction. In *The Adolescent Cat*, from 1983, she makes a rakish young ginger tomcat a metaphysical symbol rather than merely a representation of decorative style. Donald, her own grey tabby, featured in many of her later paintings.

The media-aware Pop artist Andy Warhol (1928–1987) was passionate about his cats. He produced hundreds

Purple puss
Sam by Pop Art founder Andy Warhol was created in 1954, along with other versions of the cat in differing colours.

Gerrit Greve cat
A third-generation Dutch colonial, the artist Gerrit Greve emigrated to America in 1957, settling near Chicago. His love of painting grotesque, oversized, kaleidoscopically coloured cats is no better exemplified than in this 1979 reproduction, *Yellow Cat with Blue Stripes.*

of sketches of his favourite felines in a variety of frivolous poses. While these were originally printed as presents for close friends, they were posthumously published in gift books and now adorn coffee mugs and T-shirts. Even after death, our love for cats runs deep.

Cats in fairytales, folklore, and stories

Since the earliest days of cohabitation, story tellers have been entranced by the innate qualities of the cat: its aloofness, its affection, its mystery. In every culture that it touched, tales and sayings have grown up that comment on the cat and, obliquely, on our own behaviour.

PROVERBS AND STORIES

The overwhelming prevalence of proverbs and traditional sayings involving cats testifies to the fascination they exert. From the Italian saying that "old cats mean young mice" to the German adage that "the cat cannot leave the mouse", feline habits have long been used to illuminate aspects of human behaviour.

Some of the earliest surviving oral tales featuring cats are the famous fables by the 6th century BC Greek, Aesop. In several of his morality tales, the devious, greed-motivated cat appears, often as a cipher for human defects. The French poet La Fontaine (1621–1695) created a lasting record of these stories, passed down through oral culture, wittily adapting and polishing Aesop's fables, to the delight of generations. Many pantomimes, arising out of fairytales and folklore, feature a clever

Cloaked cat
One of the best known of all cat stories is Frenchman Charles Perrault's *Puss in Boots*. A well-loved but wily trickster, *le chat botté* is illustrated here by Perrault's fellow countryman Gustave Doré (1832–1883).

CAT GOT YOUR TONGUE?

Throughout history, few other animals have provided as much scope for well-known and wise statements as the humble cat. If it's raining cats and dogs outside (pouring down) and you've let the cat out of the bag (revealed a secret by mistake), then you probably won't be feeling like the cat's whiskers (better than everyone else) and it's likely you won't have a cat in hell's chance (no chance whatever) of being forgiven. Still, there's more than one way to skin a cat (multiple ways of doing something), and if a black cat crosses your path – who knows? – you might even find yourself sitting tight in a catbird seat (in a favourable position).

LUCKY BLACK CAT

cat whose machinations aid its human friends. While the French fairytale writer Charles Perrault's (1623–1703) *Puss in Boots* and firm English favourite *Dick Whittington* are famous for their cat characters, whose wit and magic (and lack of scruples) help the heroes along to good fortune, other pantomime cats have been lost. In the original Italian version of Cinderella, the benevolent fairy godmother figure was a cat.

FAIRYTALES AND FOLKTALES

Just as *Puss in Boots* takes on human attributes and clothes, cats transforming into humans are a staple of fairytales and folktales. The Japanese myth of the wretched, vampire-like demon cat entails a creature that sucks away the lifeblood of a maiden and assumes her identity. The cat uses its human form to prey upon the girl's lover, who is saved from the brink of death by a loyal and watchful servant. Similarly, Spanish-Jewish folklore

Hat trick
First published in the United States in 1957, Dr Seuss's rhyming children's book *The Cat in the Hat* tells the story of a mischievous yet chaotically charming feline in a striped stove-pipe hat who appears from nowhere to enthral Sally and her older brother.

recounts that Adam's first wife, Lilith, became a black vampire-cat, sucking the blood of sleeping babies. This horrific myth may well lie at the root of the superstition that a cat will smother a sleeping baby or suck the child's breath.

CHILDREN'S LITERATURE
Children's stories often have their roots in fairytales and folklore. The delightfully illustrated children's books by Beatrix Potter (1866–1943) present likeable and fallible creatures in whom we can recognize our own flaws, such as the naughty but appealing Tom Kitten. American author Kathleen Hale (1898–2000) based her hugely successful series starring affable marmalade cat Orlando and his family on her own cats. The classic tale *The Cat that Walked by Himself* by Rudyard Kipling (1865–1936) recounts that the cat was never tamed, but made a mutually beneficial compact with humans, retaining its independence.

ODES TO THE CAT
Some of the best-loved children's poetry involves cats, like the comic work *The Owl and the Pussycat* by British humorist Edward Lear (1812–1888), based on his own beloved tabby, Foss. The renowned American poet TS Eliot (1888–1965) expressed his form of ailurophilia in the

Old Possum's Book of Practical Cats. These poems, which place idiosyncratic, but instantly recognizable, cats in human situations form the basis for the long-running musical *Cats*. Perhaps the most famous comic cat is the Cheshire Cat in the enduringly popular *Alice in Wonderland*, written by Lewis Carroll (1832–1898). Having the ability to disappear, leaving behind just a disembodied grin, this enigmatic character recalls the magic and sorcery long associated with cats.

Carroll's take on the cat
In Lewis Carroll's famous tale *Alice in Wonderland*, the enigmatic Cheshire Cat appears and disappears at will. This enchanting illustration, by ML Kirk, was created in 1910.

Cats in literature and entertainment

Cats have for centuries proved to be a favoured subject of the writer, appearing in fables, proverbs, stories, essays, and poems. Meanwhile, cats with successful careers in entertainment are a rarity, but those that do tread the boards always take centre stage.

PROVERBS AND PITHY PUSS SAYINGS

Cat proverbs are found in all languages. From China comes the comment, "A lame cat is better than a swift horse when rats infest the palace," while a proverb from the southern states of America has it that "The cat is mighty dignified, until the dog comes by".

A plethora of cat-loving writers have made memorable comments about their favourite felines. The British Prime Minister Sir Winston Churchill, who was awarded the Nobel Prize for Literature in 1953, reportedly said, "All dogs look up to you. All cats look down on you. Only a pig looks at you as an equal." Théophile Gautier added that "The cat is a dilettante in fur". Famous poets from Wordsworth to Baudelaire have also eulogized their feline friends.

Cat tales
The Russian playwright and writer of short stories Anton Chekhov, pictured with his wife, Olga Knipper, chose cats as the focal point of several of his stories, including *Who was to Blame?* and *An Incident*.

CATS IN PRINT

Many authors of fictional works have reconstructed their own real-life "cat experiences" to great effect. Anton Chekhov (1860–1904) wrote of the disastrous attempt his uncle Pyotr made to train Anton's kitten to kill mice, and the consequent effect this had on Anton's learning of Latin. In her short story *The Cat*, Colette recounts the story of Saha, a Russian Blue, which won the heart of his male owner after his jealous wife

attempted to kill the cat. Saki (1870-1916), whose real name was HH Munro, created the humanized Tobermory, a cat that acquired the gift of speech to devastating effect.

For those with a combined love of cats and mystery, there is a specific genre of books available – the detective novel. At the turn of the 20th century, Guy Boothby, an Australian novelist, based his books on the sleuthing skills of Dr Nikola and Apollyon, a black cat. A little later, Dorothy L Sayers (1893–1957) gave her detective Lord Peter Wimsey a distinctive crest, featuring a cat alongside the motto "As my whimsy takes me".

During the 1980s, publishers discovered that "the cat book" sells. Serious tomes, such as *The Literary Companion to Cats* and *The Cat in Ancient Egypt*, now vie for the book buyer's attention with many more recreational titles, including *The Internet for Cats*, *Testing Your Cat's IQ*, and *Yoga for Cats*.

CATS AS PERFORMERS

Historically, cats have appeared only briefly in circuses and other entertainment. In the early 19th century, the Italian Pietro Capelli's troupe of cats toured Europe, performing trapeze acts and juggling with their hindlegs. Feline stage-and-screen performers made it big in the 20th century, from Pyewacket the Siamese cat in the 1958 film *Bell, Book, and Candle* to Audrey Hepburn's beloved confidant "Cat" in *Breakfast at Tiffany's* (1961). On television, the feline character Catwoman made her first screen appearance in the 1950s' television version of *Batman*.

THE MOSCOW CAT THEATRE

Russian clown Yuri Kuklachev leads a troupe of cats that perform astounding acrobatic feats. The cats perform handstands, crawl along high wires, balance balls on their noses, jump from great heights, and even negotiate complex mazes. More than 120 cats now perform at the Moscow-based Kuklachev Cat Theatre, which was started more than 25 years ago. The cats perform six different plays in six separate weekend shows, each one lasting about two hours. Kuklachev says the secret to training cats is realizing that you can't force them to do anything.

Advertising has brought fame to many cats. In Britain, the all-white Arthur is well known for eating his food from the tin with his paw. Arthur's American equivalent, Morris, won a PATSY (an Oscar for animals) in 1973. Good advertisements appeal to our emotions and cats are ideal for representing what advertising experts classify as "female" values – warmth, beauty, capriciousness, and elegance. Cats suggest sensuality and cleanliness. With these associations, the future is bright for cats in entertainment.

The animal within

Halle Berry played the starring role in the 2004 movie *Catwoman*. In a mystical twist of fate, Patience Phillips is transformed into a woman with the strength, speed, agility, and senses of a cat.

Applause for claws
Cats – featuring the feline collective the Jellicles who attend the annual Jellicle Ball – appealed to ailurophiles the world over and was one of the longest-running theatre productions in history.

Cartoon cats

The feline image has long been used by cartoonists to portray satire and humour. From ancient Egypt to the present day, the domestic cat's image has been employed to comment on political or social matters, and has also been used to great effect in comic strips and television shows.

THE CONCEPT OF CAT CARTOONS

Cats often serve a dual role in cartoons, representing both feline and human behaviour. While the grace and elegance of the cat's movements translate effectively on to paper, it is in adapting the cat's facial features to convey human expressions – that the cartoonist can portray human characteristics in a feline guise.

HISTORICAL CARICATURES

The "cartoon cat" can be traced back to ancient Egypt, as the feline image was prominently depicted by stonemakers, sculptors, and painters not only in decoration of the tombs of the New Kingdom pharoahs, but also in satirical drawings on papyrus (reed paper). These sketches display simple cartoon drawings of cats as well as brutal commentaries on ancient Egyptian life.

In Russia, Tsar Peter the Great (1672–1725) was so unpopular that he was ridiculed by an unknown cartoonist who portrayed the despot as a large, inelegant cat, using the feline form as a particularly powerful tool in his political satire.

For centuries, Japanese artists have used the cat form in their observations, often employing feline fierceness and frailty to symbolize these same aspects of human nature. The popular Japanese artist Ando Hiroshige (1797–1858)

Early cartoon capers
This satirical scene from an Egyptian papyrus appears to turn the natural order of the animal kingdom on its head. A pair of kowtowing cats indulge the every whim of a regal-looking mouse, which sits impassively, wine glass in paw.

produced humanized cats that expressed human emotions and physical behaviour, but at the same time retained their feline features. Modern Japanese cat cartoons display a more Western influence, as seen in the popular *Doreamon* cartoon.

COMMERCIAL CARTOONS

The humanized cat was often used as a vehicle for satire in the West until the theme of sentimentality became popular in Victorian Britain. The artist Louis Wain (1860–1939), the second president of the British National Cat Club, produced much-loved caricatures of semi-human cats with particularly manlike features taking part in a variety of Victorian pastimes. Another artist, Théophile

Cat cards
These 20th-century playing cards illustrated by Austrian comic creator Manfred Deix are now collectors' items. His humorous illustrations are beautifully drawn, as exemplified in the king and ace of diamonds.

Steinlen (1859–1923), was a cat-lover who used felines in his work to advertise all manner of products, from tea and milk to cafés and veterinary clinics.

FAMILY FAVOURITES

The images of Wain and Steinlen paved the way for many other cartoon cats to entertain the public. The forerunner for this was the cheeky rogue Krazy Kat, the creation of American cartoonist George Herriman (1880–1944). The highly popular cartoon Felix the Cat, created by Otto Messmer (1892–1983), was the next to surface, and is still well loved today. Both Felix and Krazy Kat were brought to life via animation, a medium that paved the way for a host of familiar television favourites such as *Tom and Jerry*, *Top Cat*, and *Sylvester and Tweetie Pie*.

Other best-selling cat cartoons include the works of the French visual joker Siné (1928–) in which he created cleverly illustrated cat words, such as "cat alog" and "platy puss". American Bernard Kliban (1935–1990) conjured up the strongly striped and round-eyed signatory Kliban cat, while the inimitable cat

THE GROWTH OF DIGITAL ART

First there were cartoon cats. Then there were feline stars of animated film. Now it's the turn of another medium to propel cats into the limelight: digital art. Put simply, digital art is art that makes use of digital media such as computers and the Internet. Where once you could only watch Jerry hit Tom with a frying pan, now you can assist Jerry interactively.

illustrations of Englishman Ronald Searle (1920–) celebrated his fascination of his feline friends. But no cartoon cat has been as successful as the slovenly, lazy, greedy, cantankerous, self-centred, and, of course, fat *Garfield*, created by the American cartoonist Jim Davis (1945–). People all over the world instantly recognize both themselves and their cats in the character of Garfield, making the ginger whinger all the more loveable.

Corpulent kitty
Having previously made the transition from comic strip to cartoon character, in 2004 the world's idlest cat lumbered into animated film. In *Garfield: The Movie*, the lead saves his fellow pet, Odie the dog, from a kidnapper's clutches.

Cat collectables

For some people, collecting cat items is a major pastime. Due to a surge in the cat's popularity during the mid-19th century, artists, manufacturers, and later, advertisers, recognized the potential of exploiting feline imagery. This led to the emergence of a variety of cat merchandise.

MASS-PRODUCED CATS

Cultural artefacts that exemplify the role of cats in history are usually found in museums, art galleries, or in the sales of international auction houses. Whatever the case, they are inaccessible to most potential collectors. Perhaps this is why the "cat collectable" has become such big business. Modern manufacturing techniques have produced a plethora of collectable feline images that sell successfully worldwide.

It was during the 17th century that the true era of collectable cat ephemera began, as cat figurines became popular mantelpiece adornments. Those pieces made by Émile Gallé and Peter Carl Fabergé in the 19th century were in great demand, and are highly prized nowadays. Museums and collectors alike covet highly collectable cat items such as Chinese Ch'ing cats, Dutch Delftware cats, German Meissen cats, and Scottish Wemyss cats. It is possible that the craze for figurines may have resulted from the popularity of ladies' fans featuring images of cats, which originated from the East and spread across Europe from the 17th century. As the idea of the collectable took root, a profusion of cat-themed toys appeared, from the desirable Steiff soft-toy black cats, to Victorian articulated metal cats, clockwork cats from Europe, Japan, and China, and early board games from the United States.

POSTAL CATS

One of the most popular and accessible forms of collectable items is the cat postcard – an ideal starting point for any novice collector. Most countries joined the international postal system in the late 1800s, and postcards became a

STAMPS OF APPROVAL

Complementing postcards were postage stamps, another useful medium for displaying cats. The first stamp to feature a cat was issued in Spain in 1930, while the first "all-cats" set of stamps was produced in Poland in 1964. Most countries have capitalized on the collectable cat stamp, including Britain with a set of Elizabeth Blackadder's paintings of her three cats and those of her friends; Sweden with the Nordic goddess Freya; and France with a centenary stamp to celebrate the birth of its cat-loving novelist Colette.

Cat stamps
These examples of feline philately are from Holland (left) and Mongolia.

Popular puss ornaments
For those who cannot afford the fine porcelain cats of Meissen or Gallé, this charming ceramic cat pairing is a much more reasonably priced option.

fun and fashionable method of keeping in touch via the written word. Manufacturers reflected the popularity of the cat in their designs, which ranged from the dainty illustrations of Helena Maguire (1860–1909) to the caricature style of Arthur Thiele (1841–1919), and the anthropomorphization of Louis Wain (1860–1939). The various crazes have included showing cats in clothing, cat breeds, or sentimental cat pictures.

HALLOWEEN MEMORABILIA

In countries that celebrate Halloween, 31 October is a favoured date for cat-merchandise collectors. Sending special cards and decorating the house with cat designs is all part of the festival. For many centuries, black cats have been associated with witches and evil. Today, most of these negative connotations have been forgotten, with black cats now serving more decorative than frightening purposes.

CAT PROMOTIONS

Cats and kittens have figured prominently in advertising campaigns for over a century. Originally, the black cat was used, not because it was popular, but simply because the colour lent itself well to inexpensive mass production. One brand in particular

Cat pins
French designer Lea Stein has been making innovative designs in costume jewellery since the 1960s. These arresting Bacchus cat's-head pins from the early 1990s are made from a variety of colours of laminated rhodoid.

excelled, and advertisements for Black Cat cigarettes, matches, stockings, and other products can be bought for reasonable prices today. Other manufacturers have seen the potential in collectable cat advertising and have designed different labels for the same product. The makers of German wine *Zeller Schwarze Katz*, for example, also saw the potential in using a black cat to sell their wares. However, do not think that advertising remained the prerogative of the black cat. Advanced reproductive technology and changes in fashion for different breeds have resulted in a huge range of collectable items.

It is easy to start collecting any of these curios as a hobby, but for some enthusiasts the collection takes over their lives, as well as their homes. Special museums for private collections can now be found in Britain, the United States, Switzerland, The Netherlands, and Malaysia.

In a spin
Cats will chase virtually anything that moves. This postcard from early 20th-century Britain shows a curious-looking pet attempting to take the pace off a spinning top.

The cat's whiskers
Produced by Frederic Robinson's Brewery in Stockport, UK, the design on a bottle of Old Tom strong ale features the face of a winking cat. Containing a generously heady alcohol by volume content of 8.5 per cent, one wonders if this cat's had more than just the cream.

BREED DIVERSITY

DEFINING A BREED

The concept of breeds began in the mid-19th century, with the first cat shows (*see* pp.264–65). Today, over 100 different breeds and varieties of *Felis silvestris catus* are officially recognized worldwide. Some are "natural" breeds, originally indigenous to a particular country, while others have been bred selectively to perpetuate particular characteristics.

THE NEED TO BREED

It's difficult to say exactly what a breed is. Not all breeds are recognized by the same cat registries, and a breed might be named one way in one registry and differently in another. Put simply, the majority of pet cats are still random-bred – that is, their parents chose their own mates without human intervention. Pedigree cats, on the other hand, have been bred selectively by humans depending on body shape, coat colour, and any other qualities they feel best exemplify the breed. A cat with good pedigree has a large number of ancestors that reached championship status in the show ring.

Professional cat breeders understand the difference between dominant and recessive genes; for example the tabby gene is dominant over the black gene. They also have a keen grasp of the founder effect – the powerful genetic influence the first cats in a breeding programme have on their descendants. This knowledge has helped breeders to create cats with short or no tails, curled ears, shortened long bones, or with a lack of hair, as well as to breed in such a

Deceptive appearances
This Canadian Sphynx is bred for its hairlessness, but in truth it is covered in short, silky, "peach-fuzz" down.

way as to perpetuate specific desired coat colours or patterns.

Breeds are perhaps most commonly differentiated by face and body shape. For example, some Persians have flat faces while many Orientals have very long noses. Selective breeding has unwittingly led to a personality exaggeration within particular breeds: the placid Ragdoll, as an example, is now increasingly bred for its agreeable temperament.

With scientific advances, increasingly sophisticated and controversial techniques will become available to breeders. Cats have already been cloned, and geneticists say it is possible to engineer a cat that cannot produce allergies in humans. The exact definition of a breed looks set to continue to be debated for some time yet.

Bred for brushing
Ever-greater coat length is the reason behind these brown classic tabby kittens' appearance.

Out of Africa
Of Ethiopian descent, the Abyssinian is a breed renowned for being both opinionated and an attention-seeking athlete.

Feline genetics

Genetics is the study of how, in all living things, the characteristics and qualities of parents are given to their children by their genes. The basis is the same for cats as it is for humans: all the information needed for life is carried in the genes contained in each body cell.

THE ABCs OF DNA

The discovery of DNA, the genetic storage system that is the basis of life, led to a new understanding of the influence of genetics on physical characteristics, emotional behaviour, and disease. Every cell in a cat's body contains a nucleus at some stage in its development. Each nucleus contains 38 chromosomes, arranged in 19 pairs. Each chromosome is formed from deoxyribonucleic acid (DNA), which in turn is made up of thousands of genes. Each gene is made from four chemical components, called bases – A, T, C, and G. The combination of these bases provides the information for all aspects of a cat's life.

COPYING AND INHERITANCE

Each time a cell, such as a skin cell, is replaced, its chromosomes are copied. Data is passed down the generations in a different way. Egg and sperm cells contain 19 chromosomes, each one half of a pair. When cats mate, the 19 chromosomes in the egg unite with the 19 in the sperm, creating a new, unique set of 19 pairs. Specific information about a trait, like eye colour, is always carried at the same site on each chromosome: in a pair of chromosomes, the pair of sites is called an allele. If the information is the same at both sites, the instructions are homozygous; if not, they are heterozygous. Mistakes, or mutations as they are known, sometimes occur in egg or sperm cells, creating new traits.

Chromosome

X-shape
All chromosomes except for one have this shape

DNA
Tightly coiled DNA forms chromosomes

Nucleus

Chromosomes
Half come from each parent

Cell

Nucleus
Carries all information needed for replicating cell

The basis of life
Every living cell contains a nucleus, in which 19 pairs of chromosomes are stored. All chromosomes are X-shaped, except the male gender chromosome, which is Y-shaped. Each chromosome, when unfurled, is a helix of four bases. This helix is called DNA.

DOMINANT AND RECESSIVE TRAITS

Genetic variations in the characteristics of a cat, for example coat length, are called dominant if only one half of an allele is needed to show its effect, and recessive if both parts of an allele are needed. Generally, original traits are dominant and new mutations recessive.

THE FOUNDER EFFECT

In large populations of cats, genetic mutations usually vanish in a short time, but in small, isolated populations, they are far more influential as they have more chance of surviving. The long-term genetic influence of early members of a cat population is called the "founder effect". The founders have a potent influence on a new population, which explains the genetic trait of polydactyly (extra toes) in New England, as well as the tailnessness of cats isolated on the Isle of Man.

BREEDS AND GENETIC DISEASES

Breeders use the laws of genetics to select for specific features such as colour or body type. Unfortunately, they may also unwittingly select for other hidden, dangerous genes. This is how genetic disease gains a foothold within a pure-bred line. Advances in feline gene-mapping and responsible breeding will eventually reduce disease risks.

Base pairs
These split, unzipping DNA, when cells are renewed

Spine
Sugar-phosphate spine holds base pairs in sequence

Base
The DNA sequence combines four chemical compounds called bases in a unique pattern

UNDERSTANDING GENES

A kitten receives two separate genes, one from each parent. If one gene carries instructions to make the coat tabby and the other to make it black, you could be forgiven for thinking the kitten will be somewhere between the two colours. This isn't the case, however, and it's all to do with dominant genes. Looking at inheritance of dominant genes can help us understand how a litter can include a range of different coat colours and patterns. The tabby, or agouti, gene (A) is dominant over the non-tabby gene (a). Only when two copies of the recessive gene are inherited will the coat be non-tabby. So, in the example to the right, all tabby/black crosses are tabby, but because they carry recessive black genes, if they are mated amongst themselves they will produce tabbies and black cats on a 3:1 ratio.

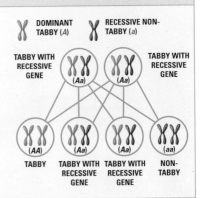

Coat colours and patterns

Whatever colour or patterns its coat displays, every cat remains a tabby in disguise. With domestication, the cat's wild, hunting camouflage was no longer essential to survival, and so today's endless variety of coat shades and patterns developed, masking the underlying "true" colouring.

THE SCIENCE OF HAIR COLOUR

Coloured hairs contain two components of melanin: phaeomelanin, which produces red and yellow, and eumelanin, producing black and brown. All colours are based on the varying amount of these pigments in the shafts of each hair. Ancestrally, cat hairs had alternating bands of pale and dark pigment in a pattern called "agouti" (*see* box, right). Cats with single-coloured, non-agouti hair are called self or solid. Self coats are recessive: the cat must carry two copies of the non-agouti gene in order to hide its true original tabby pattern.

Some cats have vibrant self coats in black, chocolate, cinnamon, or sex-linked red. This is thanks to the dense gene (D), which is dominant and ensures that each hair is loaded with pigment to give the richest colour. Other cats have lighter,

"dilute" coats in blue, lilac, fawn, or sex-linked cream. These cats have two copies of the recessive dilute gene (d), which results in less pigment in each hair: the effect is a paler shade of a dense colour.

SEX-LINKED RED

In cats, the gene for red or orange colour is located on the sex-determining X chromosome. In its dominant form (O), it makes the cat red; in its recessive form (o), it allows whatever other colour the cat is carrying to show. A male cat has only one copy of the gene, so if it carries one O it is red, and if it has one o it could be any other colour. The female cat can carry two copies of the gene. It is red if it has two copies of O, or another colour if it has two copies of o. Unlike males, a female cat can also be heterozygous (Oo).

Brown mackerel tabby and white: one of the earliest patterns

White self: blue-eyed whites are often deaf

Black self: solid colours are rare in the wild as they offer poor camouflage

White self: unlike their blue-eyed relations, orange-eyed whites aren't prone to deafness

Sex-linked red
The gene for the orange or red colour in this red classic tabby British Shorthair is dominant. In cats, this gene is found on the sex-determining X chromosome. Almost all red self cats show some faint "ghost" tabby markings.

This combination gives it a mosaic pattern of red and black known as tortoiseshell, or tortie. This combination interacts with all other colour-controlling genes, producing torties in solid and dilute colours.

WESTERN AND EASTERN COLOURS
Traditionally, Western cat-coat colours are black and its dilute blue, red and its dilute cream, their bicolour versions, and solid white. Western breeds, such as

AGOUTI ANCESTORS

The domestic cat's ancestor, the African wildcat (*Felis silvestris lybica*), is a striped tabby, camouflaged for surviving in the wild. The hair between the tabby stripes or spots contains bands of colour, almost always light at the base and dark at the tip. Other animals display this colour-banded pattern in their coats, including mice, squirrels, and the agouti, the rodent after which the pattern is named.

European Shorthairs (*see* pp.93–93), Maine Coons (*see* pp.168–71), and Norwegian Forest Cats (*see* pp.172–75), began in these colours only. The traditional Eastern colours are chocolate and its dilute lilac, and cinnamon and its dilute fawn. Some colours have been transposed from one group to another. In

Red self coats often show ghost markings on the tail, face, and legs

Brown mackerel tabby with heavy rufousing (a rich orangish-gold brown colour in the ticked hairs), which is a polygenetic trait

Coats for all seasons
The primary purpose of the cat's coat is to provide insulation against cold, heat, and wet. Cat fur comes in many guises, and selective breeding from natural mutations has led to the development of a wide range of coat colours in pedigree domestic cats that aren't seen in wild felines.

Black-and-white: the spotting gene (S) causes white blotches

Dark, symmetrical markings

White underparts and legs

Two-tone cat
A bicolour coat consists of white hair mixed with one other colour. This Ragdoll is a good example of a standard bicolour – between one-third and half its coat is white.

coloured and it passes on its colour potential to its young. A hint of a white cat's underlying colour may show on the head of a newborn kitten.

BICOLOURED CATS

Bicoloured cats are white-coated with patches of colour – tortie-and-whites are variously classified as bicolour or tricolour – and come in two types. The standard bicolour is defined as being one-third to half white, with the white concentrated on the underparts and legs. The Van pattern, originally associated solely with the Turkish Van but now also seen in other cats, consists of predominant white with solid or tortoiseshell patches restricted to the head and tail.

the UK, British Shorthairs are accepted in Eastern colours; similarly Burmese are often bred in red and cream. Conservative cat associations, however, do not accept transposed colours in these breeds.

WHITE CATS

White is dominant over all other colour genes, whether as all-over white (W), or as the white spotting gene (S). White hair contains no colour-producing pigment. Even if a white cat carries the dominant W gene, which masks the expression of all other colours, it is genetically

TAMEABILITY

The variety of feline coat colours and patterns may be more than cosmetic. Research in other animals has suggested a relationship between "tameability" and non-agouti coats. Population geneticist Dr Neil Todd studied the distribution of feline coat colours and found ever-increasing percentages of non-agouti coats along old trade routes out of Africa and up the rivers of Europe. In Britain, the end of the routes, he found the highest percentages of non-agouti cats. Todd holds that, along these routes, human selection favoured the tamest cats. Long before the registries began, owners may already have been picking their cats by colour.

The mighty white
The dominant white gene often adversely affects the inner ear structures. Thus, white cats have a tendency to deafness. The nose and ear tips of white cats can also burn easily in the sun.

DOMINANT PATTERN

Even cats with self coats carry some form of the tabby gene. The dominant agouti gene is called *A*, and any cat that inherits it from at least one parent will have a patterned coat. A cat that inherits the genetically recessive alternative to agouti (non-agouti, or *a*) from both parents will have a coat that appears solid, but careful examination may reveal tabby markings.

There are four basic types of tabby patterns, and all are variations of the same tabby gene:

■ Mackerel, or striped: narrow, parallel stripes run from the spine down the flanks to the belly.
■ Classic, or blotched: wide stripes form "oyster" swirls on the flanks, centred on a blotch.
■ Ticked, or Abyssinian: clear markings are restricted to the head, legs, and tail. The body is softly flecked.
■ Spotted: spotted body, often with striped legs and tail.

MACKEREL

CLASSIC

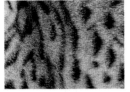

TICKED

SPOTTED

COLOURPOINT PATTERNS

The *I* gene (*see* box, left) is not the only gene to restrict colour. Restriction of colour to the extremities is called pointing. Pointed cats are light on their bodies and darker on their ears, feet, tail, and nose. A heat-sensitive enzyme in the cat's pigmenting cells controls this pattern. Normal body temperature inhibits pigment production over most of the body, but the enzyme is activated and hair pigmented where skin temperature is lower. Because it is temperature-sensitive, kittens are born white, cats in cool countries have darker coats than those in warmer climates, and all cats' bodies darken with age.

Bright, blue eyes

Dark seal-coloured tail

Clearly defined mask, matching point colour

The pointing pattern
"Colourpoint" describes a cat whose face, ears, feet, and tail are a different colour to the rest of its body, such as in this seal point Siamese. The trait is also common in longhaired breeds, and whatever colour its coat, a Colourpoint's eyes are always bright sapphire-blue.

Lighter, ivory body shade

Dense points, all matching in shade

Range of body shapes and forms

Most cat breeds are defined by their type – the distinctive shape of the face and body – and sometimes by other physical traits. A breed's type shows its origin, from the West to the East. Personality is linked to body shape: lean breeds are generally livelier than compact ones.

COLD-WEATHER CATS

The heaviest and most compact of domestic cats evolved through natural selection in cold climates. Breeds such as the British Shorthair (*see* pp.88–89) and American Shorthair (*see* pp.96–97) have large, round heads, short, broad muzzles, solid bodies with broad chests, sturdy legs and round paws, and short to medium-length, thick tails. They are built to retain as much body heat as possible.

The original longhaired cats, the Persians (Longhairs) (*see* pp.154–57), were also thickset and muscular, in order for them to withstand the harsh winters of Turkey and Iran. Other longhairs evolved in cold climates from farm cats that lived partly outdoors. Norwegian Forest Cats (*see* pp.172–75) and Maine Coons (*see* pp.168–71) have moderately long faces that make it easier for them to catch prey.

SEMI-FOREIGN BREEDS

A second group of cats has physical characteristics that fall between the muscular cats of northern Europe

A cat built for the cold
With a history of mousing and having to fend for itself in city alleyways, the British Shorthair is a robust, solid breed, designed for warmth in cold, wet winters.

Wedge-shaped, robust head

Lean, muscular body

Foreign affair
Abyssinians, like this one, and Turkish Angoras are categorized as semi-foreign, because their physical characteristics combine those of European and Asian cats.

and the more lithe cats of Africa and Asia. These lean but muscular cats are known as "semi-foreign". Breeds like the Turkish Angora (*see* pp.183–85) and Abyssinian (*see* pp.112–15) have slightly oval, slanted eyes set in moderately wedge-shaped heads, slender but muscular legs, oval paws, and long, gently tapering tails.

ORIENTAL BREEDS

Evolving in warmer climates where losing excess body heat was more important than conserving it, Oriental breeds are the most slightly built cats. With their large-eared, wedge-shaped heads, fine legs, slender bodies, and long,

FACE SHAPES

Until we began to breed cats selectively to appeal to our varying aesthetic tastes, the predominant face shape was (and still is) moderately round, with a mild wedge shape, ideal for capturing prey. In some Eastern breeds, the wedge shape has been accentuated; more recently, exceedingly so. The opposite has been achieved with some Persians, producing a flattened face, as has been done with the Pekingese breed of dog.

FLATTENED FACE (PERSIAN)

ROUNDED WEDGE FACE (BENGAL)

EXTREME WEDGE FACE (DEVON REX)

thin tails, these cats have developed maximum body surface area for their size in order to efficiently dissipate excess heat. Orientals traditionally have oval, slanted eyes, the most popular example of this being the Siamese (*see* pp.124–27).

Newer breeds have been created in the West to recreate the Oriental style. The Oriental Shorthair (*see* pp.128–29), the solid-coloured version of the Siamese, was created in the West, after non-pointed shorthaired cats from South-east Asia died out from among the original Siamese imports.

DISTINCTION OR DEFECT?

A few breeds are classified according to a single anatomical feature, often arguably a malformation. For example, the taillessness of the Manx is associated with potentially lethal medical conditions. Other cats have extra toes, a similarly unusual physical trait. The most striking change in the build of cats is the Munchkin (pictured). This is a deliberately dwarfed breed: most of the bones in the body are normal, but the long bones of the legs are dramatically shortened. The domestic cat evolved to its virtual perfection over thousands of years. Human interventions that threaten such flawless progression seem particularly arrogant and unwarranted.

NEW DEPARTURES IN BUILD

The possibility of breeding bigger or smaller cats is intriguing. However, unlike dogs, the domestic cat appears to have a genetically pre-determined, limited size range. When breeding for large or small size has been tried, the cats have reverted to normal domestic-cat size in the next generation. Only outcrossing to another species is likely to change this, although this remains a controversial move.

Large ears help to disperse heat

Cool customer
Breeds from Near, Middle, and Far Eastern countries like this Oriental Shorthair have light builds, meaning they are perfectly suited to hot climates.

Long, medium-sized body maximizes surface area

Long, slim but muscular legs

Eye colour and shape

One particularly beautiful feature of the cat is its pair of large, deep eyes that are unusually large for the size of its head. Because cats' eyes are among their most appealing attributes, many breeders strive to breed for specific eye colour, creating a range of intense shades.

EYE COLOURS

Breeding has produced many eye colours in domestic cats from blue through green to orange. Their wildcat cousins have hazel or copper eyes, and on occasion they tend towards yellow or green.

Most eye colours are not governed by coat colour, although some breed standards do link the two: silver tabbies, for example, are often required to have green eyes, but genetically they can have copper or gold eyes. The only colour that is linked to the coat colour is blue. Blue eyes are caused by forms of albinism that lead to a lack of pigmentation in both the coat and the iris and occur in cats with a lot of white in their coats. Blue-eyed white cats are often deaf, because the gene causing the lack of pigment is linked to a gene that causes fluid to dry up in the hearing receptors in the cochlea.

Siamese (*see* pp.124–27) with blue eyes – discovered by the 19th-century naturalist Peter Pallas in the Caucasus – have a different source that may be associated with poor three-dimensional vision rather than with deafness. Early Siamese often squinted to compensate for this detriment, but breeding has removed the squint.

EYE SHAPE

Wildcats' eyes are oval and slightly slanted. While some North American standards are leaning towards rounder eyes, breeds regarded as close to the "natural" cat, such as the Maine Coon (*see* pp.168–71), have these "wild" eyes. Breeding has altered natural shape in two ways: eyes may be rounder, or more slanted. Old Western breeds, such as the Chartreux (*see* p.94), have round, prominent eyes. Almond-shaped, slanted eyes are most common in foreign or Oriental breeds although some Eastern cats, the Burmese (*see* pp.132–35) for example, do exhibit rounded eyes. Extremes of shape can lead to problems. Prominent eyes in flat faces are prone to tear overflow and infection, while extremely slanted eyes tend to retain mucus, increasing the chance of infection.

Round eyes
Relaxed margins make this blue-cream British Shorthair's eyes appear spherical. Regardless of aperture size, all cats' eyes are spherically shaped.

Wild looks
This domestic cat has eye colouring close to the wildcat's hazel or copper eyes. These hues are still probably the most common colours seen in the eyes of pet cats, adding a form of camouflage in keeping with the animals' natural coat colour.

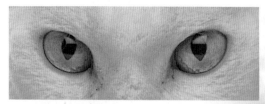

Almond-shaped, slanted eyes
A long face creates tension on the upper eyelid. This white Devon Rex's eyes are elliptically shaped – the so-called foreign look.

COLOUR VARIATIONS

Eye colour is controlled genetically. Pigment cells in the iris carry particles of brown, black, or yellowish colouring matter. Blue and green eyes arise from the scattering of reflected light through other colour pigments.

BLUE EYES
The lack of pigment in blue eyes allows higher absorption of sunlight, used by the body to produce vitamin D. This is why blue eyes are usually found in light-starved regions. Blue eyes vary considerably in depth.

YELLOW-TONED EYES
These eye colours are closest to those of wildcats. Many green eyes go through an early brown or yellow stage before they mature to their adult colour. Copper eyes may "fade" with age, while yellow-gold eyes can vary greatly in appearance.

GREEN-TONED EYES
Green eyes have become common in random-bred cats, and pure greens of varying shades define several breeds. The Chinchilla Longhair's sea-green eyes may be another route for breeders to achieve blue eyes in their cats.

Changing colours
Kittens are born with blue eyes, and their eyes change colour as they mature. Adult cats have eyes in shades of coppery brown, orange, yellow, green, and, occasionally, blue.

The future of breeding

Cat breeders increasingly aim to create eye-catching pets that are content to laze about as our household companions. Provoking ethical discussions, cloning is already a reality, and genetic advances mean breeding cats for a shopping list of characteristics will soon be possible.

CATS – THE NEW DOGS?

Cats may have replaced dogs as our most popular household companions, but that does not mean dogs have fallen out of favour. Changes in the way we live just make it more difficult to keep dogs, and cat breeders have, knowingly or otherwise, responded. The trend towards creating breeds, or at least describing new breeds, with dog-like traits looks set to run. In the future, cats will continue to be bred to greet you when you come home, to enjoy being walked on a lead, to be content to enjoy a relaxed indoor life, to be, in effect, small, indolent dogs that miaow rather than bark.

GENETICS AND BREEDING

The concept of parentage testing and DNA fingerprinting (from a simple buccal swab) in cats was originally developed with the help of Havana Brown breeders who were interested in the genetic diversity of their breed.

Fruits of scientific labour
In August 2004, a Californian-based cloning company created Peaches, above, a clone of Mango, an orange tabby cat two years older than Peaches. The ethical implications behind this science continue to cause debate.

Cloned cats on display
Two-year-old Bengal Tahini (right) and her one-year-old clone Baba Ganoush (left) make an appearance at a technology fair. Baba Ganoush is one of the first cats produced using a technique called chromatin transfer technology.

The Feline Genome Project, a worldwide operation set up in an effort to develop feline specific genetic tools and resources to improve feline and human health, yields ever-increasing quantities of data. As a result of the project's findings, breeders will be able to use new genetic information to breed more accurately for physical attributes. For example, polydactylism (extra toes) is a simple, genetically dominant trait that breeders

may wish to perpetuate in future by utilizing genetic testing to select their breeding stock. The flip side of these findings is that pernicious traits that would not survive naturally, such as hairlessness and dwarfism, will continue to be selected for.

THE CLONING CONUNDRUM

Cat cloning has been commercially available since 2004. Typically, all that is needed from the cat for it to be cloned is a small skin sample. Living cells within this sample contain DNA in their nuclei. The nuclei are removed and preserved by freezing in liquid nitrogen. Eventually, a nucleus is thawed and inserted into a feline egg that has been cleansed of its own DNA material. Using an electrical or chemical "shock", the nucleus and the egg are "fused". The lab then manipulates events so that the egg divides and becomes an embryo. The difference between this "fertilized" egg and a naturally fertilized type of egg is that its DNA comes from one source only, the donor, rather than from mother and father. Once the embryo is developing properly, it is inserted into the uterus of a "host mother". Cloning creates a genetic copy, the equivalent of an identical twin, but it does not produce copycat personalities.

HYBRID CATS

Incidences of domestic cats mating with a number of other small cat species, to produce healthy, fertile descendants, are on the increase. The Bengal, created by crossing the domestic cat with the Asian leopard cat, is already Britain's fourth most popular breed. Hybrid cats are banned from many cat registries, but breeding for cats that look like they just walked in from the wilderness is booming and shows no signs of slowing down in the foreseeable future.

CATS THAT DON'T INDUCE ALLERGY?

Many of us are allergic to cats, specifically to an allergen in their saliva and dander called Fel d1. But this is set to change. Using gene-silencing technology, geneticists plan to breed "hypoallergenic cats", individuals we are unlikely to be allergic to, starting in 2007. Over 1,500 of these British Shorthairs have been ordered. While this genetic manipulation would certainly benefit us, many people question exactly what role Fel d1 plays in the cat's life and are concerned about the consequences of eliminating a trait that evolution actively selected for in the feline family.

Coat reveals origins of mating between domestic cat with Asian leopard cat

Wild at heart
Many new breeds emulate wildcats. The Bengal was the first breed produced by mating a domestic cat with a wild species. This hybrid was followed by the Chausie (see p.121).

Siamese dream
This Siamese, an Oriental breed, developed in a warm climate. A physique combining short coat, large ears, and slender body means it is perfectly adapted to ridding itself of excess heat.

SHORTHAIRED CATS

The earliest varieties of cats were moderately sized, lean, and fine coated, much like the African wildcat from which they descended. Short hair was practical in temperate climates, and as cats have evolved, shorthaired breeds remain the most numerous. The density of short hair varies enormously, from luxuriously thick to positively naked.

THE SHORTHAIRS' SUCCESS STORY

The cat's coat consists of shiny, thick guard hair and duller, thinner insulating down. As shorthaired cats were transported out of Africa into the cooler climes of central and northern Europe, survival of the fittest was key: only individuals with denser, insulating, waterproof downy hair, thick guard hair, and stocky or cobby bodies would prevail. These cats later developed into the British and European Shorthair breeds (see pp.88–89 and 92–93). In turn, their descendants were taken by European explorers and immigrants to the New World where they formed the basis for such breeds as the American Shorthair (see pp.96–97).

In warmer climates, natural selection favoured small cats with thinner, sparser coats of guard hair and minimal – or even an absence of – insulating down. This coat helped to radiate excess heat. These cats grew lither and leaner than their ancestors, and are now known as foreign or, if extremely slender, Oriental breeds. The most popular cat of this type is the Siamese (see pp.124–27). Mutations in hair type have always occurred, but without human intervention they die out. It is only through selective breeding that breeds such as the American Wirehair (see p.98) and rexed cats (see pp.144–47) have flourished. Shorthairs also include the relatively hairless or even the totally bald (see pp.148–49).

The rex effect
In rexed cats, long- or shorthaired, the growth of hair is genetically retarded. This Cornish Rex has no guard hairs.

Best of British
The striking coat pattern of this British Shorthair Silver Spotted Tabby was one of the earliest variants to appear, in the 1880s.

EXOTIC

DATE OF ORIGIN 1960s
PLACE OF ORIGIN United States
ANCESTRY Persian, American Shorthair
WEIGHT RANGE 3.5–7kg (8–15lb)
COLOURS All self and tortie colours and bicolours in solid, smoke, shaded, and tipped, and classic tabby pattern
BREED REGISTRIES GCCF, FIFé, CFA, TICA

The Exotic is the result of an experiment that went wrong. Breeders were trying to produce an American Shorthair (*see* pp.96–97) with the shimmering coat and green eyes of a silver shaded Persian (*see* p.154): instead they got the Persian in a short coat. At first, it was proposed that these shorthaired silver cats could be developed under the name "Sterling" (a name that has also been suggested for silver Persians themselves), but more colours emerged and the Exotic was born instead. Similar crosses of Persians and British Shorthairs (*see* pp.88–89) were also made, and other cats used in the

development of the breed are known to have included the Burmese (*see* pp.132–35) and even Russian Shorthairs (*see* p.95), but once the shorthaired coat had been achieved, these crosses were always bred back to Persians for type. In the early stages there was some resistance from

Large, broad face with full cheeks

BLUE POINT COLOURPOINT

MISTAKEN IDENTITY

The Exotic is a classic example of a breed created by accident. Although the handsome results are not what was desired, demand for Exotics is strong and prices paid are generally high. The high value of members of the breed has tempted some people to crossbreed Exotics with cats possessing, for example, striking coat colours. The kittens are sold with falsified papers. Professional breeders call the activity "paperhanging". These deceptions often go unnoticed unless the cross accidentally produces kittens of dramatically different type. Some authorities claim this practice is of particular concern within breeds such as the Exotic.

Medium to large, cobby body, carried low on legs

Dense, plush coat, standing out from body

Compact cat
The Exotic's body is both cobby and muscular. Its other distinguishing features are its exaggerated flat face and eyes.

Short, bushy tail, normally carried uncurled

SHADED GOLDEN

Large, round,
prominent eyes

BLACK

Persian breeders, but the Exotic is now accepted in all major registries and is one of the most popular breeds in both Europe and North America.

FORM AND CHARACTER

Because the longhaired trait is recessive, the Exotic still produces longhaired variants (*see* p.167). The shortened face means that Exotics can suffer the same breathing problems as their longhaired cousins, and polycystic kidney disease is also present in the breed. Tear-duct conditions are common too, caused by lubricating tears failing to drain down the nasolacrimal duct into the nose and then overflowing down the face. When exposed to air, clear, colourless tears stain a deep mahogany colour. This is more an aesthetic than a medical problem.

The breed's soft, plush coat is thicker and somewhat longer than many shorthair coats, and it benefits from a little additional grooming to keep it looking its best. The coat, the flattened face, and the generally rounded, cobby build have led to Exotics being likened to teddy bears, an image that has contributed to their popularity. They have soft, quiet voices, and while they are generally more active than Persians they remain self-contained and easy-going pets.

Small ears with
rounded tips

CREAM-AND-BLUE

Large, round,
firm paws

BRITISH SHORTHAIR

DATE OF ORIGIN 1880s
PLACE OF ORIGIN Great Britain
ANCESTRY Household, street, and farm cats
WEIGHT RANGE 4–8kg (9–18lb)
COLOURS All self and tortie colours and bicolours, in solid, smoke, and tipped, in Western tabby patterns and pointed pattern
BREED REGISTRIES GCCF, FIFé, CFA, TICA

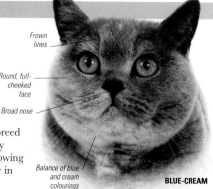

Frown lines

Round, full-cheeked face

Broad nose

Balance of blue and cream colourings

BLUE-CREAM

The original founding stock for this breed was drawn from the best of the sturdy everyday cats of Britain when the showing and breeding of cats became popular in the late 19th century. It was the most popular breed in the very first British cat shows. The founder of the Cat Fancy (*see* p.264) in Britain, Harrison Weir, bred British Blues. Nonetheless, the breed lost favour in the early part of the 20th century, and had almost died out by 1950. A concerted effort by breeders using cats from all over the Commonwealth revived its fortunes. By the 1970s, its future was secure and the British Blue had even become popular in North America. Today, the British Shorthair is the most popular pedigree cat in its native country. One curious trait that sets British Shorthairs

apart is that almost half of all cats in the breed have Type B blood, a particularly rare trait in the cat population at large.

FORM AND CHARACTER

The word most used to describe the British Shorthair is "cobby". This is a breed derived from robust farm cats, mousers, and street brawlers, and its looks remain true to its origins. A strong, muscular body is carried low on sturdy legs, and the broad, full face has a short, straight nose. The dense, crisp coat is weatherproof and practical, although it requires a little help from time to time to keep it looking its best. The classic Blues, Tortoiseshells, and Tabbies are still popular today, but the crosses made to revive the

Medium-sized ears with round tips

Dense coat, with crisp feel

Good width in shoulders

Short, strong legs

Compact, firm, and round paws

SILVER SPOTTED TABBY

breed brought in new genes. The result is that today a wide range of exotic colours and patterns is recognized in the breed in its homeland, reflecting the increased diversity of the domestic cat population in general. This remains, however, a stereotypically British breed: reserved and self-contained. It is gentle, but prefers only limited handling. Not known for its acrobatics or turn of speed, the British Shorthair is still a competent hunter when the opportunity arises.

TRUE COLOURS

Non-agouti, or solid-coloured cats, such as this white British Shorthair (below), became predominant in European domestic populations, as opposed to the sandy, ticked pattern of the original Egyptian cat. So great is this prevalence that Britain now has the highest proportion of solid-coloured cats. Why this is remains uncertain, although population geneticist Dr Neil Todd suggests that these cats may have been more tractable than other breeds, and thus more popular with cat owners.

British Blue
The British Blue is the most familiar of all British Shorthairs, not only because of its stunning looks, but also because it has featured regularly in popular TV commercials for cat food.

MANX

DATE OF ORIGIN Before 1700s
PLACE OF ORIGIN Isle of Man
ANCESTRY Household cats
WEIGHT RANGE 3.5–5.5kg (8–12lb)
COLOURS All self and tortie colours and bicolours, in solid, smoke, and tipped, in Western tabby patterns and pointed pattern
BREED REGISTRIES GCCF, FIFé, CFA, TICA

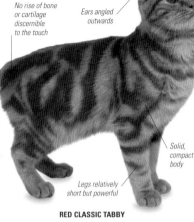

No rise of bone or cartilage discernible to the touch

Ears angled outwards

Solid, compact body

Legs relatively short but powerful

RED CLASSIC TABBY

Taillessness in cats usually dies out, but in the small, isolated cat population of the Isle of Man, this dominant mutation, unrelated to any of the other short-tailed breeds, persisted and became famous. The Manx was exhibited at shows in the 19th century and later exported in the early 20th century, becoming established in all major registries, although the CFA allows only traditional Western colours. The longhaired Manx, or Cymric (*see* p.177), is not as widely recognized. Manx come in four basic models: longies have almost normal, but often kinked, tails; stumpies have stubby tails; risers have a nub or cartilage; and rumpies have completely smooth rears or even a dimple. Show cats are all rumpies (except in FIFé), but are bred to the others to avoid potentially lethal deformity. The long hindlegs contributed to myths of rabbit hybridization, but although friendly, Manx are not bouncy, having the even-tempered personality typical of British cats.

CABBITS

In his publication *An Historical and Statistical Account of the Isle of Man* of 1854, writer Joseph Train described the existence of a cabbit, a cross between a female cat and a buck rabbit. The implicit suggestion was that it was a Manx cat that spawned this freakish offspring. "Cabbit" is now the name for a type of animal in Japanese animation.

Striking a balance
In spite of the absence of tail, the Manx breed has no problems with balance. Their longer-than-normal hindlegs may help to compensate.

SCOTTISH FOLD

DATE OF ORIGIN 1961
PLACE OF ORIGIN Scotland
ANCESTRY Farm cat, British and American Shorthairs
WEIGHT RANGE 2.5–6kg (6–13lb)
COLOURS Traditional Western self and tortie colours and bicolours in solid, smoke, shaded, and tipped, and traditional tabby patterns colours
BREED REGISTRIES CFA, TICA

Small ears, tightly folded to head

Large, round eyes, sweet in expression

BLUE-CREAM DOUBLE FOLD

The Fold mutation was first seen in Susie, a farm cat from Tayside. William Ross and his wife Mary bred a female kitten, Snooks, to a British Shorthair (*see* pp.88–89), and in 1971 sent some Folds to the United States, where development continued using American Shorthairs (*see* pp.96–97). North American registries now recognize both shorthairs and longhairs (*see* p.177), and TICA allows traditional Eastern colours and the pointed pattern. However, the breed is not accepted in Europe, in part due to the potentially crippling effects of the dominant gene if two Folds are bred together. The ears may have anything from a tight "triple" fold in show cats to a much looser "single" fold, where the ears bend forwards, in the cats generally sold as pets. Apart from its distinctive ears, the Scottish Fold has inherited a compact, sturdy build and a rounded head from the breeds used in its development. Modestly confident, these cats have generally retiring personalities and quiet voices.

TORTIE-AND-WHITE SINGLE FOLD

Folded ears, with rounded tips

Rounded head, with broad, short nose

Long, tapering tail preferred

Short, dense coat

Medium-length, fairly muscular legs

Medium-sized, sturdily built body

Neat, round paws

BLUE-AND-WHITE DOUBLE FOLD

EUROPEAN SHORTHAIR

DATE OF ORIGIN 1982
PLACE OF ORIGIN Mainland Europe
ANCESTRY Household cats, British Shorthair
WEIGHT RANGE 3.5–7kg (8–15lb)
COLOURS Traditional Western self and tortie colours and bicolours, in solid, smoke, and Western tabby patterns
BREED REGISTRIES FIFé

While there have been shorthaired cats in mainland Europe for almost two thousand years, the characteristic pedigrees were initially classified within the British Shorthair (*see* pp.88–89). In 1982, FIFé created a new category for this breed, which started with an established type and a large breeding stock of cats from documented backgrounds. Since then, the breed has diverged from the British type, and crosses to British Shorthairs are not permitted. However, it has failed to win either great popularity or widespread recognition beyond its original registry. The reason for this lack of renown may be that there is little that is novel or extraordinary about the breed.

FORM AND CHARACTER

Physically, the European Shorthair is a faithful reflection of the characteristics of free-breeding domestic cats that have populated Europe for centuries, and although more exotic colours and patterns have not been completely bred out of the pedigree lines, they cannot be shown. The breed's

Close to its roots
The looks, demeanour, and size range of the European Shorthair reflect its origins in mainland Europe's self-sufficient cats.

appearance is moderate in all respects. It has a medium to large, well-muscled body, but is not as heavily built or cobby as the British Shorthair. The broad head is triangular to rounded, with large, round eyes and medium-sized, upright ears. The coat is short but dense, springy, and insulating, making this a sturdy, all-weather, all-purpose cat. The nature of the breed is also typically that of a European household cat. Intelligent, but generally quiet and calm, and content in its own company, this cat neither demands nor receives a great deal of attention.

BLUE POINT

Triangular to rounded head, with well-defined muzzle

Short, dense coat, standing away from body

Medium to large body, well muscled, but not cobby

Medium-length tail tapers at base

Medium-length, well-muscled legs

BLACK SILVER MACKEREL TABBY

SMOOTH OPERATORS

The genes for short hair are dominant over the ones for long hair, meaning that if you spot a cat in the street, it is most likely to be sporting a naturally close-cropped coat. These cats have always enjoyed evolutionary advantages: short hair never tangles or catches on branches, wounds can be easily tended, and parasites don't find short hair such a welcoming environment in which to settle. So while longhaired cats may flaunt their hirsute handsomeness, in purely coat terms, it is svelte shorthairs who generally have the upper paw.

CHARTREUX

DATE OF ORIGIN Before 1700s
PLACE OF ORIGIN France
ANCESTRY Household cats
WEIGHT RANGE 3–7.5kg (7–17lb)
COLOURS Blue self only
BREED REGISTRIES FIFé, CFA, TICA

Blue or grey cats are said to have been brought to Europe from Syria during the Crusades. By the 18th century, the Chartreux was so well established that it had its own scientific name, *Felis catus coeruleus*, and was described as "the cat of France" by the naturalist Georges-Louis Leclerc, Comte de Buffon.

Natural colonies existed throughout France, but numbers were never very high and by the end of World War II,

the Chartreux was almost extinct. Breeders worked to preserve it, crossing with breeds such as the British Shorthair (*see* pp.88–89) to broaden the gene pool. Initially, FIFé included the Chartreux with the British Shorthair, but later they were separated.

Like most traditional European breeds, the Chartreux is a self-contained, stolid cat, less vocal than most and content to remain in the background. The stocky body is carried on surprisingly slender legs and clothed in a plush, dense coat that has a velvet sheen when properly groomed.

CAT FOOD

The Chartreux suffered a significant drop in numbers during World War II. Populations of all cat breeds were affected in some way, but times were even harder for cats without pedigrees. Cats are about the same size and build as rabbits, and rabbits for the pot were traditionally sold with the paws still attached, to prevent unscrupulous substitution. Where the English expression "to pull the wool over your eyes" describes an act of deception, the Germans, Spanish, and Portuguese all use phrases that refer to selling a cat as a hare or rabbit. Wartime food shortages meant some people could not be particular; cats were seen as a source of protein, and nicknamed "roof rabbits".

Large, round eyes, gold or copper in colour

Short to medium-length coat

Robust, densely muscled body

Short, sturdy but slim legs

Thick tail tapers at base

Home on the range
The Chartreux's coat gives little camouflage on grass, but provides superb cover for hunting in an urban setting.

RUSSIAN SHORTHAIRS

DATE OF ORIGIN Before 1800s
PLACE OF ORIGIN Russia
ANCESTRY Household cats
WEIGHT RANGE 3–5.5kg (7–12lb)
COLOURS Blue, black, white
BREED REGISTRIES GCCF, FIFé, CFA, TICA

RUSSIAN BLACK

The Russian Blue has long been accepted as a naturally occurring blue breed, like the Chartreux (*see* opposite) or Korat (*see* pp.142–43). It declined in the early 20th century, but was revived in the 1950s.

More recently, it has been claimed that the blue colour was not central to the breed in Russia. In the 1970s, Australian Mavis Jones bred from a white Russian cat, which had black and tabby genes. The Russian Black and Russian White are now accepted in Australia, New Zealand, and Britain, but not widely elsewhere. The Russian Tabby has progressed less.

In all coats, the Russian is a muscular, elegant cat with a long face, large ears, and limpid green eyes. It is a gentle and reserved breed, but dislikes change and stress, preferring a quiet home.

Large, almond-shaped, widely spaced eyes

Double coat, with very dense undercoat

Moderate-length tail, tapering to rounded tip

RUSSIAN BLUE

SELKIRK REX (SHORTHAIR)

DATE OF ORIGIN 1987
PLACE OF ORIGIN United States
ANCESTRY Rescued domestic cat, Persian, Exotic, British and American Shorthairs
WEIGHT RANGE 3–5kg (7–11lb)
COLOURS All colours and all patterns
BREED REGISTRIES GCCF, CFA, TICA

This newest of the rexed breeds has a Scottish-sounding name, and a build close to the British Shorthair (*see* pp.88–89), but it came into being in the US state of Montana. A female kitten with curly hair was born at For Pet's Sake, a rescue shelter run by Kitty Brown. Adopted by breeder Jeri Newman and named Miss DePesto of NoFace, she went on to produce more curly coated kittens, showing the gene to be dominant. The breed was named after the nearby Selkirk Mountains, and both shorthaired and longhaired (*see* pp.178–79) versions are now accepted in all major registries.

The Selkirk's thick coat forms random "clumps" rather than regular waves. It is unique among the recognized rex breeds in having a broad, full-cheeked head and substantial build, with sturdy legs that are similar to those of the British Shorthair. It is also typically Western in character, being a quiet, self-contained breed that is content to be the sole cat in a household.

Soft coat, falling in loose, individual curls

Muscular, rectangular body with slight rise to hindquarters

Large paws

BLUE-CREAM

AMERICAN SHORTHAIR

DATE OF ORIGIN 1900s
PLACE OF ORIGIN United States
ANCESTRY Domestic cats
WEIGHT RANGE 3.5–7kg (8–15lb)
COLOURS Traditional Western self and tortie colours and bicolours, in solid, smoke, shaded, or tipped, and classic or mackerel tabby
BREED REGISTRIES CFA, TICA, TCA

VAN PATTERN TABBY

American Shorthairs developed from ancestors of the British and European Shorthairs, which were taken to the US by the early settlers. Domestic cats are known to have arrived in North America with the first settlers as early as the 1500s, and they have been present in substantial numbers as working household and farm animals since the 1700s. It was only at the very end of the 19th century that showing and planned breeding of cats were taken seriously and American breeders realized that the characteristics of their domestic cats were worth preserving. The Domestic Shorthair, as it was at first called, was the result. The founding litter of the breed, born in 1904, was from a mating of American cats and British Shorthairs with known and stable genetic traits, and for a long time any American cat that met the standard could be registered, giving this breed a large gene pool. It was renamed the American Shorthair in 1966, and remains popular in Canada and the United States but uncommon elsewhere.

EARLY CAT SHOWS

Although cats had been shown in one way or another for centuries, the "beauty contest" style of modern shows and the registering of breeds goes back no further than the late 19th century. The first major show was held in Britain in 1871; the first American show in Madison Square Gardens, New York, in 1895. From the start, cats could command high prices, and at the second show in New York the following year a brown tabby American shorthair was offered for sale for $2,500. The Cat Fanciers' Association (CFA) was established in 1906 with five registered breeds, of which the Domestic Shorthair was one.

Showstopper
Beauty isn't always a guarantee of success in the show ring: an artist's impression from the 1870s of a champion half-breed wild cat.

FORM AND CHARACTER

The pressures of the North American environment, with a wider range of natural predators and prey than in Europe, ensured that the domestic cat evolved into a larger animal than its Old World counterparts, with a powerful body set on well-muscled legs. Size among

Medium-length, heavily muscled legs

Medium-length tail tapers to a rounded tip

American Shorthairs varies considerably: large males are often more than twice the size of females. In addition to this potential to be bulky, neutered cats have a tendency to obesity and their diet should be monitored. The breed's short coat is thick and hard in texture to provide protection against the cold, wet, and minor injuries. It is still bred to look like the cream of domestic cats, and is robust and long-lived, helped by an exemplary breed standard that disqualifies "any feature so exaggerated as to foster weakness". It is not an overly vocal or busy cat, but an even-tempered, amiable breed with a relaxed and no-nonsense approach to life.

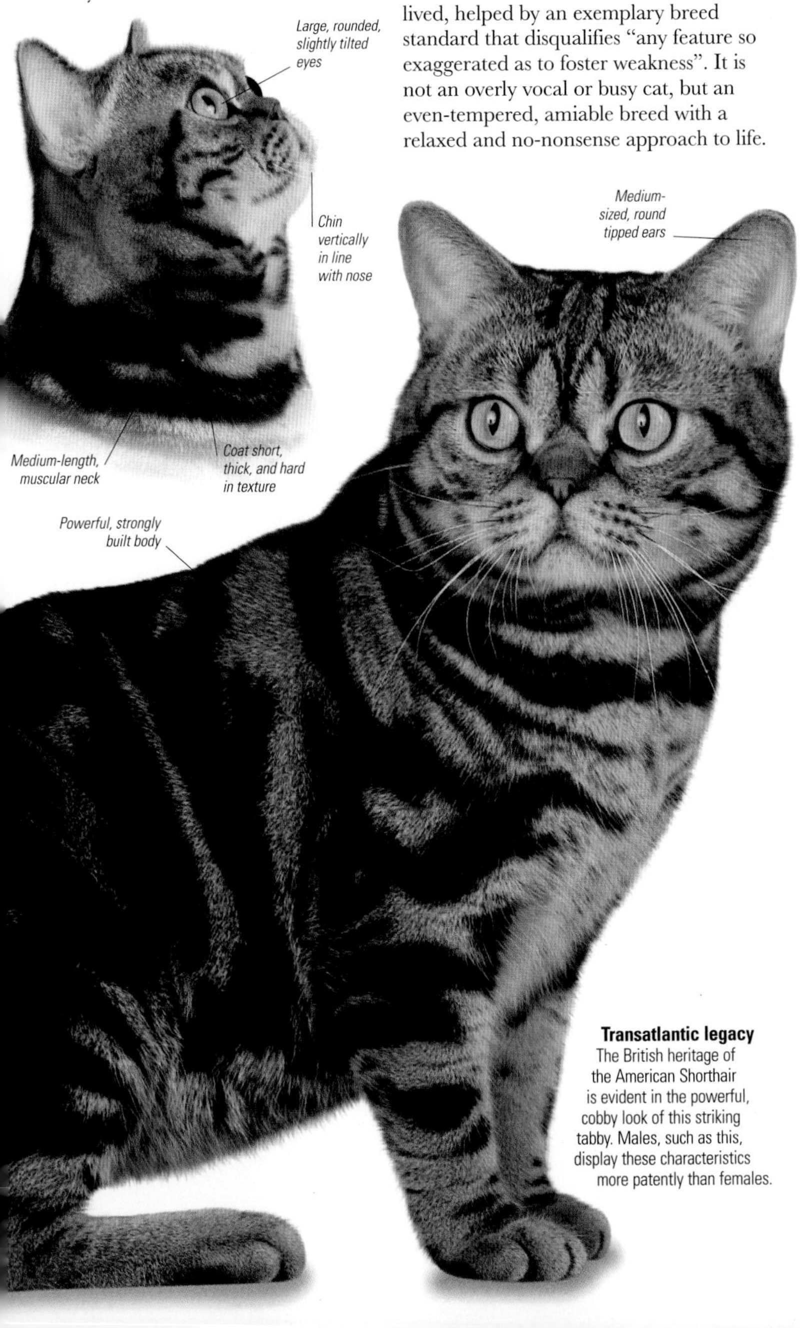

Large, rounded, slightly tilted eyes

Chin vertically in line with nose

Medium-sized, round tipped ears

Medium-length, muscular neck

Coat short, thick, and hard in texture

Powerful, strongly built body

Transatlantic legacy
The British heritage of the American Shorthair is evident in the powerful, cobby look of this striking tabby. Males, such as this, display these characteristics more patently than females.

AMERICAN WIREHAIR

DATE OF ORIGIN 1966
PLACE OF ORIGIN United States
ANCESTRY Farm cats
WEIGHT RANGE 3.5–7kg (8–15lb)
COLOURS Traditional Western self and tortie colours and bicolours, in solid, smoke, shaded, and tipped, and classic or mackerel tabby pattern
BREED REGISTRIES CFA, TICA

CREAM-AND-WHITE

The Wirehair coat is a dominant mutation first seen in a single kitten (named Council Rock Farm Adams of Hi-Fi), born to a litter from a farm in upstate New York in 1966. Wirehairs were developed using the American Shorthair (*see* pp.96–97), and in TICA the two are still classed as types of a single breed group. In the CFA, however, the Wirehair has its own separate classification. TICA also accepts all coat colours and patterns.

The coat of the Wirehair is hard, springy, and resilient with crimped or hooked hairs. The hardest coats look most striking, but can be brittle and fragile.

Longhaired kittens are occasionally produced, but these are not eligible for showing and have been unflatteringly described as "dust bunnies". Although not a particularly vocal breed, the Wirehair is friendly and active, and according to its advocates "knows no strangers".

Tortie-and-white
The white patches in tortie-and-white (also known as tricolour or calico) cats seem to be influenced by the dominant white spotting gene (*S*).

REX PROBLEMS

Curled, or rexed coats (pictured close-up, below), such as those of wirehaired breeds, can carry problems. The Wirehair has a tendency to allergies and the coat may be brittle, but it seems free of more serious conditions. Thankfully, most of these kinds of problems usually die out or remain limited in free-breeding populations. Some rexed coats have little or no undercoat, making them poor insulators. Others are inclined to bald patches, and at least two cases have been reported in which a female's hair fell out when she had kittens and grew back without any curl. The whiskers, an important part of the cat's sensory array, may be absent.

LAPERM (SHORTHAIR)

DATE OF ORIGIN 1982
PLACE OF ORIGIN United States
ANCESTRY Farm cats
WEIGHT RANGE 3.5–5.5kg (8–12lb)
COLOURS All colours, shades, and patterns
BREED REGISTRIES GCCF, CFA, TICA

The founder of this breed was born hairless in a litter of farm cats in The Dalles, Oregon. When she finally grew a coat, some eight weeks later, it was soft and curly. The owner, Linda Koehl, called her Curly and over the next five years produced more rexed kittens, the foundation of this breed. The gene responsible for the curly coat is dominant, so a wide gene pool can be established while still producing rexed kittens. The breed is now at least provisionally accepted in registries worldwide, and outcrossing is allowed to non-pedigree cats and, in Britain, a range of predominantly Oriental breeds.

This was the first longhaired rex breed, and it has been remarkably successful in gaining recognition. Examples of other recorded rexed longhairs have been mutations of established breeds, such as

Broad head with prominent muzzle

Short, thick, silky coat, with moderate undercoat

Long, tapering tail, with wavy hair

CHOCOLATE TABBY

the Bohemian Rex, a variant of the Persian (*see* pp.154–57), or the Maine Wave, a variant of the Maine Coon (*see* pp.168–71). These may have failed to win acceptance as much on political as on health grounds.

The type is elegant, with a wedge-shaped head and long legs, but it is far more moderate than either the Cornish Rex (*see* pp.144–45) or Devon Rex (*see* pp.146–47). Unlike those breeds, the short, silky coat of the LaPerm is thick, with a moderate undercoat. Although inquisitive and sociable, the breed is not one of the most conversational.

Busy body
The LaPerm sprang from robust farm rat-catchers, and early standards called for "excellent hunters". This requirement has now been dropped, but they are not idle lap cats.

AMERICAN CURL (SHORTHAIR)

DATE OF ORIGIN 1981
PLACE OF ORIGIN United States
ANCESTRY Household cats
WEIGHT RANGE 3–5kg (7–11lb)
COLOURS All self and tortie colours and bicolours, in solid, smoke, shaded, or tipped, and all tabby and pointed patterns
BREED REGISTRIES FIFé, CFA, TICA

The first American Curl was a stray, or street cat, from California, named Shulamith by Joe and Grace Ruga when they adopted her in 1981. When a breeding programme began a couple of years later, the trait was determined to be dominant and apparently without harmful side-effects. By the 1990s, the Curl was fully recognized in North America as both shorthair and longhair (*see* p.181). It has more recently spread to Europe, although it is still not accepted by the GCCF.

The distinctive feature of this breed is, of course, the ears, which are shaped in a curl by firm cartilage. Straight at birth, they develop to anything from a slight tilt to a complete curl with the tips pointing down at the back of the head; how they will turn out in any kitten is unpredictable. The American Curl is moderate in build, with a fine, close coat and a generally wedge-shaped head. Possibly due to some Oriental heritage, Curls are outgoing, playful, intensely curious, and sociable.

Ear furnishings desirable

Eyes have oval upper rim and rounded lower rim

SILVER TABBY

NOVEL MUTATIONS

While dog breeds have for centuries encompassed a wide range of sizes, shapes, faces, and ear types, such diversity in appearance is very new in the world of the domestic cat. Cats were not carefully bred selectively until the 19th century, and, unlike dogs, they have never been bred for a particular purpose, so the older breeds are defined largely by a general conformation or colour. This is changing rapidly, however, and there has been a tendency in recent decades to preserve, and perhaps even to seek out, novel mutations, such as curled coats, curled ears, or other marked physical differences. When such features are selected as a reason for breeding, it always causes controversy, and the results divide the opinions of breeders, registries, and cat lovers, but such breeds are here to stay.

Tail equal to length of body, wide at base, tapering to tip

Semi-foreign body shape, moderately muscled

Ears curve at least 90° in smooth arc

Wedge-shaped head with gentle curves

Soft, close-lying coat

BROWN SPOTTED TABBY

Medium-length legs

MUNCHKIN (SHORTHAIR)

DATE OF ORIGIN 1980s
PLACE OF ORIGIN United States
ANCESTRY Household cats
WEIGHT RANGE 2.5–4kg (6–9lb)
COLOURS All colours and all patterns
BREED REGISTRIES TICA

Short-legged cats are known to have appeared several times in the 19th century, but they usually disappeared without trace. The same might have happened in the 1980s in Louisiana, but this time the mutation got a helping human hand from Sandra Hochenedel, who adopted a short-legged black stray and used her kittens as the foundation of this breed. The long bones of the legs are stunted by the dominant gene; the shortest Munchkins are called "rughuggers".

It may be that the flexibility of the feline spine averts the sort of problems that are suffered by short-legged dogs, and breeders do claim that these are healthy, happy cats. Nonetheless, Munchkins are not widely accepted; they are banned by many registries in Europe and where they are accepted, they have had to undergo rigorous health investigations.

Aside from the extremely short legs, the Munchkin is moderate in appearance – its head is a rounded wedge shape with large,

WHITE

walnut-shaped, slightly tilted eyes, and its medium-length body is well-rounded but not thickset. There is also a longhaired version (*see* p.180).

Owners say they are lively and inquisitive, and that an accelerating Munchkin resembles a sports car, but their small stature makes an outdoor life comparatively risky for them.

Head almost triangular

Moderately large ears, wide at base

Medium-thick tail set high, tapering to rounded tip

TORTIE-AND-WHITE

Well-muscled legs, short but not misshapen

Short-changed
The Munchkin is bred selectively for dwarfism, a disproportionately short stature that does not survive without human intervention. Munchkins are not accepted by most cat registries.

AMERICAN BOBTAIL (SHORTHAIR)

DATE OF ORIGIN 1960s
PLACE OF ORIGIN United States
ANCESTRY Uncertain
WEIGHT RANGE 3–7kg (7–15lb)
COLOURS All colours and all patterns
BREED REGISTRIES CFA, TICA

Broad head with curved contours

Semi-cobby body, with substantial muscling

Tail must be present, but stops above the hock

Resilient double coat

SPOTTED TABBY

The American Bobtail traces its ancestry back to Yodie, a wild-looking stray tom picked up in Arizona by John and Brenda Sanders from Iowa. Early breeding efforts were aimed at creating something like a short-tailed Snowshoe (*see* p.139), but attempting to fix this complex pattern led to high levels of inbreeding and unhealthy cats. In the 1980s, the focus shifted to producing a wild-looking tabby based on Yodie's appearance, and the Bobtail finally won acceptance in the major North American registries, although it remains rare. The longhaired version (*see* p.197) was the first to be recognized as a breed.

Like the Manx (*see* p.90), Bobtails can have tails of varying lengths, or no tail at all; however, tailless cats are rare, and the mutation appears to be separate. The Bobtail, which is slow to mature, has a muscular build and hard coat that may look slightly shaggy. Despite the wild look that is aimed for in the breed standard, they are tolerant and friendly companions.

Adaptable pet
Bobtails are large and dramatic-looking cats, but they have playful and clownish natures that make them good family pets. In keeping with their wild look, they are a quiet breed, limiting their conversation to soft chirps and trills.

HYBRID CATS IN THE WILD

Whenever a short-tailed cat turns up in North America, there are rumours that it is a hybrid with the native bobcat (below) as one parent. Inevitably, this turns out to be no more than fancy. Such hybridization is highly unlikely, because the offspring would almost certainly suffer partial or complete sterility and be the first and last generation. Hybrid cat breeds are developed at the cost of time, patience, and a plenty of disappointment, and do not persist in the wild. The exceptions are the European wildcats, such as the Scottish wildcat, which are closely related to the domestic cat. The offspring cannot be domesticated, but the wildcat population may now contain many hybrid individuals.

BOBCAT

PIXIEBOB (SHORTHAIR)

DATE OF ORIGIN 1980s
PLACE OF ORIGIN United States
ANCESTRY Farm cats
WEIGHT RANGE 4–8kg (9–18lb)
COLOURS Brown spotted tabby
BREED REGISTRIES TICA

In North America, there is an anecdotal tradition of domestic cat to wild bobcat matings, with the offspring being known as "legend cats". When it appeared, the short-tailed Pixiebob was thought to be just such a hybrid, and it can be traced back to two "legend cats" acquired in 1985 by Carol Ann Brewer in Washington State, and their offspring Pixie. Similar "legend cats" were also used in its development. The breed was recognized by TICA in the 1990s, but remains a North American phenomenon. There is also a longhaired version (*see* p.197).

The aim in breeding Pixiebobs is to achieve a likeness of the bobcat. The tail must be short but present, and ideally not kinked, but the likeness must also extend to a certain amount of white around the eyes and tufts of hair on the tips of the ears. The personality of the breed, however, is utterly domestic; this is a cat

BROWN TABBY

that prefers a peaceful and stable home life. They have been likened to a faithful dog and seem to prefer to be an only cat, in a house where they can rule the roost.

Wild thing
Although the Pixiebob gives a good impression of a wild animal that has wandered into the garden, there is no genetic evidence that it originated from a hybrid cat.

AMERICAN RINGTAIL

DATE OF ORIGIN 1999
PLACE OF ORIGIN United States
ANCESTRY Household cats
WEIGHT RANGE 3–7kg (7–15lb)
COLOURS All colours and all patterns
BREED REGISTRIES Working with TICA

*Head slightly
longer than
it is wide*

*Medium-sized,
well-muscled,
firm body*

BLUE-AND-WH▶

In 1998, American breeder Susan
Manley was given Solomon, a two-
day-old kitten found in Fremont,
California, who carried his tail in a
ring with the tip centered over his
back. This trait, which is occasionally
seen in cats, was relatively common
in the locality, and was inherited
by Solomon's offspring.

The curl is not due to fused bones;
the tail moves normally. The muscles
at the base are larger and stronger than

*Forelegs
slightly shorter
than hindlegs*

*Long, distinctive,
flexible tail*

CURLED TAILS

Curly tails in cats have been recorded for decades.
They range from a loose circle to a spiral, and it is not
certain whether the same genes are involved in every
case. The curl seems harmless and is quite unlike the
kinked tail of breeds such as the Japanese Bobtail, in
which the bones are fused. It is, nonetheless,
sometimes seen as a deformity, and
may lead to the tail being
amputated. Curled tails would
be a fault under most pedigree
cat standards, but since the
American Ringtail appeared
and curly tails became
interesting, breeders have begun
to report a trait they might
otherwise have overlooked.

usual, and breeders allege that
Ringtails curl their tails around
things, like monkeys.

Ringtails are lean and
muscular, with a short plush coat;
a longhaired version is planned.
Gregarious, highly active, and curious,
they may be destructive if kept indoors
without company and entertainment.
The breed briefly rejoiced in the
title Ringtail Sing-a-Ling,
referring to the cats'
greeting "trill", but
is now more
soberly named.

*Large ears set
low on head*

*Tail substantial,
not whippy*

*Strong,
athletic legs*

BLUE

ANTIPODEAN

DATE OF ORIGIN 1990s
PLACE OF ORIGIN New Zealand and Australia
ANCESTRY Household cats
WEIGHT RANGE 3.5–7kg (8–15lb)
COLOURS Traditional Western self and tortie colours and bicolours in solid, smoke, shaded, tipped, and tabby patterns
BREED REGISTRIES CATZ Inc

Medium-sized head

Muscular build

Extra toe(s) on forepaws and hindpaws

CLIPPERCAT

This breed was at first known as the New Zealand Shorthair: the name change reflects both the inclusion of a longhair standard and the increased work that has been done on the breed in Australia. The Antipodean is drawn from typical household and working cats, descended from the cats that travelled with early settlers from Europe. It is on the way to full recognition by registries in its homelands, including the New Zealand-based CATZ Inc.

The Antipodean is moderate in all ways, being medium-sized, of muscular build, and with a gently rounded, wedge-shaped head. There is a subset of the breed, known as the Clippercat, which is essentially an Antipodean with extra toes. This harmless trait, called polydactyly, is found in cats across the world, but is not very widely permitted in pedigree breeds. The genetic heritage of both cats is that of robust, long-lived felines that are intelligent, adaptable, and equally able to fend for themselves or fit into family life. As a newly established breed, the Antipodean still accepts for registry any domestic cats that meet the breed criteria, regardless of unknown parentage. This provides the breed with a wide genetic base right from the beginning.

Seasonal colour
Black cats often turn "rusty" in strong sunlight, and can look more like dark chocolates. Keeping a cat jet black for the show ring can be difficult in Australia's sunny climate, so many breeders choose to keep their cats indoors.

AUSTRALIAN MIST

DATE OF ORIGIN 1975
PLACE OF ORIGIN Australia
ANCESTRY Abyssinian, Burmese, non-pedigree shorthairs
WEIGHT RANGE 3.5–6kg (8–13lb)
COLOURS Traditional Eastern colours in spotted tabby pattern
BREED REGISTRIES ACFA

Australia's first "home-grown" breed was developed by Dr Truda Staede in New South Wales. As well as having household cats, Dr Staede owned and showed Burmese (*see* pp.134–35) and Abyssinians (*see* pp.112–15), and a hybrid mating gave her the idea for developing an attractive cat with a ticked and spotted coat overlaid with sepia shading, and possessing the

LILAC

home-loving, people-orientated Burmese personality. Paying rigorous attention to genetics, she created a breed that is now well-established in Australia, but remains extremely rare everywhere else.

At first, the new breed was called the Spotted Mist, but the introduction of a second pattern, the Marbled, made a change of name inevitable. Since 1998, it has been called the Australian Mist, the name Dr Staede always hoped for. New breeding lines are still being introduced to give the cat the best possible genetic base for health, as well as to improve the coat.

FORM AND CHARACTER

The short, close Australian Mist coat is a spotted or marbled tabby pattern with added Abyssinian ticking, which gives a soft, misty effect; the sepia pointing further lightens the coat, except at the extremities. Breeders also select for "rufous" or warm coat colours, aiming for the rich reddish shades of the Abyssinian,

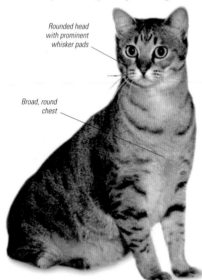

Rounded head with prominent whisker pads

Broad, round chest

BROWN SPOTTED

CATS AND WILDLIFE

The effects that cats have on wildlife often produce heated arguments, but they are not always rational. In Australia, the perceived problem has led to suggestions that all cats be kept under curfew at night, allowed outside only on a lead at any time, declawed, culled, or banned outright. Cats can be highly efficient predators, but it seems that some studies behind these suggestions lack a sound statistical base. Where wildlife, including the kookaburra (pictured) and other birds, is under threat, cats may not be the main culprits: a range of factors, such as roadkill, farming practices, and human encroachment are usually also involved. Changing these requires considerable effort from the whole population; the cat may be a relatively small part of the overall problem, but it is a very easy target.

rather than the cool colouring of the similarly ticked Singapura (*see* pp.110–11). Brown, blue, chocolate, and lilac are all recognized and named as in other breeds, but the cinnamon and fawn shades are sufficiently light and warm that, in this breed, they are known as gold and peach.

The Mist is sociable, and a gentle and affectionate family cat that will happily share its home with children or other cats. Many in Australia hoped it would have a diminished hunting instinct, and would be happy with life indoors, but while its relaxed character makes it amenable to staying indoors, the hunting instinct is not fully eradicated. This cat also has masses of energy, so those who choose the Mist as an indoor cat must be prepared to provide it with plenty of entertainment.

Keeping young
With the aim of producing long-lived cats, these Australian Mist kittens have been bred deliberately for late sexual maturity using domestic tabbies.

Dense, glossy coat

Firm, muscular body with rounded contours

Legs strong but not thickset

Long, thick tail, with almost no taper

PEACH SPOTTED

SINGAPURA

DATE OF ORIGIN 1975
PLACE OF ORIGIN Singapore and United States
ANCESTRY Disputed
WEIGHT RANGE 2–4kg (4–9lb)
COLOURS Sepia agouti (black in ticked tabby pattern with sepia pointing)
BREED REGISTRIES GCCF, CFA, TICA

Slender tail with blunt tip

Cats answering the general description of the Singapura have long been present in the free-breeding feline populations of Singapore. They are a distinctive strain among the feral cats of Singapore city, where they are known as "longkang", or drain cats. The founding stock of the recognized breed was shipped from Loyang, east of the city, to North America by Hal Meadows, whose wife Tommy bred Abyssinians (*see* pp.112–15), Siamese (*see* pp.124–27), and Burmese (*see* pp.132–35). It took just seven years for the breed to be recognized in North America, but much longer in Europe, where it remains rare. In its homeland, the Singapura has more recently been adopted as the mascot of the Singapore Tourist Board and declared a national treasure under the name of Kucinta, or "love cat".

FORM AND CHARACTER

The Singapura has a ticked tabby coat, like that of the Abyssinian, overlaid with the sepia pointing pattern of the Burmese to give a colouring called sepia agouti. Tommy Meadows already kept both these other breeds, which naturally made this new cat interesting to her, but this fact has also raised questions about whether they might have made any genetic contribution to the Singapura.

The size of the Singapura has also been a matter of some controversy. When these cats first caught the eye of Western breeders and the media, their diminutive stature was fancifully said to be a genetic adaptation as a result of living in small drains. However, the breed standard calls for a cat of small to medium size, and Western Singapuras are larger than the feral cats of Singapore.

Straight, broad muzzle

Warm coat colour

Legs muscular at the top, tapering elegantly to the paws

CAT SIZE

When the diminutive Singapuras first came to the West, they seemed to hold the promise of miniaturized breeds. That this failed to materialize highlights an interesting trait of the domestic cat: its size range is remarkably small. At its limits are breeds such as the large Maine Coon (*see* pp.168–69) and the small Singapura. One reason for this may be that selective breeding of cats has only occurred in last 200 years. More tellingly, attempts to breed giant cats from the largest breeds have not succeeded, and even hybrids become the size of an average domestic cat within a few generations, suggesting that cat size is genetically very stable.

Eyes large and widely spaced

Some say this points to a hybrid origin for the breed, but this overlooks the fact that a pet will have a markedly better diet than a feral cat, which, in turn, will tend to make it larger. The breed is also said to have a retiring nature, and this has been attributed to its feral background, which favoured the ability to escape undue attention. There may be some truth in this, as Singapuras, although affectionate, are generally less vocal and demanding than many other Oriental breeds.

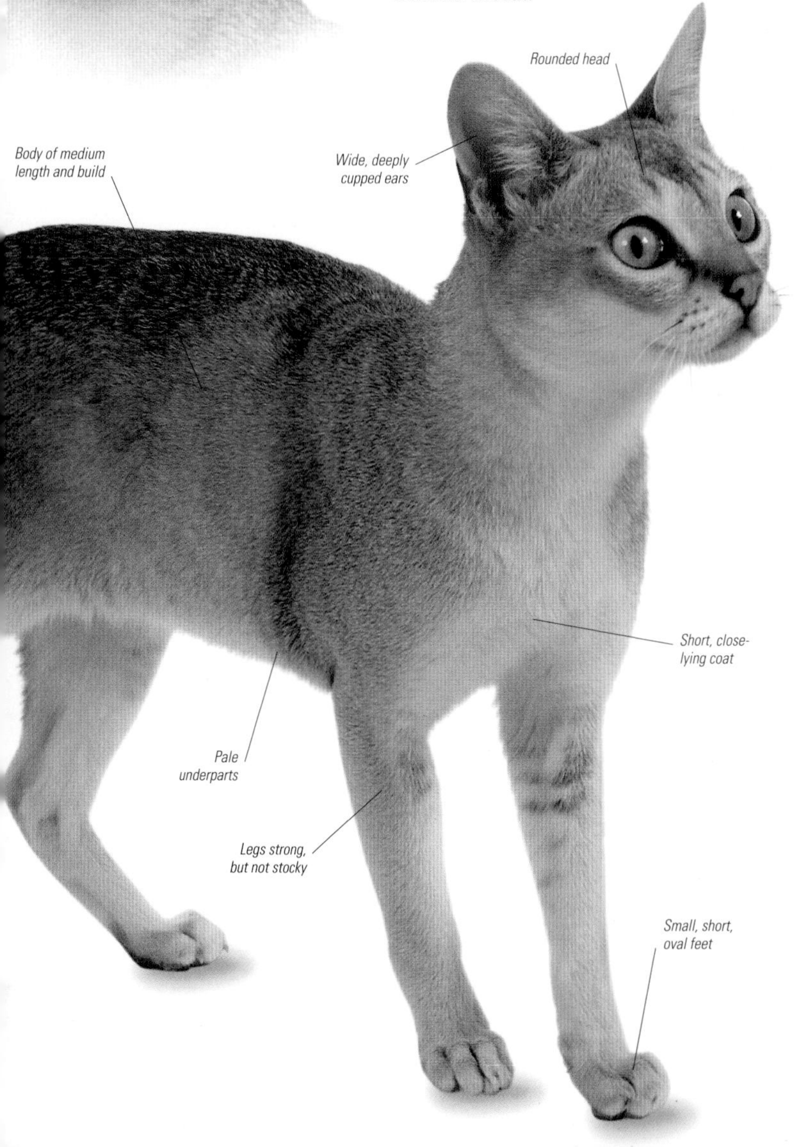

Rounded head

Wide, deeply cupped ears

Body of medium length and build

Short, close-lying coat

Pale underparts

Legs strong, but not stocky

Small, short, oval feet

ABYSSINIAN

DATE OF ORIGIN 1860s
PLACE OF ORIGIN Ethiopia
ANCESTRY Household and street cats
WEIGHT RANGE 4–7.5kg (9–17lb)
COLOURS Traditional Western and Eastern colours in solid and shaded, in ticked tabby pattern
BREED REGISTRIES GCCF, FIFé, CFA, TICA

Today, the Abyssinian is the fifth most popular breed in North America, but it is a breed with a somewhat chequered past. The founding cats, including one called Zula, were brought to Britain from Abyssinia (now Ethiopia) in 1868 after the Abyssinian War, and the breed was accepted by 1882. It was almost extinct by the early 20th century, but recovered to become recognized on both sides of the Atlantic by the 1930s. Today, it is

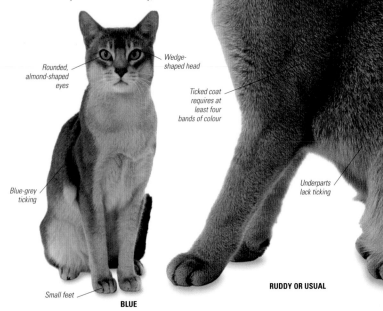

Nose and chin align vertically

Chin should be cream but may be white

Rounded, almond-shaped eyes

Wedge-shaped head

Ticked coat requires at least four bands of colour

Blue-grey ticking

Underparts lack ticking

Small feet

BLUE

RUDDY OR USUAL

KITTEN COLOURS

Abyssinian kittens are all born with similar dark coats that, with time, start to lighten in colour. Ticking is not present at birth, but gradually develops over the first few weeks of life. The final coat colour can take months to become apparent, although it is usually evident by the time a kitten leaves its mother in search of its new home. As it ages, the kitten's coat colour brightens at the root and matches the colour on its undersides and the insides of its legs. This kitten (right) still displays dark patches on its young coat.

firmly established among the top ten registered cat breeds in the United States, although it has never gained quite the same level of popularity in Britain.

The Abyssinian carried the recessive longhaired gene from the beginning, and there is now a longhaired version, the Somali (*see* pp.186–87). The original colours accepted in the breed were the Ruddy or Usual (previously also called Normal in Britain), which is a black tabby, the Sorrel, which is in fact genetically a cinnamon, and their dilutes. The more conservative registries still accept these colours only, while other organizations embrace a wider range.

"Mascara" lines

Soft, glossy, dense coat

Slender, elegant, and moderately long legs

USUAL SILVER

FORM AND CHARACTER

There is a strong similarity between the Abyssinian and cats portrayed in ancient Egyptian images, and it is likely the ticked coat mutation (*see* below) occurred thousands of years ago. The almost translucent coat pattern is a perfect camouflage, especially in the North African desert, and has probably been present in the domestic cat from the start, but other tabby patterns were more popular as the cat spread across Europe. Ticked tabbies spread eastwards instead, and this coat is commonly seen across Asia.

In personality, the Abyssinian is often almost silent, but this does not mean that it is a reserved breed: on the contrary, the Aby is a playful and attention-seeking cat, a natural, curious athlete, and is happiest with a devoted owner or in a multi-cat household. The Abyssinian can suffer from inherited forms of retinal atrophy, an eye problem seen more often in dogs.

Medium-sized, muscular body

Gently tapering tail, same length as body

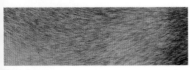

Ticked coats
The Abyssinian's ticked tabby pattern is shared with the domestic cat's ancestor, the African wildcat (*Felis silvestris lybica*). The pattern is controlled by a single gene and gives each hair alternating light and dark bands that result in a shimmering effect as the cat moves. The Abyssinian's coat should be short and very thick, which makes grooming relatively easy, with a soft and silky feel to it.

SORREL

An Ethiopian offering
Elegance personified, the Abyssinian is one of the oldest breeds and bears a striking resemblance to the cats that featured in the paintings and sculptures of Ancient Egypt.

EGYPTIAN MAU

DATE OF ORIGIN 1950s
PLACE OF ORIGIN Egypt, Italy
ANCESTRY Egyptian street cats, Italian household cats
WEIGHT RANGE 2.5–5kg (6–11lb)
COLOURS Bronze spotted tabby, silver spotted tabby, and in black smoke without tabby pattern but with strong "ghost" markings
BREED REGISTRIES GCCF, FIFé, CFA, TICA

Mau is the Egyptian word for cat, and of all the breeds in existence, the Mau probably bears the closest resemblance to the original domestic cats of ancient Egypt. This look is not due to careful recreation using diverse breeds or strains, but to the breed's descent from Egyptian street cats that may have lived in the same region and looked essentially the same for millennia. If the appearance of this strain is taken as the date of origin for the breed, it is by far the oldest in the world. More recently, the Mau as a pedigree breed is the creation of Nathalie Troubetskoy, an exiled Russian living in Italy after World War II, who imported cats from Cairo. She bred from these and showed the resultant kittens in Europe, registering them in the United States where she settled in 1956. Full recognition of the breed took another 20 years, and longer in Britain, where it was hindered by confusion with similar spotted tabbies, which were once called Maus but became part of the Oriental Shorthair (*see* pp.128–29), and by its similarity to the Ocicat (*see* pp.118–19).

FORM AND CHARACTER

The Mau is very similar to cats depicted on Egyptian walls and scrolls, with a long, athletic body and spots that follow no discernable pattern. It also has a "belly flap" of skin at the back of the abdomen, an unusual feature that allegedly gives great mobility and is said to contribute to the Mau's incredible turn of speed. The only other breed said to have this flap is the American Keuda.

The eyes of the Mau differ from the ancient images, which show narrow, wild-looking eyes, while those of the Mau are wide, rounded, and look slightly worried. Breeders have worked to give the Mau the docile temperament valued in cats today, but it remains independent, intelligent, and a ferocious hunter. If deprived of entertainment or freedom, it may choose to hunt and destroy inappropriate targets.

"Mascara-lined", worried-looking eyes

Forelegs shorter than hindlegs

BRONZE SPOTTED TABBY

SPOTTED TABBIES

The spots on cats often follow the vertical lines of the mackerel tabby, leading to a theory that they are the result of a dominant modification that "breaks" the lines. The coats of the Egyptian Mau and the Ocicat lack such a pattern, but these breeds produce classic tabby variants, so their spotting might be a broken classic pattern. Some experts hold that there is at least one dominant gene that produces a spotted tabby pattern independently of any other pattern. There may be more to the spotted tabby than broken lines, but if it is due to the influences of many genes, it will be hard to determine.

Coat silky, but not too short

Random spotting pattern

SILVER SPOTTED TABBY

Facial features
The face of the Mau is a rounded wedge shape, flowing smoothly into the muzzle, and the nose is the same width throughout its length. Its expression is strong, focused, and intelligent.

OCICAT

DATE OF ORIGIN 1964
PLACE OF ORIGIN United States
ANCESTRY Siamese, Abyssinian, American Shorthair
WEIGHT RANGE 2.5–6.5kg (6–14lb)
COLOURS Brown, cinnamon, blue, or fawn solid and silver spotted tabbies
BREED REGISTRIES GCCF, FIFé, CFA, TICA

Although its name seems to imply that it belongs among the wild-cat hybrids, the Ocicat is a happy accident dating back to long before the hybridizing trend. Virginia Daly, a breeder from Michigan, crossed a Siamese (*see* pp.124–27) with an Abyssinian (*see* pp.112–15), in the hope of creating a Siamese with ticked tabby points. The first generation of kittens resembled Abys, and when crossed back to a Siamese produced the hoped-for Aby-pointed second generation. This litter also included a spotted kitten, however, which Daly's daughter dubbed an "ocicat" for its resemblance to an ocelot (*see* p.18). This kitten was neutered and sold as a pet. But when the mating was repeated and the result was another such kitten, she

was named Dalai Talua, becoming the foundation female of this still-rare breed. Another breeder, Tom Brown, introduced American Shorthair lines some years later. The Ocicat was first recognized in 1986 by TICA, and is now accepted in most major registries.

CHOCOLATE

The coat is short and fine, and clothes a powerful but elegant, athletic build with muscular legs. The broadly wedge-shaped head has large ears and slightly slanted eyes, giving a moderately Oriental appearance. The Ocicat also shows its Siamese ancestry in its personality, being playful, talkative, and responding well to training when young. It is a sociable breed, and is not suited to prolonged solitude.

BLUE SILVER

Wedge-shaped head with broad muzzle

Large, almond-shaped eyes

Large, powerful, yet graceful body

Short, fine, close-lying coat

Graceful, arching neck

Medium-length, well-muscled legs

Long, tapering tail

CINNAMON

TABBY PATTERNS

The tabby pattern is defined as a solid colour alternating with lighter-coloured agouti fur. The Ocicat is a spotted tabby, but this is only one of several tabby patterns, which include ticked, striped, and mackerel – these three being mutations of the tabby gene. The genetics of spotted tabbies, however, are not so clear. Some believe this is another distinct mutation of the tabby gene, and point to wild cats with consistent spotted patterns as evidence. Others say it is caused by different genes modifying the tabby gene, and point to variant kittens in domestic spotted cat breeds.

Domestic animal
The Ocicat may have a coat pattern that is reminiscent of the wild ocelot, but its temperament is pure domestic cat. Ocicats often exhibit their Siamese heritage in their talkative behaviour.

BENGAL

DATE OF ORIGIN 1983
PLACE OF ORIGIN United States
ANCESTRY Asian leopard cat, household cats, Egyptian Mau, Indian street cats
WEIGHT RANGE 5.5–10kg (12–22lb)
COLOURS Brown marbled and spotted tabby and pointed tabby
BREED REGISTRIES GCCF, FIFé, TICA

High cheekbones

Large, muscular body

CLASSIC TABBY

This is the earliest of the hybrid cat breeds. In 1981, Californian breeder Jean Sugden acquired eight hybrids that had been produced for studying the Asian leopard cat's resistance to feline leukaemia virus (FeLV). She crossed them with non-pedigree cats, Egyptian Maus, and with other pedigree cats with useful coats. The result, the Bengal, is now one of the top ten breeds in Britain, although the CFA will not recognize it due to its hybrid origins.

Unique to the Bengal is the dusting of "glitter" on its coat, which is short to medium, soft, and very thick. The wide range of cats used in early development

HYBRIDIZING CAT SPECIES

Many species in the cat family will produce healthy offspring when crossed, and circuses and zoos have had big cat hybrids over the years caused by accidental or deliberate matings. In most cases, either the male or the female offspring are partially or completely infertile, making further development of the hybrid line difficult. Wild cat hybrids remain controversial: some say the wildness can never be bred out, some hold it is cruel to the animals involved, and some fear that wild coat patterns on domestic cats will fuel the fur trade.

brought in the pointed gene, which gives the dramatic blue-eyed "snow" tabbies. The Bengal's large size and very muscular build reflects the breed's hybrid past. Its unusual voice has a wide range of sounds.

Temperament
The first generations of hybrids are generally highly strung. However, Bengals have since been selected for temperament and are an alert but tractable breed.

CHAUSIE

DATE OF ORIGIN 1990s
PLACE OF ORIGIN North America
ANCESTRY Jungle cat, household cats, Abyssinian
WEIGHT RANGE 5.5–10kg (12–22lb)
COLOURS Brown ticked tabby, black solid, and silver tipped only
BREED REGISTRIES TICA

Hybrids of the domestic cat and the jungle cat (*Felis chaus*) were made as long ago as the 1960s, but virtually all males were sterile and it was only in the 1990s that the Chausie developed enough to be recognized. The allowed coat patterns reflect those of the jungle cat – a ticked tabby with occasional black or silver-tipped sports. The Chausie inherits a tendency to a somewhat shorter tail from the jungle cat, but is never bobtailed or tailless. It is generally more lithe than its wild ancestor, possibly due to the influence of Abyssinian (*see* pp.112–15) genes. Like most hybrid cats, this is an adventurous, highly active breed, and definitely a high-maintainance pet.

Strong, full muzzle

Large, athletic body

BROWN TICKED TABBY

Tail somewhat short

SAVANNAH

DATE OF ORIGIN 1980s
PLACE OF ORIGIN North America
ANCESTRY African serval, household cats
WEIGHT RANGE 5.5–10kg (12–22lb)
COLOURS Black solid and smoke, brown-spotted tabby, and silver-spotted tabby only
BREED REGISTRIES TICA

This breed, which began as a cross of an African serval and a domestic cat, was made in the 1980s by Judee Frank, a breeder of Bengals (*see* opposite). In the 1990s, Patrick Kelley and Joyce Sroufe used a descendant of this original cross, along with new hybrids and spotted domestic shorthairs, to develop the Savannah, which is named after the serval's natural habitat. This rare breed is lean and long-legged, with a standard that aims to mimic the serval in miniature. The serval is a relatively sociable wild cat, and the further these cats are from the original cross, the more domestic they are in character. Despite this, the Savannah is an active, curious breed, and not a suitable pet for collectors of crystal and china.

Large ears set high on the head

Wide, rounded nose with low-set nostrils

Thick, spotted, cheetah-like coat

BROWN SPOTTED TABBY

TOYGER

DATE OF ORIGIN 1990s
PLACE OF ORIGIN United States
ANCESTRY Bengal, household cats, street cats
WEIGHT RANGE 5.5–10kg (12–22lb)
COLOURS Brown tiger-striped tabby
BREED REGISTRIES TICA (not full recognition)

The somewhat quirkily named Toyger is the brainchild of Judy Sugden. In the late 1980s, she began using her Bengals (*see* p.120), along with a mackerel tabby household cat, and a cat from India, to create a tiger in miniature. At first called the California Toyger, the cat she produced has been exported to Britain and Australia, and seems to have a good chance of wider acceptance.

In the breed standard, every part of the Toyger – from the nose to the tail – is described as "muscular". The short, thick, orange coat has an overlying sheen of "glitter", like that of the Bengal, and the striking striped pattern lacks the curved lines and dorsal stripe of a mackerel tabby. Still a breed in progress, the Toyger should gradually become ever more tiger-like in looks.

In character, Toygers should be gregarious but relaxed, intelligent, and trainable.

Long neck; carried horizontally when walking

Long body with smooth lines

Large-boned legs

Tail is long and not thick

Small, rounded, well-furred ears

Striped coat with no spotting

Very dark markings preferred

White area on belly and chest

CALIFORNIA SPANGLED

DATE OF ORIGIN 1971
PLACE OF ORIGIN United States
ANCESTRY Abyssinian, Siamese, British and American Shorthairs, Manx, Persians, African and Asian street cats
WEIGHT RANGE 4–7kg (9–15lb)
COLOURS Traditional Western colours in solid, smoke, and silver in tabby pattern only
BREED REGISTRIES TICA

In 1971, Californian Paul Casey set out to create a wild-looking, spotted cat, in part to highlight the plight of the big cats being poached to extinction in Africa. Ironically, when it was launched in 1986, the Californian Spangled was listed in a catalogue that also contained fur coats. The breed remains rare. It was a victim of its own success: the high-profile launch alienated many in the cat-breeding and conservation worlds, while the demand for the cats depleted breeding stock. It has only recently been recognized by TICA. The Spangled is a strong, lithe cat that moves with a hunter's gait. It is given to stalking its toys, but, nevertheless, makes an amiable house cat.

Oval eyes slightly slanted

Long, muscular body

Medium-length legs

CLASSIC TABBY

SOKOKE CAT

DATE OF ORIGIN 1978
PLACE OF ORIGIN Kenya
ANCESTRY Forest cats
WEIGHT RANGE 3.5–6.5kg (8–14lb)
COLOURS Brown blotched tabby
BREED REGISTRIES FIFé

In Swahili, this cat is called Kadzonzo, which translates as "looks like tree bark". It originated in the Sokoke Forest, Kenya, which is home to a number of rare and endemic animals. In 1978, Jeni Slater found a litter of kittens living in her coconut plantation. They were slender in build, with the classic or blotched tabby pattern, unlike the cobby, spotted tabby local cats. In 1984, specimens of the Sokoke Cat were brought to Denmark, where breeding has continued. It has been suggested that they either come from a previously unknown wildcat strain, or are the originator of the classic tabby pattern; the recent appearance of blue-eyed, "snow" Sokokes indicates that they carry the pointing gene.

Close to its roots
Only a few generations from its free-ranging forest ancestry, the Sokoke is not a docile lap cat. Although friendly and vocal, it is also an independent and curious breed.

SIAMESE

DATE OF ORIGIN Pre-1700s
PLACE OF ORIGIN Thailand (formerly Siam)
ANCESTRY Household and temple cats
WEIGHT RANGE 2.5–5.5kg (6–12lb)
COLOURS All solid self and tortie
colours and tabbies, with Siamese pointed pattern
BREED REGISTRIES GCCF, FIFé, CFA, TICA, TCA

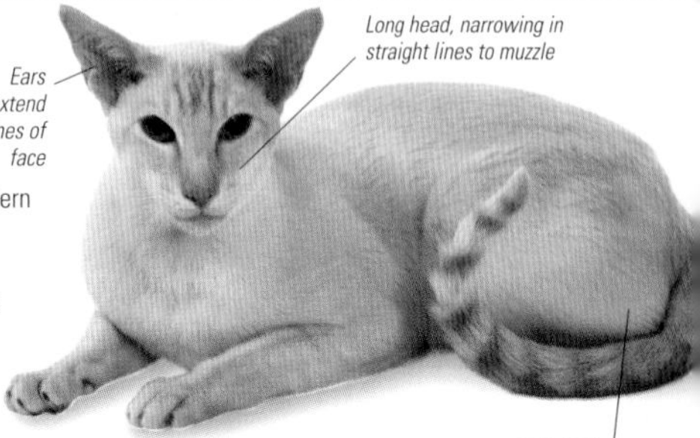

Long head, narrowing in straight lines to muzzle

Ears extend lines of face

Very short, fine coat

RED TABBY POINT

The Siamese is arguably one of the most instantly recognizable cat breeds in the world. Its pointed coat pattern originated as a mutation somewhere in Asia at least 500 years ago. How widespread the pattern was at this time is not clear, but it has become most strongly associated with the Far East and especially Thailand. These striking cats were kept by royal families and in temples. Over the years, they also attracted the admiration of visitors from overseas, and they were brought to the West in the late 19th century.

At first, both pointed and solid-coloured cats from the East were known as Siamese, but the name was always more closely associated with the classic blue-eyed, pointed type. By the 1920s, it had been decided that only cats that had this pattern could be called Siamese, and solid cats eventually became known as Oriental Shorthairs (*see* pp.128–129).

Red point
The coats of red and cream points darken more slowly than those of melanistic colours, often not being definite until the cat is mature.

Siamese cats also occasionally produced long-haired kittens, and these have been developed into the Balinese (*see* pp.190–91).

FORM AND CHARACTER

The looks and identity of the Siamese remain a matter of dispute. Over the years, the show Siamese has become progressively lighter-boned and elongated, with a more accentuated wedge-shaped head, particularly in North America. Some breeders, however, preserve the older type, which has a heavier build and a round or "apple" head. In colour, the most conservative registries recognize only black (called seal), chocolate, blue, and lilac points; red, cream, and traditional Eastern colours, as well as tortie and tabby points, are accepted as Siamese in Europe, but called Colorpoint Shorthairs in North America. Whatever their colours and names, all these cats share the typical Siamese temperament of a playful, outgoing chatterbox who craves attention and companionship. This is not a solitary cat, but needs either an attentive owner or another feline companion, and ideally both.

CHANGING FASHIONS

Tastes change down the years, and selective breeding can gradually change the look of any breed, written standards notwithstanding; coats become longer or shorter, the particular shade of a colour may become deeper or lighter, and even body build can change. Early breed standards for the Siamese called for crossed eyes, a kinked tail, and legs that were "a little short", all features common in the early examples imported from Thailand. These characteristics are now generally no longer to be seen, and in shows, crossed eyes or a kinked tail are a disqualifying fault.

Old-fashioned face
This look is controversial among many breeders who feel the Siamese is meant to have an extremely long, narrow head.

Wide-based ears with pricked tips

Oriental-shaped, blue eyes, set at a slant

Medium-sized, long, svelte body

Long, tapering, tail, free of kinks

SEAL POINT

Legs slim in proportion to body

Top cat
Elegant and graceful in appearance, spirited, vocal, and demanding by temperament, the Siamese remains consistently one of the most popular of all shorthaired breeds of cat worldwide.

ORIENTAL SHORTHAIR

DATE OF ORIGIN 1950s
PLACE OF ORIGIN Great Britain
ANCESTRY Siamese, Korat, Persian, Shorthairs
WEIGHT RANGE 4–6.5kg (9–14lb)
COLOURS All colours, patterns, and shades, except pointed sepia, and mink; many colours have special names
BREED REGISTRIES GCCF, FIFé, CFA, TICA

There were solid and tabby colours among the first cats brought to the West from Siam (modern Thailand), but in the 1920s the Siamese Club of Great Britain declared that the name Siamese (*see* pp.124–27) should only apply to blue-eyed, pointed cats, and the other coat colours fell into decline. After World War II, work on a solid chocolate led to the recognition of the Chestnut Brown Foreign in 1957, and this was the start of both the Oriental Shorthair and the Havana Brown breeds (*see* p.137). In CFA in North America the Oriental Shorthairs and Oriental Longhairs (*see* pp.192–93) are combined under the single name, Oriental. Many of the coat colours have also had individual names down the decades, leading to some confusion over identities.

FORM AND CHARACTER

There is no mistaking the qualities of these elegant felines. The coat is very short and fine, with a glossy sheen, and needs next to no care, but it provides little

Green eyes, like those of all Orientals

Long, svelte, medium-sized body

Necklaces are acceptable

Long, slim, but muscular legs

Small, oval paws

SILVER SPOTTED TABBY

BLACK

RED MACK TABB

insulation in cold weather. Lean and lithe in build, Oriental Shorthairs have large, pricked ears on a characteristic long, triangular head, and a svelte body carried on long, slender legs. Despite their delicate appearance, these are long-lived cats with a median life expectancy of over 17 years.

The breed has a typically Oriental character that matches its looks; it is active, playful, athletic, and notoriously gregarious. An Oriental's favourite spot is almost always between you and whatever you may be trying to do, and these vocal flirts will chat up anyone who seems likely to repay the effort.

These cats thrive on companionship, and if you cannot lavish attention on your Oriental for much of the day, it may be better to keep two so that they can admire and entertain each other.

Ears wide at base

Triangular face

BLUE

Hindlegs longer than forelegs

Long tail tapers to a point

COLOUR CATALOGUE

The *Tamra Maew*, or *Cat Book Poems*, is a historical manuscript describing and illustrating the many types of cat found in Thailand. Dating back to the Ayudha period (1350–1767), it was recopied in monasteries over the centuries. Although the striking pointed pattern now known as Siamese captured the imagination when cats from the Far East were first brought to the West, the *Tamra Maew* shows that there has always been a variety of coat colours – including the chocolate tortie (right) – and patterns in Oriental cats. It describes a wide range of solid, bicoloured, tabby, and shaded cats, including the intriguing Ninlarat, which is poetically claimed to be black in every part, including claws, eyes, tongue, and teeth.

CHOCOLATE TORTIE

TONKINESE

DATE OF ORIGIN 1960s
PLACE OF ORIGIN United States and Canada
ANCESTRY American Burmese and Siamese
WEIGHT RANGE 2.5–5.5kg (6–12lb)
COLOURS All self and tortie colours except fawn and cinnamon, in solid and all tabby patterns, in mink pattern
BREED REGISTRIES GCCF, CFA, TICA

One of the most popular breeds in North America, the Tonkinese is a hybrid of the Siamese (*see* pp.124–25) and the American Burmese (*see* pp.132–33). Such hybrids have existed as long as the two pointing mutations have been around, and they may in fact reveal the true identity of the "Chocolate Siamese" recorded in the 1880s. The founder of the Burmese breed, Wong Mau, is now recognized to have been a natural Tonkinese, because she produced kittens of both coat patterns. It was not until the 1950s, however, that breeders began to work on deliberately creating and refining hybrids. The breed was developed and first recognized in Canada, and today is accepted by major registries on both sides of the Atlantic.

Medium-sized eyes set wide apart

LILAC POINT

Ears slightly taller than wide

Mischievous personalities
With its alert features, this cat exhibits the inquisitive nature of the breed. It is less vocal than the Siamese, but equal to any Burmese in its inherent ability to command attention.

Moderate, wedge-shaped head with slight nose break and whisker pinch

Long, slim, elegant legs

Forelegs slightly shorter than hindlegs

RED POINT

although some registries still dispute whether the "Tonk" is truly a breed. Because the characteristic coat is a blend of two genetic patterns, the genes for both are present in all Tonkinese cats, and every mating may produce some kittens of the Siamese or Burmese pattern. This is not the only breed to produce variants, however, so the debate is more a matter of degree than principle.

FORM AND CHARACTER

The Tonk coat pattern is known as "mink". The genes for the Siamese and Burmese patterns are both recessive, and neither dominates the other, so a cat with one copy of each shows this third level of shading halfway between the two. This subtle pattern on a silky coat covers a build that is in every way moderate and balanced, and complemented by the striking blue-green eye colour. Gregarious and fun-loving, Tonkinese have the affectionate nature typical of Oriental breeds, but are less stridently vocal than most, and have a greater-than-average life expectancy. It is surprising that this healthy and sociable breed has never gained a high level of popularity outside North America. While on that continent it is one of the ten most popular breeds, it remains relatively uncommon in Europe and Australasia.

Most cat owners claim their cats are particularly intelligent, and Tonk owners are no exception. While there is no evidence that one breed is more "intelligent" than another (*see* pp.226–27, *Cat intelligence*), the Tonkinese, like its parent breeds, is acknowledged to behave at the extrovert end of the feline behaviour spectrum. One consequence of this is that the Tonkinese is particularly favoured by families who want their cats to be as dog-like as possible.

Tail equal to body in length, neither heavy nor thin

Short, soft, and close-lying coat

WHAT MAKES A BREED?

The Tonkinese showcases the best qualities of both the Burmese and the Siamese breeds, but whether the Tonk can itself be acknowledged truly as a breed is the subject of much debate. Purists will argue that if it had been realized at the time that the first Tonkinese was a hybrid, it would never have been recognized as a breed. But that fact wasn't realized, and matings resulted in litters in which some kittens looked like the parents while others resembled the founding breeds. Breeders were quick to breed from Tonkinese cats that looked like the parents, showing the characteristic mink coat pattern (below). Thus, they were able to produce cats to a Tonkinese breed standard, but genetically the Tonk remains a hybrid of the Burmese and Siamese.

LILAC COAT COLOUR

Dainty, oval paws

CHOCOLATE TORTIE

AMERICAN BURMESE

DATE OF ORIGIN 1930s
PLACE OF ORIGIN Myanmar (formerly Burma)
ANCESTRY Temple cats, Siamese crosses, household cat crosses
WEIGHT RANGE 3.5–6.5kg (8–14lb)
COLOURS Sable, champagne, blue, and platinum (CFA), all solid self and tortie colours (TICA), in sepia pattern
BREED REGISTRIES CFA, TICA, TCA

Ears tilt forwards

Short and broad muzzle, with a rounded chin

CHAMPAGNE

The origins of all Burmese cats can be traced back to a single female. Although cats of the Burmese pattern were widely known in their homeland, and possibly even shown as a type of Siamese in Britain in the late 19th century, the founder of the recognized breed was Wong Mau. She was brought from Burma (now Myanmar) to America in 1930 by US Navy psychiatrist Joseph Thompson. Ironically, Wong Mau was not a Burmese. When she

was bred with a Siamese (*see* pp.124–25) the litter she produced contained kittens with the typical Siamese pointed pattern and some with darker, more subtly pointed coats, some so subtle as to be hardly pointed at all. This means she carried the genes for both pointing patterns and was, in fact, what is now called a Tonkinese (*see* pp.130–31).

The mostly subtly pointed kittens were the ones that resulted in the Burmese we know today. The breed was recognized within a few years, but caused some disagreement within the cat breeding community and, as a result, was dropped by the CFA a few years later. Dedicated

Rounded tips

Medium-sized, widely spaced ears

Pleasingly rounded head, with full cheeks

Rounded, golden-yellow eyes

Medium-sized, muscular, and compact body

Legs moderate in bone structure and length

Medium-length tail

SABLE

work by breeders led to the Burmese being reinstated in the 1950s, and until recently it was among the top ten registered breeds.

FORM AND CHARACTER

The Burmese is defined mainly by the extremely subtly shaded pattern of its fine, satin-like coat, which is known as sepia. It has a muscular body that is surprisingly heavy for its size, leading to the cat being fondly described as "bricks wrapped in silk". Its distinctive huge, round eyes are enormously expressive.

For many years the only colour allowed in the American Burmese was sable (genetically black). Kittens of other colours – blue, chocolate (known as champagne), and lilac (known as platinum) – were occasionally born and the CFA put them in a separate category, called Mandalays, until 1984. At the other extreme, the TICA accepted all colours.

Although they are quieter and more relaxed than most other Orientals, Burmese cats still crave company; some owners call them "Velcro cats" because of their propensity to cling.

Kitten colours
Like all cats, Burmese have blue eyes when they are born. The characteristic golden hues only start to develop when the kittens are several weeks old, and will take months to reach their full brilliance. The coat colours are also always paler in kittens than in than adults.

WHEN GENETICS COMES TO A HEAD

Some breeds have a small gene pool, in which any inherited diseases may spread through much of the population and be hard to eradicate. Generally, this does not appear to be a problem for the Burmese, which was drawn from a large number of cats in the early decades of its development. However, a problem arose in the 1970s when breeders selected for an altered head shape, favouring an extremely round look. This "contemporary" head has held sway in the CFA show ring for many years, but carries with it malformed jaws and lethal skull deformities. As a result, North American Burmese have been banned from British and some other breed registries, for fear of importing this genetic defect. Some North American breeders have abandoned the lines favoured in the CFA and now breed either Traditional or Classic Burmese, using American lines that do not carry the trait, or Foreign Burmese, which include European Burmese in their breeding. All have a more wedge-shaped head.

EUROPEAN BURMESE

DATE OF ORIGIN 1952
PLACE OF ORIGIN Myanmar (formerly Burma)
ANCESTRY Temple cats, Siamese crosses, household cat crosses
WEIGHT RANGE 3.5–6.5kg (8–14lb)
COLOURS All self colours with Burmese pointing pattern
BREED REGISTRIES GCCF, FIFé

The European Burmese has the same origins as the American Burmese (*see* pp.132–33), dating back to Wong Mau, a cat brought from Burma to America in 1930. American cats, descended from Wong Mau, were imported into Britain and the brown colour was recognized in 1952, but after this the breed diverged to take different forms on opposite sides of the Atlantic. In Europe, breeders preferred a more typically Oriental look, and were also interested in a wider colour range. The blue colour, a recessive trait carried by the cats imported from America, was accepted within a few years. Red-based colours and tortoiseshells, resulting from an accidental

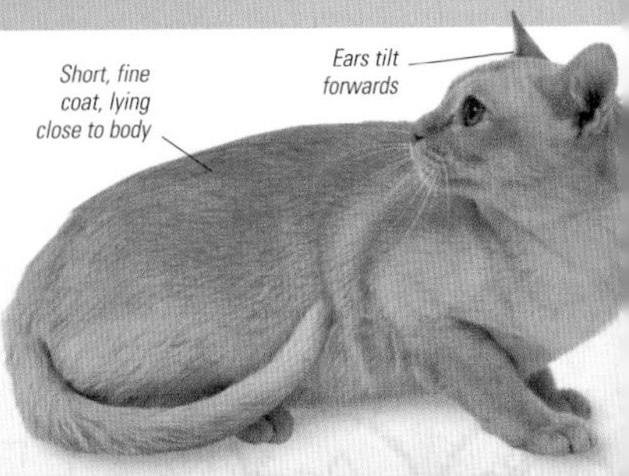

Short, fine coat, lying close to body

Ears tilt forwards

RED

Coat shades
The shading of the pointing pattern varies with age and climate. In this cat the mask and paws are noticeably darker.

consistently appears among the most popular breeds, but it is most highly ranked in Europe, where shorthairs hold more sway than longhaired cats.

FORM AND CHARACTER

The European Burmese, like the American cat, is characterized mainly by the sepia pattern of its coat, shading gradually to the darker points and solid to the roots, with no tabby markings. The coat is short and fine, lying close to the body and needing no day-to-day care. The slender legs carry a fairly lean but muscular body, which is surprisingly heavy for its size. The head is the feature in which the European Burmese differs most from the American type. It is a short wedge shape and the muzzle is blunt; the eyes are widely placed, rounded, and only slightly slanted.

This is a typically gregarious cat, and happy to be part of a busy, multi-cat household. It is less vocal and less active than some other Oriental breeds, making it a more peaceable companion.

Burmese eyes
The eyes are typically rounder than those of other Oriental breeds. Their ideal colour is clear golden-yellow, although the shade varies with coat colour and in different lights.

outcrossing, had been recognized by the 1970s. Cats from Britain were exported to Europe, Africa, Australia, and New Zealand in the 1950s. As a result, the breed in these countries follows the European type. Green eyes are allowed by FIFé, but are seen as a fault by the GCCF.

On both sides of the Atlantic, the Burmese still

Short, blunt, wedge-shaped head

Strong, muscular, surprisingly heavy body

SABLE

Hindlegs longer than forelegs

ORIENTAL MUTATIONS

Although the Siamese and Burmese pointing patterns have come to be associated with two quite separate geographical areas, mutations are rarely completely isolated. The Siamese pattern was carried by Wong Mau, the founding cat of the Burmese breed, and the Burmese pattern was probably also present in Thailand. Many breeders point to the Thong Daeng, or copper-coloured cats, mentioned in the Thai manuscript *Tamra Maew*, or *Cat Book Poems*, as an early record of the Burmese, although Tonkinese breeders also claim these cats as their breed's progenitors. Since Wong Mau was a Tonkinese, their claim has some validity.

Medium-sized ears, rounded at tips

Blunt muzzle, with deep chin

BLUE

BOMBAY

DATE OF ORIGIN 1960s
PLACE OF ORIGIN United States
ANCESTRY Black American Shorthairs and sable Burmese
WEIGHT RANGE 2.5–5kg (6–11lb)
COLOURS Black
BREED REGISTRIES CFA, TICA

Head rounded in all aspects

Large, rounded, and widely spaced eyes

The Bombay is the creation of Kentucky breeder Nikki Horner, who set out in the 1950s to produce a black panther in miniature. Using black American Shorthairs (*see* pp.96–97) for their colour and sable Burmese (*see* pp.132–33) for their build, she succeeded in producing muscular cats with glossy rich black coats and copper eyes by the 1960s, and the breed was formally recognized in 1976. However, the Bombay, which is still rare, especially outside North America, has not been recognized by registries in Europe, and in Britain the name Bombay refers to a black Asian Shorthair (*see* pp.140–41).

Medium-length, moderately thick tail

In looks, the Bombay has diverged from its original Burmese appearance, particularly in the shape of the head: this may be a result of breeding to avoid the lines associated with skull deformities in the Burmese. The short, close coat has the same fine, glossy qualities, however, and is easy to care for. The gregarious Bombay seeks out warm locations and human company whenever it can, ideally by installing itself on someone's lap. It has a pleasant and distinctive voice.

Close-lying coat, with satin-like texture

Medium-sized, surprisingly heavy body

LITTLE BLACK CATS

Striking black cats, such as this black Asian Smoke cat (below), have often occured in breeding programmes. However, with the advent of wild-cat hybrids, there has been a growing trend for panther look-alikes. The Bengal (*see* p.120) produces occasional black kittens, the basis of the Pantherette and Black Panther experimental breeds. The Serengeti, also an offshoot of the Bengal, includes a solid black sometimes called Black Panther, while the Machbagral is created from fishing cats (*Felis viverrina*) and black domestic cats. Internet claims of hybrids with wild black panthers do not appear credible.

Medium-length, sturdy legs

Rounded paws

HAVANA BROWN

DATE OF ORIGIN 1950s
PLACE OF ORIGIN Great Britain and United States
ANCESTRY Siamese, Russian Blue, household cats
WEIGHT RANGE 2.5–4.5kg (6–10lb)
COLOURS Chocolate
BREED REGISTRIES CFA, TICA

Oval, green eyes

Large ears, wide-set but upright

Medium-length body, carried level

Short, smooth, and shiny coat

CHOCOLATE

In the cat world, the word Havana has two different meanings. In Britain, a solid chocolate cat of Siamese type (*see* pp.124–27) was developed in the 1950s; the colour was called Havana, but the breed itself was registered as Chestnut Brown Foreign, and eventually became part of the Oriental Shorthair (*see* pp.128–29). Chestnut Brown Foreigns were also exported to the United States, where they became the foundation of a separate breed, called the Havana Brown.

The Havana Brown, which remains very rare, is slender and elegant, with a long body and head, but is less extreme in form than the Oriental Shorthair. The Russian Blue was used in the development of the breed, which still more or less follows the Russian lines. The sleek, close coat is a warm, rich brown. Due to the influence of the recessive dilute gene of the Russian Blue, lilacs are sometimes born, although they are not recognized for showing. This gregarious, lively breed is less vocal than most Oriental types.

Havana head
The long, slender head narrows to a slim muzzle with a distinctive "pinch" just behind the whisker pads. The chin has a strong profile and the whiskers are brown or lilac to complement the coat colour.

KURILEAN BOBTAIL (SHORTHAIR)

DATE OF ORIGIN Before 1700s
PLACE OF ORIGIN Kuril Islands, Russian far east
ANCESTRY Domestic cats
WEIGHT RANGE 3–4.5kg (7–10lb)
COLOURS Traditional Western self and tortie colours and bicolours, in solid, smoke, shaded, and tipped, and with traditional tabby patterns.
BREED REGISTRIES FIFé

Although the gene for the short tail of the Kurilean Bobtail has undoubtedly existed for centuries, the breed was little heard of in the West until the 1990s. Wider recognition may now be on the way, although those registries that recognize the Japanese Bobtail may be reluctant to accept another breed that has the same mutation.

Although the first cats seen in the West were longhairs (*see* p.198), this shorthaired version is not an afterthought, but a strain that has always been present. The

Kurilean is heavier than the Japanese, with a shorter, deeper body, a distinction that is most apparent in the shorthaired version. The breeds also differ in personality, with the independent-minded Kurilean being somewhat less of a prima donna.

Broad head, with gentle nose break

Short, curled tail, carried high

Sturdy legs, but not heavy for build

JAPANESE BOBTAIL (SHORTHAIR)

DATE OF ORIGIN 1800s
PLACE OF ORIGIN Japan
ANCESTRY Household cats
WEIGHT RANGE 2.5–4kg (6–9lb)
COLOURS All self and tortie colours and bicolours in solid and traditional tabby patterns
BREED REGISTRIES FIFé, CFA, TICA

It is hard to pinpoint when cats arrived in Japan, but they were in Southeast Asia by about AD 400. The mutation for stumpy or "bobbed" tails probably arose before they reached Japan,

but largely died out elsewhere, gaining prominence due to the restricted gene pool of the Japanese population and possibly with human help in selection. The first breeding programme outside Japan was established in 1968 by American breeder Elizabeth Freret. The breed is also recognized in Europe and there is a longhaired version (*see* p.199).

The Bobtail is slender but not dainty, although it is lighter-boned in the West than in its homeland. The most prized coat is white with red and black patches, but all other colours are allowed, except by the CFA, which, somewhat curiously, only accepts Western colours.

The Bobtail has the archetypal Oriental personality, being vocal, inquisitive, and sociable; it is happiest when it has an attentive owner or a feline companion.

Face and body
The Japanese Bobtail's face is an equilateral triangle with high cheekbones, and widely spaced eyes. It is lightly built with long legs.

SNOWSHOE

DATE OF ORIGIN 1960s
PLACE OF ORIGIN United States
ANCESTRY Siamese, American Shorthair
WEIGHT RANGE 2.5–5.5kg (6–12lb)
COLOURS All self and tortie colours and all tabby patterns, in pointed pattern and with white spotting only
BREED REGISTRIES GCCF, FIFé, TICA

Many of the early Siamese (*see* pp.124–27) had white toes or other markings, which were bred out over the decades. Then, in the 1960s, Philadelphia breeder Dorothy Hinds-Daugherty crossed Siamese with American Shorthairs (*see* pp.96–97) to create a new breed that was based around the white toe "fault". The Snowshoe has been accepted by most major registries, despite opposition from Siamese breeders, who had worked hard to eradicate this type of feature from their breed.

The Snowshoe used to be described as a shorthaired Birman (*see* pp.160–61), but that title is now claimed by the Templecat (*see* p.161), and was never very appropriate. The Snowshoe is lighter in build than the Birman, with a more wedge-shaped head, and white is allowed on the body especially in an inverted V on the face.

While fairly content to be the sole cat in a household, the Snowshoe has an outgoing and sociable character, and is talkative, with a pleasant, soft voice.

Moderate body size

Short, smooth, and close-lying coat

SEAL MITTED

Medium to medium-large ears

Body has semi-foreign build

Legs in proportion with body

BLUE MITTED

Broad, modified wedge-shaped head

Medium-sized, oval, blue eyes

No noticeable undercoat

SEAL MITTED

ASIAN GROUP

DATE OF ORIGIN 1981
PLACE OF ORIGIN Great Britain
ANCESTRY Burmese, Chinchillas, non-pedigrees
WEIGHT RANGE 4–7kg (9–15lb)
COLOURS Traditional Western and Eastern self and tortie colours in solid, smoke, and shaded, and tabby and sepia patterns; some colours have special names
BREED REGISTRIES GCCF, FIFé (some variants recognized)

The Asians are sufficiently varied to be recognized by the GCCF registry not as a single breed but as a group of four: Shaded or Burmilla; Smoke; Self and Tortie; and Tabby. There is also a semi-longhaired variety, the Tiffanie (*see* p.195).

It all began back in 1981, with the accidental mating of a European Burmese (*see* pp.134–35) and a Chinchilla Longhair, which produced attractive silver-shaded kittens of Burmese type. The owner was Miranda von Kirchberg, who had bought the Chinchilla for her husband. Using these kittens, she began a breeding programme and the Asian Shaded was accepted by the GCCF in 1989 and (with different breeding lines) the FIFé in 1994. The other divisions are still recognized only by the GCCF.

The Asian Shaded, or Burmilla, is like the European Burmese in form and has a short coat, combined with the colour and the striking "mascara" around the eyes found in the Chinchilla. The Asian Smoke, once called Burmoire, appeared

Eyes any colour from gold to green

Lighter colour on body due to pointing gene

SELF CREAM VARIANT

in the second generation of crosses from the Asian Shaded. It possesses a white undercoat that shows as a shimmer in a coat slightly longer than that of the Burmese. The Asian Self resulted from the inclusion of breeding lines aimed at

Medium to large ears, widely spaced, and angled slightly outwards

Medium length legs with oval paws

Ticked tabby kitten
The Asian Group's unique heritage means that it is one of a very few cats recognized in Britain in the ticked pattern (pictured) as well as classic, mackerel, and spotted tabby.

LILAC SHADED (BURMILLA)

producing a black Burmese; the black Asian Self, called Bombay, should not be confused with the American breed of the same name (*see* p.136). Unlike the others, sepia-pointed Asian Selfs cannot be shown. This is to ensure they remain separate from the Burmese. Asian Tabbies appeared in the second generation of crosses from the Asian Shaded, and are one of the few breeds to be accepted in all four tabby patterns in Britain.

The Asian personality is consistent across the four divisions: all are more relaxed than the typical Burmese. More outgoing and sociable than Persians, Asians always appreciate company, but refrain from talking too much.

THE NAMING OF CATS

When TS Eliot jokingly suggested that a cat must have three names, he had no idea how close to the truth he was. The Bombay is a colour in Britain and a breed in North America, and the same is true for the Havana and its near namesake the Havana Brown. The confusion between the Tiffanie and the Tiffany (now mostly called the Chantilly) has helped neither breed, and Persians have been called Longhairs in Britain, but have always been Persians in America, except when they are Himalayans. Even the same coat pattern may have different names in different breeds, a problem the FIFé registry has sought to overcome with a system of numerical codes.

Asian Smoke coat should show ghost tabby markings

Medium to long tail, tapering to rounded tip

CHOCOLATE SMOKE

Shading varies from medium to heavy tipping

Medium-sized, firmly muscled body

KORAT

DATE OF ORIGIN Before 1700
PLACE OF ORIGIN Thailand
ANCESTRY Household cats
WEIGHT RANGE 2.5–4.5kg (6–10lb)
COLOURS Solid blue self
BREED REGISTRIES GCCF, FIFé, CFA, TICA

Large, flat forehead

Firm, rounded muzzle

The *Tamra Maew* or *Cat Book Poems* (1350–1767) of Thailand distinguishes the frosted silver Si-Sawat from other blue cats. Today, this cat is known as the Korat, after the province of Thailand that is its homeland. When it first came to the West is unclear. A "blue Siamese" shown in London in 1882 may have been either a Korat or a blue Oriental Shorthair (*see* pp.128–29). Modern Korats were introduced to the United States in 1959 and were recognized in 1965. They were brought to the UK in 1972

Luminous, prominent, and rounded eyes

Glossy, fine, and close-lying coat

Coat "breaks" over spine

and recognized later that year. A recessive genetic neuromuscular disorder affects a few individuals, but a screening programme is in place to eliminate it.

Korats are sturdily built cats with a densely muscled body on strong legs. The short, fine coat is tipped with silver, an effect called "sea foam" in Thailand.

Playful and outgoing, the Korat is happy in a multi-cat household, but be warned: this is a bossy breed that likes to have its own way and will grumble loudly if it does not get it.

LUCKY CATS IN THAILAND

Different cats in Thailand have different kinds of good or bad luck associated with them, but there are also traditional rituals involving cats for the times when simply having them in your home was not enough. The Hae Nang Maew festival is still sometimes held in May or June in years when there has not been adequate rainfall. A cat is caught and put into a basket (pictured) and the villagers carry it around from house to house to the accompaniment of a traditional folk dance. At each house they sprinkle water onto the cat to symbolize the rain that is needed. The cloud-coloured Korat breed is said to be particularly associated with this festival.

Tail heavy at base, tapering to round tip

Face and eyes
The Korat's face is heart-shaped, with gentle curves and rounded eyes. The eyes' limpid green colouring may take two years to develop fully.

CORNISH REX

DATE OF ORIGIN 1950s
PLACE OF ORIGIN Great Britain
ANCESTRY Farm cat
WEIGHT RANGE 2.5–4.5kg (6–10lb)
COLOURS All colours, shades, and patterns
BREED REGISTRIES GCCF, FIFé, CFA, TICA

In 1950, a curly-coated kitten appeared in a litter born on a farm near Bodmin in Cornwall. The owner, Nina Ennismore, recognized this as similar to the "rex" mutation in rabbits, and bred the kitten, Kallibunker, back to his mother, Serena. The mix of kittens in the resulting litter showed that the trait was recessive, and breeding rex-to-rex produced all-rex offspring. Burmese (*see* pp.134–35) and British Shorthairs (*see* pp.88–89) were used to develop the breed in Britain, while Siamese (*see* pp.124–27) and Oriental Shorthairs (*see* pp.128–29) were introduced into the bloodlines in North America, where the cat arrived in 1957. This has resulted in a different style of cat on either side of the Atlantic.

CINNAMON POINT

FORM AND CHARACTER

The breed founder, Kallibunker, may have had some Oriental genes judging by both the looks and the character he bequeathed: the Cornish Rex does not resemble a typical British farm cat, but

Shining through
The curl of the Cornish Rex coat and the lack of concealing guard hairs make the white undercoat of this black smoke-and-white very apparent.

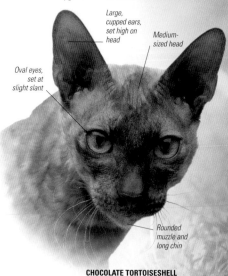

Large, cupped ears, set high on head

Medium-sized head

Oval eyes, set at slight slant

Rounded muzzle and long chin

CHOCOLATE TORTOISESHELL

has a generally foreign appearance, with long legs and an arched spine. Beyond this and the defining characteristic of the curly coat, the breed has developed differently in Europe and North America. In Europe, the build is typically muscular and the head is wedge-shaped, with a straight nose. In North America, the trend has been towards a more greyhound-like build with a distinctly tucked-up belly, and the head is more rounded, with a Roman nose.

There is also a German Rex. Rexing, found in German cats as early as 1946, was confirmed as the same mutation, but the German Rex has not enjoyed the success of the Cornish.

Active, adventurous, and even acrobatic, Cornish Rexes tend to be vocal and gregarious.

THE HYPOALLERGENIC MYTH

As well as being the first recognized rexed breed, the Cornish Rex was also the first to be touted as a "hypoallergenic" cat, less likely to make allergy-sufferers sneeze. Because the coat has no guard hairs, it is held that there is less to shed, and some people claim the curled coat will hold onto loose hairs until they are groomed out, like the coat of a Poodle, rather than shedding them around the house. Sadly, the evidence does not seem to bear out these hopes: hairs will be shed, allergens are not solely carried on hairs, and owners tend to be in such close contact with their cats that they will be affected anyway. Grooming is far more important than breed choice in controlling allergies.

Small to medium body, with fine bones

Slender, elegant neck

TORTIE-AND-WHITE

DEVON REX

DATE OF ORIGIN 1960
PLACE OF ORIGIN Great Britain
ANCESTRY Feral and household cats
WEIGHT RANGE 2.5–4kg (6–9lb)
COLOURS All colours, shades, and patterns
BREED REGISTRIES GCCF, FIFé, CFA

Large ears very wide at base, tapering to round tip

Wedge-shaped head, with a well-defined chin

BLACK SMOKE

In 1960, Beryl Cox, an RSPCA (Royal Society for the Prevention of Cruelty to Animals) worker, took in a litter of feral kittens, one of which had a waved coat just like that of a familiar feral tom in the area. She kept this kitten and named it Kirlee. The curly-coated Cornish Rex (*see* pp.144–45) had been bred for a decade in the neighbouring county, and it was at first assumed that this cat showed the same mutation. When test matings were carried out, however, all the resultant kittens had straight coats. Further experimental breeding revealed that the Devon Rex coat is a recessive trait, just as it is in the Cornish Rex, but that it is caused by a quite different mutation.

In Britain, the Devon Rex was recognized as a separate breed within the decade, but it was not separated from the Cornish Rex in North America until 1979. Early inbreeding to establish the type showed up a genetic spasticity syndrome in the breed; this is being studied as part of the Feline Genome Project, and breeders have worked hard to eliminate it. To improve the gene pool, a number of different breeds are allowed as outcrosses in North America and Europe.

FORM AND CHARACTER

The coat of the Devon Rex is very short and soft; it lacks guard hairs, and its overall effect is of close rippling. Like all rexed coats, this shows off smoke and silver shades particularly well.

The looks of the Devon are often described as elfin, and the broad head with its oversized, widely

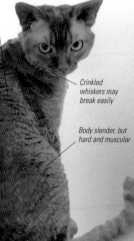

Very short, soft, rippled, swirling coat

Crinkled whiskers may break easily

Body slender, but hard and muscular

Rex appeal
Wide outcrossing in the development of the Devon Rex has given it almost limitless patterns and colours. The curl shows up shaded colours well, as in this example, and softens the markings.

RED TABBY

OUTCROSSING

The Devon Rex is one of many breeds to benefit from outcrossing, a practice that makes it possible to select for particular genetic traits. Whether to allow mating outside the breed is always a vexed question for registries. Without new lines, the gene pool of a breed can become dangerously small, leading to a higher incidence of inherited diseases and not enough cats to breed away from the lines carrying them. On the other hand, every outcrossing carries the risk of losing the breed's distinctive type.

DEVON REX KITTEN

also have a broad chest, which can give them the appearance of being bow-legged when viewed from the front, but they do not suffer from any skeletal deformities.

The Devon Rex is chatty, alert, and sociable, and, for a cat, it is reasonably trainable: it may be this last trait, as much as its striking looks, that landed the breed a role as pet in the film *Dune*.

spaced ears and large eyes is certainly somewhat otherworldly. Although they have a slender body and long legs, these cats are not delicate and are usually too active and busy to appear elegant. They

SPHYNX

DATE OF ORIGIN 1978
PLACE OF ORIGIN North America, Europe
ANCESTRY Street and household cats, Devon Rex
WEIGHT RANGE 3.5–7kg (8–15lb)
COLOURS All colours and all patterns
BREED REGISTRIES FIFé, CFA, TICA

Tapering, whip-like tail

Rounded, hard, and muscular body

Firm and muscular legs

Short coat consists of fine down

Hairless cats have been documented for over a century. The Sphynx can be traced back to a recessive mutation in Toronto, Canada, in 1978, although the same mutation may have surfaced there in the 1960s. The Sphynx was developed using the Devon Rex (*see* pp.146–47) and is accepted by most major registries. However, the GCCF only records Sphynxes to ensure the mutation does not slip into the Devon Rex breeding lines.

Not truly hairless, the Sphynx usually has a light down, particularly on the extremities. A wrinkled appearance is preferred, and the Devon Rex heritage is obvious. Breeders describe Sphynxes as energetic, gregarious show-offs.

CARING FOR HAIRLESS CATS

These breeds have no coat to absorb oil, so they need to be washed regularly, something that must be begun in kittenhood if the cat is to accept it. Allergy sufferers may find a regularly bathed and hairless cat easier to live with than an unbathed, furred cat. Although vulnerable to sunburn and the cold, their mutations were first found in street cats in countries with cold winters, so these cats might be tougher than they look.

MINSKIN

DATE OF ORIGIN 2000
PLACE OF ORIGIN United States
ANCESTRY Munchkin, Sphynx
WEIGHT RANGE 2.5–4kg (6–9lb)
COLOURS All colours and all patterns
BREED REGISTRIES Registered but not yet recognized by TICA

Paul McSorley of Boston began work on producing the Minskin in 1998. He used the Sphynx for its lack of coat and the Munchkin (*see* pp.101–103) for its short legs. The first cat that fulfilled his brief was I Am Minskin Hear Me Roar, born in 2000. The breed remains rare.

The Minskin generally resembles a Munchkin, but for the coat. It is not completely hairless, but is described as "fur pointed", as it has fine fur on the face, feet, and tail, where a pointed cat would show a darker colour, and a soft down on the rest of the body. Minskins are generally playful, gregarious, and outgoing.

Muted colours
Hairless or downy cats show all the basic coat colours and patterns on their skin, although the colours are softer than they would be on a full coat.

DON HAIRLESS

DATE OF ORIGIN 1987
PLACE OF ORIGIN Russia
ANCESTRY Street and household cats
WEIGHT RANGE 3.5–7kg (8–15lb)
COLOURS All colours and all patterns
BREED REGISTRIES TICA

Although it is sometimes called the Don, or Donskoy, Sphynx, this breed is unrelated to the Sphynx, having its origins in a separate, dominant mutation. The founding female was a cat named Varya, who was rescued in the town of Rostov-na-Donu. At first she was thought to be bald due to a fungal infection. The breed has been developed using household cats and European Shorthairs (*see* pp.92–93).

Like the Sphynx, the Don has very wrinkled skin and may have a light fuzz, especially on the extremities or in winter. They differ in their curly whiskers and their generally more European physique. They are intelligent, outgoing, and apparently healthy cats.

PETERBALD

DATE OF ORIGIN 1994
PLACE OF ORIGIN Russia
ANCESTRY Street and household cats, Siamese
WEIGHT RANGE 3.5–7kg (8–15lb)
COLOURS All colours and all patterns
BREED REGISTRIES TICA

In 1993 a breeder mated an Oriental-type cat and a male Don Hairless of relatively light build. This male was also bred to Russian Blues and the kittens from these matings have been used to develop the Peterbald. The absence of coat is the same as in its parent Don breed. However, it is more Oriental, with a slender body, a triangular head, and large ears.

Very large ears, wide at base

Head longer than it is wide

Slight hair growth visible

Firm body

DOWNY

HAIRLESS

NON-PEDIGREE SHORTHAIRS

DATE OF ORIGIN Before 2000 BC
PLACE OF ORIGIN Egypt
ANCESTRY African wildcat
WEIGHT RANGE 2.5–8kg (6–18lb)
COLOURS All colours and all patterns
BREED REGISTRIES Most registries have
a household cat class for showing

*Coat colour
and pattern
unpredictable*

BROWN TORTIE TABBY-AND-WHITE

Although cats have lived with humans for thousands of years, they have until very recently been almost entirely free-ranging animals that have chosen their own mates; selective and controlled breeding is a relatively new phenomenon. The basis for the first breeds evolved over centuries through such natural selection. Different traits became predominant in different areas of the world because they were useful in local conditions; a light build and a fine coat are advantageous in a warm climate, for example, as both enable a cat to regulate its body temperature more effectively. Even today, with a proliferation of breeds to suit every taste, the vast majority of pet cats are still random-bred moggies. Most of these are shorthaired, in part because it is a dominant genetic trait. Random-bred shorthairs can show any kind of coat, from the thick plush of a

British Shorthair (*see* pp.88–89) to the fine sleekness of a Siamese (*see* pp.124–27), and as the occasional pedigree breedline enters the wider population, foreign colours and other traits are spread, although they remain rare. The colours and exact conformation of a random-bred cat are less predictable than those of pedigree breeds, but most cats inherit the general looks and personalities of their parents, through genetics or as a result of early socialization.

BROWN MACKEREL TABBY

*Lithe, supple,
muscular
body*

*Strong,
sturdy legs*

BLACK-AND-WHITE

Fit for life
Over centuries, natural selection has ensured that the non-pedigree cats are perfectly suited to an active and independent life, being capable of living alone or with a human family.

The lure of a longhair
A big cat with beautiful, long, lustrous, waterproof fur and a winter neck ruff, the Maine Coon is the oldest feline breed in North America. It makes for an ideal companion cat.

LONGHAIRED CATS

Longhaired cats do not exist readily in nature because the trait is genetically recessive. However, a single, and therefore simple, genetic mutation governs long hair. This has made it relatively easy for breeders to perpetuate the characteristic by breeding longhair to longhair and then continue the trait by breeding only from descendants with long hair.

MORE THAN JUST A FASHION ACCESSORY

The domestic cat inherited from its wild ancestors the genetically recessive trait for long hair. While in most regions of the world this attribute never took hold, in what is now eastern Turkey, northern Iraq, the North Caucasian republics, and Iran, longhaired cats survived and multiplied. The reason for this successful acclimatization is probably that the bitterly cold winter climate in these mountainous regions favoured cats with the best thermal insulation. In the 1500s, small numbers of these cats were brought to Europe, initially to Italy and France, and a little later to Britain as well. Known originally as Russian or French cats, by the late 1800s they were called Persians and Angoras. The Persians (*see* pp.154–57) were for a time called Longhairs, while the Angora is now known as the Oriental Longhair (Angora) (*see* pp.188–89). Other breeds of longhaired cats developed elsewhere in northern latitudes: the Maine Coon in New England (*see* pp.168–71), the Norwegian Forest Cat in Norway (*see* pp.172–75), and the Siberian Forest Cat in Russia (*see* p.176). It is likely that these breeds evolved from the descendants of the Central Asian longhaired cats brought to Europe centuries earlier.

Longhairs have full coats of both long guard and long down hair. Cats that have semi-long, silky coats make up another group within the longhaired-cat section, but the development of this type of coat is genetically different from the true longhairs. Perhaps the most striking of all longhaired breeds are the rexed longhairs, with a curl to the coat, such as the LaPerm (*see* p.196) and the Selkirk Rex (*see* pp.178–79). In addition, breeders continue to import the longhair gene into shorthair breeds, creating an ever expanding variety of these hairiest of felines.

Ruff stuff
The coat of a longhaired cat can look spectacular. The one major disadvantage of owning such a breed is grooming.

An American tail
The American Curl is instantly recognizable by its curled-back ears, but its full-plumed tail — as long as the cat's body — is an equally dramatic feature.

PERSIAN

DATE OF ORIGIN 1800s
PLACE OF ORIGIN Great Britain
ANCESTRY Longhaired Middle Eastern cats
WEIGHT RANGE 3.5–7kg (8–15lb)
COLOURS All self and tortie colours and bicolours in solid, smoke, shaded, and tipped, and classic tabby pattern
BREED REGISTRIES GCCF, FIFé, CFA, TICA, TCA (Doll-Faced)

Kitten colours
Almost all red self cats show some faint "ghost" tabby markings. These are often more pronounced in kittens, making it hard to tell a show quality cat until it is mature.

Longhaired cats from the Middle East have been status-symbol pets ever since they first arrived in Europe. They were brought from Persia into Italy by Pietro della Valle and from Turkey into France by Nicolas-Claude Fabri de Peiresc, both in the early 17th century, and have had a variety of names since. In the late 19th century, the fledgling cat fancy in Britain began to develop these cats under the name Persian, according to the first written guidelines created by Harrison Weir. The Persian was one of the first breeds recognized in Britain, and by 1900 it was accepted in all registries that still exist today. For some time, however, it was called the Longhair, which led to occasional confusion. There is a high incidence of polycystic kidney disease and retained testicles in the breed.

FORM AND CHARACTER

The Persian was one of the most popular cat breeds worldwide throughout the 20th century. It remains by far the most popular breed in North America, although its lead has diminished in the last few years, and it recently lost the top spot in Britain. Always a sturdy

CREAM

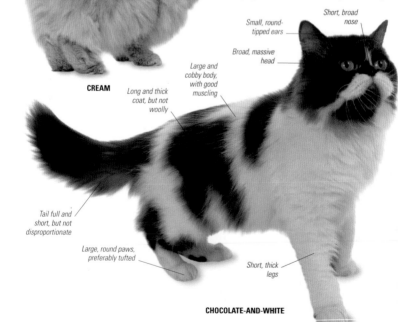

Small, round-tipped ears

Short, broad nose

Broad, massive head

Large and cobby body, with good muscling

Long and thick coat, but not woolly

Tail full and short, but not disproportionate

Large, round paws, preferably tufted

Short, thick legs

CHOCOLATE-AND-WHITE

feline, the Persian has a cobby body with short, thick legs and a broad chest. The head is round, and the ears small, with plentiful tufts of fur at the base. The widely spaced eyes are large and round. The noses of early Persians were less compressed than those seen in today's show cats, and cats in Europe still tend to have longer noses than those bred in North America, where concern about health problems has led some breeders to move away from the mainstream and deliberately breed "doll-faced" Persians instead. Conversely, the coat has become longer over the generations, and can be up to 12cm (5in) long in top show cats.

Often rather idle, the Persian is usually an indoor dweller. Its long coat makes it very high-maintainance, demanding a considerable investment of time in daily grooming. The rising popularity of the Exotic (*see* p.167) may be at its expense.

The Triumphant Traditional
The ultra-type Persian, with very short nose and very long coat, holds sway in the show ring but is not unchallenged. Breeders of Traditional Persians aim for a cat with a longer nose, like this blue self. Although less distinctive, this type is less prone to health problems.

LONG HAIR AND BEHAVIOUR

A long coat in cats is the result of a recessive mutation of one gene, which slows the rate at which the hair is shed. The difference between the thick, extraordinarily long coat of the Persian and the finer, less extravagant coats of other breeds is down to the modifying effect of other genes, selected for over decades. Outside the showing season many Persian breeders clip their cats to reduce the grooming burden, and a side-effect is that these usually placid cats can become markedly more active and involved in life once free from their warm, heavy coats.

Persian perfection
An unmistakable appearance: a show-quality Persian has an extremely long, thick coat, short legs, a wide head with the ears set far apart, large eyes, and a typically foreshortened muzzle.

COLOURPOINT PERSIAN

DATE OF ORIGIN 1950s
PLACE OF ORIGIN Britain and United States
ANCESTRY Siamese
WEIGHT RANGE 3.5–7kg (8–15lbs)
COLOURS Traditional Eastern and Western self and tortie colours in pointed pattern
BREED REGISTRIES GCCF, FIFé, CFA, TICA

BLUE POINT

As long ago as the 1920s, experimental crosses between Persians (*see* pp.154–55) and Siamese (*see* pp.124–27) in Europe, resulted in a breed called the Khmer and, some say, the Birman (*see* pp.160–61). This was possibly the first deliberate crossing of two breeds. In the 1930s, geneticists in the United States also crossed Persians and Siamese to investigate inherited traits. They called the resulting pointed, longhaired offspring Himalayan, after a similarly patterned type of rabbit. These cats were recognized in Britain in 1955 as Colourpoint Longhairs (the Persian was called the Longhair in Britain at that time). This was the first recognition of a breed that had "imported" the pointed pattern. In Europe the name Khmer gave way to the name Colourpoint. In North America the cats were recognized in 1957 as a new and separate breed, the Himalayan. They are now generally included in the Persian breed, although the pattern is still referred to as

Himalayan. Some breeders feel the type differs, but there is also the problem that once the recessive pointing gene is in a bloodline, breeders aiming to produce solid-coloured kittens can never be sure whether a cat carries the trait or not.

FORM AND CHARACTER

The Colourpoint Persian has the build, face, and coat of a Persian with the colouring of a Siamese. The round head has the same full cheeks and short nose as the Persian. The pointed coat looks somewhat different on a longhaired cat and the eyes are generally

Shading develops on older cats

Short, cobby body

SEAL POINT

Long, thick, and silky coat, with no wooliness

CREAM POINT

POINTED PATTERNS

The first cat to be shown in the West with restriction of colour to the extremities or "points" of the body was the Siamese (*see* pp.124–27), but this mutation was probably not confined to the Far East. Peter Pallas (1741–1811), the naturalist who gave his name to the wild Asian Pallas's cat (*Felis manul*), encountered a cat with just such a coat pattern in an area near the Caspian Sea. He described and illustrated it in his book *Travels Throughout the Southern Provinces of the Russian Empire*, published in 1793. It wasn't until well over a century later though that geneticists crossed Siamese and Persians, and unintentionally created the Colourpoint Persian.

COLOURPOINT PERSIAN

less intensely blue than in the Siamese. The differing personalities of the two parents result in a cat that is more outgoing than one, while more relaxed than the other. The main demand that the Colourpoint places on its owner is the time needed to care for the long coat.

Split personality

The Colourpoint Persian may have the body and facial features of the Persian, along with a fairly laid-back character, but it also inherits some Siamese traits, making it more likely to live an active, energetic life.

BIRMAN

DATE OF ORIGIN Unknown, recognized 1925
PLACE OF ORIGIN Myanmar (formerly Burma) or France
ANCESTRY Uncertain
WEIGHT RANGE 4.5–8kg (10–18lb)
COLOURS All self and tortie colours and tabbies, in pointed pattern with white mittens
BREED REGISTRIES GCCF, FIFé, CFA, TICA

Medium-sized, well-spaced ears

"Mitten" ends below ankle

RED POINT

Birmans have for generations been bred as companion cats; the breed's loving and affectionate nature competing with a truly beautiful coat as its most attractive quality. Tradition has it that the Birman is descended from Sita, a temple cat shipped from Burma (now Myanmar) in 1919 to August Pavie and Major Russell Gordon in France. She was said to be one of a pair sent by the Khmer

Enduring perfection
These Blue-point Birman kittens combine stunning visual presence with striking personality. Friendly to humans, they also enjoy the company of other animals.

people as a gift of thanks for saving temples during Brahmin uprisings. The legend behind the pattern is that a white cat named Sinh in a temple honouring the blue-eyed, golden goddess Tsun-Kyan-Tse took on these colours as he stood over the fallen body of a monk during an attack on the temple, a sight that inspired the monks to spirited defence. While it is likely that the pointed gene was

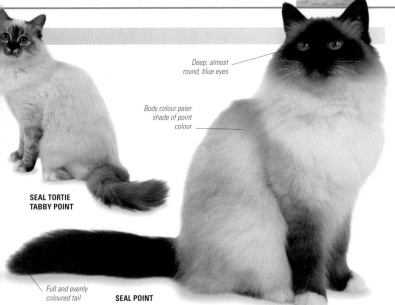

Deep, almost
round, blue eyes

Body colour paler
shade of point
colour

**SEAL TORTIE
TABBY POINT**

Full and evenly
coloured tail

SEAL POINT

present in the feline population of
Myanmar (and the pattern may therefore
originate there), another suggestion is
that the Birman resulted from the same
experimental breeding that created the
Colourpoint Persian (*see* pp.158–59).
That breed was at first called the Khmer
in mainland Europe, which might lend
credence to such a theory, but this white-
footed breed has from the start been
known as the Sacred Cat of Burma, or
the Birman, from "Birmanie", the French
for Burma. It was almost extinct in the
West at the end of World War II, when
only two individuals remained in France.
These were outcrossed with other cats
to perpetuate the breed, increasing the
genetic base and introducing the potential
for a variety of point colours. Happily,
its fortunes recovered steadily thereafter

to the extent that it
is now one of the most popular breeds of
cat in both Europe and North America.

FORM AND CHARACTER

The Birman is in many respects halfway
between Colourpoint Persians and the
sleek, longhaired Oriental breeds. It is
strongly built but not cobby, with medium-
length legs and a long body, and its head is
neither elongated nor shortened. The silky
coat is not as thick and prone to matting
as that of the Persian, but daily grooming
is still essential for Birmans. Inbreeding
may concentrate hereditary problems,
but only rare skin and nerve disorders are
hereditary in this breed. While generally
quiet and relaxed, Birmans believe their
place is naturally at the centre of their
owner's attention, and can be bossy.

THE TEMPLECAT

This shorthaired equivalent of the Birman was created by
New Zealand breeder June Mateer. Her first cross of a
Birman and a cinnamon tabby Oriental Shorthair (*see*
pp.128–29) produced a seal-pointed kitten, showing that
the Oriental luckily carried the recessive pointing gene.
Once the dominant shorthair trait had been introduced,
crosses were all back to Birmans to develop the desired
conformation and markings. Provisionally called the
Birman Shorthair, the breed (right) was recognized by the
new registry CATZ Inc in New Zealand in 2001 under the
name Templecat. It is not yet accepted in other registries.

RAGDOLL

DATE OF ORIGIN 1960s
PLACE OF ORIGIN United States
ANCESTRY Unclear
WEIGHT RANGE 4.5–9kg (10–20lb)
COLOURS All self and tortie colours (excluding cinnamon), and bicolours, in solid and tabby with pointed pattern
BREED REGISTRIES GCCF, FIFé, CFA, TICA

Ragdolls have possibly the strangest and most controversial history of any breed. In the 1960s, American breeder Ann Baker began producing cats from Josephine, a white, probably non-pedigree, longhaired cat, and her Birman-type son, Daddy Warbucks. What was most remarkable about this new breed was Baker's claim that after being injured in a road accident Josephine produced extraordinarily placid kittens that flopped like ragdolls when they were handled. She registered the Ragdoll name as trademark and formed a breed society, the International Ragdoll Cat Association (IRCA), in 1971. She then declared: "If you do not have an IRCA registered kitten, you do not have a true Ragdoll". However, Baker's own cats did not win wider acceptance. It was other breeders, working with her lines, who eventually won recognition for the Ragdoll. This appreciation was achieved in Britain by 1990, and in 2000, the Ragdoll won full CFA acceptance. The Ragamuffin (*see* p.166), recognized only in North America, is related to the Ragdoll.

FORM AND CHARACTER

The Ragdoll has become one of the most popular breeds in Britain and North America. It is a large, surprisingly heavy cat with a long body and a rounded face. The coat is medium length, dense, silky, and flowing, and comes in pointed

DESIGNING BREEDS

The genetics of cat coat colours, patterns, and length have been pieced together painstakingly over more than a century of selective breeding. How much genes influence behaviour is much less understood, but few breeders would claim that injuries to a parent cat could be inherited by their offspring. Ann Baker was an exception to the rule. The traits of Ragdolls were said to be the result of the founding female's involvement in a road accident or government experiments, and the related Honeybear was supposedly created from a cat injected with manipulated skunk genes. Such unorthodox and unproven theories are generally unhelpful for the health and well-being of the breeds involved.

pattern, mitted pattern, and bicolour, which is somewhat similar to the mitted pattern but with more white.

Ann Baker claimed that Ragdolls differed in character from other breeds in three key ways: their tendency to go limp in

Long, muscular body

Non-matting, moderately long fur

SEAL BICOLOUR

Medium-sized, round-tipped ears

Medium-length, dense, and silky coat

Long, bushy, slightly tapered tail

BLUE MITTED

a person's arms when held, and a higher pain threshold and lower self-preservation instincts than normal. The breed does have a relaxed personality and is easy to handle, but the other claims have caused some problems for the Ragdoll. Breeders have spent many years trying to dispel the myth that these cats are tolerant of pain, for obvious reasons, and the breed's survival instincts seem to be as robust as those of any other cat. The Ragdoll's reputation for being more than happy to live indoors and indifferent to hunting has helped it to gain popularity in Australia, where environmentalists are concerned over cats preying on wildlife.

Basic instincts
Although Ragdolls are laid-back and more tolerant of a life indoors than other breeds, they will patrol and defend their territory just like other cats if allowed outside.

Living doll
Mostly known for its famously placid disposition, the Ragdoll also boasts a surprisingly heavy build, a receptiveness to training, and a pair of commanding azure eyes.

RAGAMUFFIN

DATE OF ORIGIN 1994
PLACE OF ORIGIN United States
ANCESTRY Unclear, but in part Ragdolls
WEIGHT RANGE 4.5–9kg (10–20lb)
COLOURS All self and tortie colours, and bicolours in all patterns except pointed
BREED REGISTRIES CFA

Broad, modified-wedge head

Rounded chin and muzzle

Large body, with broad chest and shoulders

According to the CFA breed profile, "The exact development and early history of the RagaMuffin breed is clouded. The full story will likely stay a mystery forever." This is a delicate description of a messy story. The RagaMuffin could be called the "alternative" Ragdoll (*see* pp.162–65). Breeding Ragdolls was not always easy, with breeder Ann Baker keeping tight control over breeding decisions, information, and finances, and making strange claims about the breed's origins. When she delayed her retirement, exasperated breeders opted to break away, renaming their version of the breed to avoid legal problems.

Large, rounded, and tufted paws

Long and fully furred tail

Early promise
The RagaMuffin is a large cat, and kittens may take a few years to reach full adult size. All kinds of bicolour markings are allowed, with no importance attached to symmetry.

The shared history of the Ragdoll and the RagaMuffin continues to cause some difficulties, partly as there is a continuing perception that the breeds are one and the same, although they are likely to become more distinct as time passes. The RagaMuffin is still a relatively obscure breed, but with CFA recognition it is beginning to increase in popularity.

Like the Ragdoll, the RagaMuffin is a large, heavy cat with a luxuriant, silky coat. It has a sweet expression and a mellow character to match; these cats are relaxed and patient with children and will tolerate indignities, although not abuse.

LONGHAIRED EXOTIC VARIANT

DATE OF ORIGIN 1960s
PLACE OF ORIGIN United States
ANCESTRY Persian, American Shorthair
WEIGHT RANGE 3.5–7kg (8–15lb)
COLOURS All self and tortie colours and bicolours in solid, smoke, shaded, and tipped, and classic tabby pattern
BREED REGISTRIES FIFé, TICA

Perhaps confusingly, this is the longhaired variety of a shorthaired version of a longhaired breed. The Exotic (*see* p.167) is essentially a Persian (*see* pp.154–57) in a short coat, developed by crosses primarily to American Shorthairs (*see* pp.96–97) and British Shorthairs (*see* pp.88–89), bred back to Persians for type. The longhaired gene is recessive, and longhaired Exotics are still often born. The problem of how to categorize these has been approached differently by different registries: in FIFé and TICA they are shown as Persians, while the CFA and GCCF class them as variants of the Exotic.

WHAT'S IN A NAME?

More than any other cat, the longhaired variant of the Exotic raises the question of what makes a breed: its genes, its appearance, or its history? Genetically, these cats are extremely close to Persians, and they carry no risk of producing unexpected shorthairs. Many people hold that there is now no perceptible difference between them and Persians, beyond the usual variation of quality and appearance found within any breed, or indeed any litter of kittens. On these grounds, some breed registries allow these cats to be shown as Persians; this also occurs with some breeds that have distinctive traits, where any cat with the trait can be registered. But to other registries the most important factor is the history and the pedigree, and here it seems the longhaired Exotics will find no place.

The distinction between this cat and the Persian is disputed. Some say the coat is not of quite the same texture, the conformity not identical, or the character more lively; others maintain that the Exotic is a perfect shorthaired Persian, and the coat length is the only true difference. Outside the show ring, the continuing dispute over the exact status of these cats is more or less irrelevant, but their existence does mean that anyone looking for a pet Persian may find a source in breeders of Exotics.

Distinctively long whiskers

Black smoke and white
Almost all colours and bicolours must have brilliant copper-coloured eyes. The exceptions are the whites, which may have blue eyes, and shaded or tipped black selfs or tabbies, which have blue-green eyes.

MAINE COON

DATE OF ORIGIN 1860s
PLACE OF ORIGIN United States
ANCESTRY Farm cats
WEIGHT RANGE 4–7.5kg (9–17lb)
COLOURS Traditional Western self and tortie colours and bicolours in solid, smoke, and shaded, and in classic and mackerel tabby patterns
BREED REGISTRIES GCCF, FIFé, CFA, TICA

WHITE

The Maine Coon is distinguished by two features above all others: its long coat and its large size. In the harsh winters of eastern North America, cats that had lengthy insulating coats and were large enough to hunt hares and see off other predators enjoyed distinct survival advantages. The Maine Coon is one such naturally selected breed. Exactly how and when the longhaired gene first arrived in North America is not clear, but it could easily have been brought in by cats on ships arriving from Scandinavia or Russia in Maine's ports. The first Maine to be noted at shows, in 1861, was called Captain Jenks of the Horse Marines, and the breed enjoyed popularity for a while as the Maine Shag before being supplanted in the public's affections by the more luxuriant Persians (*see* pp.154–57) at the end of the century. It survived this hiatus because it was simply an excellent farm cat: a voracious mouser that continued to thrive as such. Interest was rekindled after World War II, and the Maine is now second only to the Persian in popularity

Heavy coat
This well-insulated individual has the look of confidence that is typical of the breed. The Maine Coon remains an independent spirit, comfortable indoors, but at its best in the natural world.

Large, slightly
slanted eyes

Very large,
long, and well-
muscled body

Plume-like
end to tail

Long,
glossy coat

Large, round
paws

in its homeland. The
breed arrived with
something of a feline
fanfare in Britain in the
mid-1980s, and this
gentle giant of a cat
has gained popularity
steadily to become a well-
established companion.

Medium-length,
strong legs

BRITISH LOOK SILVER TABBY

FORM AND CHARACTER

The Maine build is large, solid,
and muscular, but claims of cats as
big as dogs are exaggerated. Maines
displaying the British look have broad
faces with oval eyes, and the body and legs
are correspondingly stocky. TICA prefers
the alternative look, with a slightly more
angular face and rounder eyes. The
thick coat is water-repellent and
needs less maintenance than
some of the softer longhair
coats. Originally, only
the tabbies were called
Coons, because of their
passing resemblance

to raccoons, and today tabbies are still
favoured because they seem to reflect
the barn-cat origins of the breed.
Although in many ways a self-contained
and independent cat, the Maine differs
from many Western breeds in being vocal,
with a distinctive chirping trill used in
greeting. An active and outgoing cat, like
the Norwegian Forest Cat (*see* pp.172–75),
individuals have been known to enjoy
fishing and even swimming.

SHIPS' CATS

The idea that the Maine Coon
journeyed by ship from Europe to
the US certainly holds water. The
domestic cat spread from North
Africa first with the Phoenicians
and the Romans, and later crossed
the Atlantic with Europeans bound
for the New World, on ships such
as the *Mayflower* (right). It made
sense to keep cats on ships to
safeguard food supplies from mice
and rats and boost crew morale.
Plus it meant an extra source of
protein if times were really hard.

Maine attraction
Powerful, even-tempered, and luxurious to both look at and touch, the Maine Coon has become an extremely popular companion. Not just any old longhair, true Maines comply to rigorous standards.

NORWEGIAN FOREST CAT

DATE OF ORIGIN 1930s
PLACE OF ORIGIN Norway
ANCESTRY Farm cats
WEIGHT RANGE 3–9kg (7–20lb)
COLOURS Traditional Western self and tortie colours and bicolours in solid, smoke, shaded, and tipped, and Western tabby patterns
BREED REGISTRIES GCCF, FIFé, CFA, TICA

Black selfs have eyes of either green or gold

All that is certain about the Norwegian Forest Cat is that it is an old breed. Legend has it that it may be none other than the troll cat of Scandinavian fairy-tales, but history suggests otherwise.

The domestic cat is known to have reached Norway by about AD 1000. As well as arriving via the gradual spread of felines across Europe in the preceding centuries, cats came to Scandinavia as a result of the direct trade between the Vikings and the Byzantine empire. Evidence of this movement is apparent in some coat colours that are common in Turkey and Norway, but rare across the rest of Europe. This link raises the

BLACK

BLUE TORTIE TABBY-AND-WHITE

possibility that the longhaired gene arrived in Norway by the same trading routes. A long coat conferred a distinct advantage in the harsh northern winters, and it became a widespread trait in household and especially farm cats in Norway. The Skogkatt, or Skaukatt, as it was also known, was not regarded as a breed in its homeland until the 1930s, and it was only some decades later that planned selective breeding was undertaken. Since

Ears open, wide at base, and set high on head

Large body, with good bone and muscle structure

Long and bushy tail, equal in length to body

Legs long but not delicate

Large, round paws, with tufts between toes

SILVER TABBY-AND-WHITE

COAT SCIENCE

All cats, including the ancestors of the Norwegian Forest Cat, carry either a gene called "L" that is responsible for a short coat, or a companion gene called "l" that selects for a long coat (*see* pp.74–77). The short coat gene "L" is dominant. Only one copy of "L" is necessary to produce shorthaired cats. If, however, both parents carry the "l" gene, their kittens are longhaired. In the survival of the fittest it is these "ll" kittens that survived and multiplied, producing the ancestors of the Norwegian Forest Cat.

then, however, the Norwegian Forest Cat has won recognition at home and abroad, though it is still less well-known than the Maine Coon (*see* pp.168–71), another longhaired cat from a similar background.

Long, water-resistant guard hairs covering woolly, thick underfur

SILVER TABBY

FORM AND CHARACTER

This breed, also known as the Wegie, still reflects its origins as a free-living farm cat, and breeders sometimes refer to it as their "little lynx". It is large, robust, and muscular, and the triangular head is defined by a long nose. The glossy coat has a smooth and distinctly water-repellent top coat over a dense, insulating undercoat. The personality remains that of a farm cat, too. These cats are lithe and agile, excellent hunters, and have been known to fish. While they do make gentle, quiet companions, they are self-contained and tend to be quite spirited in defence of their territory, and a Norwegian will live happily as the sole cat in a household.

Making a mark

This Norwegian Forest Cat is in its element as it sharpens its claws on a fallen tree. This act helps to both mark and defend its territory.

Vikings' cat
Originating in the harsh conditions of Scandinavia, the Norwegian Forest Cat has a woolly undercoat that is covered by a water-repellent uppercoat – essential protection in freezing temperatures.

SIBERIAN

DATE OF ORIGIN 1980s
PLACE OF ORIGIN Eastern Russia
ANCESTRY Household and farm cats
WEIGHT RANGE 4.5–9kg (10–20lb)
COLOURS Traditional Western self and tortie colours and bicolours in solid, smoke, shaded, and tipped, with traditional tabby patterns
BREED REGISTRIES GCCF, FIFé, CFA, TICA

Like other large, shaggy cat breeds, the Siberian is a result of the harsh climate of its homeland favouring the hardiest hunters with a coat that would keep out the cold. It was overlooked as a breed until the 1980s, but then spread rapidly, being exported to Europe and North America in the 1990s, initially under the name Siberian Forest Cat. It is now accepted by the major breed registries, but its name has been changed to avoid confusion with the Norwegian Forest Cat (*see* pp.172–75). The pointed version of the breed, called the Neva Masquerade, is not widely recognized.

Although there are some variations in the standard internationally, they agree in broad points. The Siberian is a powerful, muscular cat with a heavy-set body and substantial legs. The wild-looking coat has a water-repellent, slightly oily top coat, and a dense, insulating undercoat that is designed to keep out piercing cold.

The breed reflects its past in character as much as in appearance. While it is sociable and steady, it is also active and resourceful and so ill-suited to the role of lap-cat. Contrary to claims, the Siberian is no less allergenic than other cats.

RED SHADED TABBY

Medium-sized ears with rounded tips, angled out

Long coat, with a slightly oily top coat

Short and sturdy neck

Medium-length, thick tail, with a rounded tip

Females, like this one, are finer-boned than males

BROWN SPOTTED TABBY-AND-WHITE

SCOTTISH FOLD (LONGHAIR)

DATE OF ORIGIN 1961
PLACE OF ORIGIN Scotland
ANCESTRY Farm cat, British and American Shorthairs
WEIGHT RANGE 2.5–6kg (6–13lb)
COLOURS Traditional Western self and tortie colours and bicolours in solid, smoke, shaded, and tipped, and traditional tabby patterns colours
BREED REGISTRIES CFA, TICA

The Longhaired Scottish Fold shares its breed history with the shorthaired version (*see* p.91). The longhair gene has been present from the start, but remains rare because other shorthaired breeds have been used in the Fold's development. In the longhair, a soft, medium-long coat clothes a sturdy body. Folds have a lovely character, being quiet and peaceable with a sweet expression; a healthy Fold makes an enjoyable and undemanding pet.

Small ears, tightly folded to head

Large, round expressive eyes

Very large and fluffy tail

BLUE-CREAM AND WHITE

CYMRIC

DATE OF ORIGIN 1960s
PLACE OF ORIGIN Canada and United States
ANCESTRY Household cats
WEIGHT RANGE 3.5–5.5kg (8–12lb)
COLOURS All self and tortie colours and bicolours, in solid, smoke, and tipped, in Western tabby patterns and pointed pattern
BREED REGISTRIES FIFé, CFA, TICA

The Manx (*see* p.90) has always produced occasional longhaired kittens, which were not accepted for showing. In the 1960s, breeders in North America worked to have these variants recognized, and succeeded by the 1980s. The CFA includes the Cymric with the Manx and allows only Western colours.

RED TABBY AND WHITE KITTEN

Like the Manx, Cymrics can have various lengths of tail or smooth rears. In North America only tailless cats, "rumpies", are shown, but in FIFé all four have their own classes; concentrating on achieving complete taillessness can have serious health implications for the cat. Distinctively sturdy in build, with long hindlegs, the Cymric is friendly and steady, like its shorthaired forebear.

Pure white coat, with no hint of yellowing

Rounded head with gentle dip from forehead to nose

ORANGE-EYED WHITE

SELKIRK REX (LONGHAIR)

DATE OF ORIGIN 1987
PLACE OF ORIGIN United States
ANCESTRY Rescued domestic cat, Persian, Exotic, British and American Shorthairs
WEIGHT RANGE 3–5kg (7–11lb)
COLOURS All colours and all patterns
BREED REGISTRIES GCCF, CFA, TICA

The mutation behind this rexed breed may be traced back to a single female kitten born in For Pet's Sake, a rescue shelter run by Kitty Brown in Sheridan, Montana. Although there were seven kittens in the litter, she was the only one with curly hair and curly whiskers. The kitten was adopted by Jeri Newman, a breeder with a keen interest in genetics, and named Miss DePesto of NoFace. When she was mated to a Newman's Persian (*see* pp.154–57), "Pest" produced some ordinary and some curly kittens, showing the gene to be dominant. The breed was named after the Selkirk Mountains in Canada, and both the longhaired and the shorthaired (*see* p.95) Selkirk are accepted in all major registries.

The breeds used in the creation of this breed have given it a conformation that is close to the British Shorthair (*see* pp.88–89).

Full cheeks and whisker pads

Eyes round and widely spaced

CREAM BICOLOUR

The coat is thick, like that of the British Shorthair, but differs in that it is randomly curled, with the breed standards calling for "ringlets". This effect is most readily produced in cats that have one rexing gene and one straight-haired gene. The head of the Selkirk is full-cheeked and short-muzzled, with a Western character, rather than the Oriental look that is favoured for other rexes.

This eye-catching, soft-coated breed is calm, steady, and patient. It does not demand attention.

Rounded head with short muzzle

RED-SHADED TABBY

Muscular and rectangular body

Soft coat falls in loose, individual curls

Slight rise to hindquarters

Medium-length legs with large paws

Thick tail tapers to rounded tip

BLUE-CREAM

Persian influence
While Persian genes have helped give the Selkirk a strong, rounded head, the breed standard specifies a muzzle half as long as it is wide, avoiding the very short nose of the Persian.

MUNCHKIN (LONGHAIR)

DATE OF ORIGIN 1980s
PLACE OF ORIGIN United States
ANCESTRY Household cats
WEIGHT RANGE 2.5–4kg (6–9lb)
COLOURS All colours and all patterns
BREED REGISTRIES TICA

The Longhaired Munchkin has the same origins as the shorthaired type (*see* pp.101–103). Whether Blackberry, the original female cat rescued by Sandra Hochenedel in Louisiana, carried the longhair gene is not recorded, but the subsequent wide variety of outcrosses to both pedigree and non-pedigree cats would have brought it into the breed at an early stage, along with probably every coat colour and pattern known in the feline world.

The Longhaired Munchkin possesses a semi-long, silky coat with a moderate undercoat. The coat is described as "all weather", although an indoor life is recommended for this diminutive cat by most breeders. In other respects, the longhaired variety closely resembles the shorthaired version, having a medium-

Never going to grow up
The short legs of the breed are apparent from birth. The Munchkin gene is dominant, making it clear which kittens in a litter have the trait; long-legged kittens do still appear.

sized body and rounded, wedge-shaped head with large eyes. Despite their small stature, they are reputedly active, with a curious nature and lively personality.

Over the years, the Munchkin has been crossed with many other breeds to create a variety of cats of novel appearance. Breeders have used it with the Persian (*see* pp.154–57) to produce the Napoleon, the Sphynx (*see* p.148) to create the Minskin (*see* p.148), and the LaPerm (*see* p.196) to produce the Skookum, a rexed Munchkin.

Tail tapers to the tip

Triangular, moderately large ears

Spine level or rises slightly from shoulder to rump

Legs short but straight

TORTIE-AND-WHITE

AMERICAN CURL (LONGHAIR)

DATE OF ORIGIN 1981
PLACE OF ORIGIN United States
ANCESTRY Household cats
WEIGHT RANGE 3–5kg (7–11lb)
COLOURS All self and tortie colours and bicolours, in solid, smoke, shaded, or tipped, and all tabby and pointed patterns
BREED REGISTRIES FIFé, CFA, TICA

RED TABBY-AND-WHITE

The founding mother of the American Curl was a stray cat adopted by Joe and Grace Ruga in California 1981. A black longhair, she was named Shulamith by her new owners, who began a breeding programme with her a couple of years later. By the 1990s the Curl was fully recognized in North America. While the breed is known in Europe, it has still not been accepted by the GCCF.

Although Shulamith had long hair, there were also short-coated kittens among the earliest litters, and as a result this was the first breed in the CFA with two coat lengths (*see* also p.100).

The breed has been developed with a standard written around Shulamith's own appearance. She had a moderate build, being lithe but not overly slender. The ears, the key feature of the American Curl, have firm cartilage, more like that in the human ear than the softer ears typical in the cat. All kittens are born with straight ears, and what degree of curl they will develop is still unpredictable. Curls have a pleasing personality, being outgoing and sociable, playful and intensely curious.

Distinctive curled ears

Plumed tail same length as body

Moderately muscled body

SPOTTED TABBY-AND-WHITE

Medium-length legs

Semi-foreign build

TURKISH VAN

DATE OF ORIGIN Before 1700s
PLACE OF ORIGIN Turkey
ANCESTRY Household cats
WEIGHT RANGE 3–8.5kg (7–19lb)
COLOURS Traditional Western self and tortie colours in solid or tabby patterns, as bicolour only
BREED REGISTRIES GCCF, FIFé, CFA, TICA

The Van is a naturally occurring cat strain breeding in relative isolation in the mountainous Lake Van region of eastern Turkey, where it has been recorded for centuries. It became known further afield when two individuals were brought to Britain in 1955; Vans reached North America only in the 1970s. In Britain, the all-white version, Turkish Vankedisi, also sometimes called Van Kedi, has embarked on its progress towards recognition by the GCCF, but it remains virtually unknown in North America.

The striking coat pattern of this cat, with the colour being restricted to ears and tail, is now known simply as van. The strict colour standards extend to the eyes, which must be amber or blue or one of each, the last being the "classic" look for the breed. Although elegant and silky-haired, with a sweet expression, the Turkish Van is not a lap-cat but an active and independent feline, famed in its homeland for its ability to fish and swim.

Large ears set high on head

Large and oval eyes

VAN FACE

Coat "breaks" readily

Bushy tail, as long as body

CREAM

Short, wedge-shaped head with long, straight profile

Long and silky coat with no undercoat

Long and sturdy body

Medium-length legs, with neat, rounded paws

BLUE

TURKISH ANGORA

DATE OF ORIGIN 1400s

PLACE OF ORIGIN Turkey

ANCESTRY Household cats

WEIGHT RANGE 2.5–5kg (6–11lb)

COLOURS Traditional Western self and tortie colours and bicolours in solid, smoke, shaded, classic and mackerel tabby and silver patterns

BREED REGISTRIES FIFé, CFA, TICA

The first longhaired cats came to Europe from the Middle East centuries ago, and at least some of them came from Turkey. By the early 20th century, indiscriminate breeding had led to this type becoming almost extinct: it is reputed to have been saved by a breeding programme in Ankara Zoo. More recently, in Britain, it has suffered from confusion with the Angora, now the Oriental Longhair (Angora) (*see* pp.188–89), a name change which may improve the Turkish breed's fortunes.

In the Turkish Angora, a shimmering coat with almost no undercoat clothes a lithe body. Quick off the mark, this cat is as close as a cat ever gets to exuberant.

Classic colour

White cats of the Turkish Angora type have appeared in paintings for centuries. In all coat colours, the eyes may be any colour from copper through gold and green to blue.

Large, slightly pointed ears set high

Large, oval eyes

Slim, graceful neck

Long, slender, but muscular body

BLUE TABBY

LONGHAIR ORIGINS

Although the Persian was the first longhaired breed to be widely established in the West, the Turkish Angora may have a better claim to being the "original" longhaired cat. Mapping the historical spread of the longhaired trait seems to indicate that it arose as a mutation in the domestic cat, most likely in an isolated population in central Asia. It was once suggested that the trait was the result of Tartars domesticating the Pallas's cat (*Felis manul*) and taking it to Turkey, where it bred with local shorthairs. But the Pallas's cat's intractable nature and a tendency to sterility in hybrids make this unlikely.

Turkish delight
Graceful and athletic, this Turkish Angora kitten is a protected breed in its homeland. When the coat is shed in summer, the cat's silver colouring becomes more apparent, especially on the face.

SOMALI

DATE OF ORIGIN 1963
PLACE OF ORIGIN Canada and United States
ANCESTRY Abyssinian
WEIGHT RANGE 3.5–5.5kg (8–12lb)
COLOURS Traditional Eastern and Western self and tortie colours, in solid and shaded, in ticked tabby pattern
BREED REGISTRIES GCCF, FIFé, CFA, TICA

BLUE-SILVER

One common belief about Somalis is that they are direct descendants of the Sacred Cat of Egypt. The truth, however, may be somewhat less fascinating. Basically a longhaired Abyssinian (see pp.112–15), the Somali has an identically patterned coat, but with medium-long, slightly shaggy fur.

From its very early days, the Abyssinian produced the occasional fuzzy, longhaired kitten. In the 1940s, breeder Jean Robertson exported Abys to North America, Australia, and New Zealand, and in 1963 a longhaired descendant was shown by Canadian breeder Mary Malling at a local show. The judge, Ken McGill, was so taken with it that he asked for one to breed from, and the first "official" Somali was his May-Ling Tutsuta. Meanwhile, in the United States, breeder Mary Mague was also developing longhaired Abys, which she called Somalis. Canadian breeder Don Richings began working with her using McGill's breeding stock, and by the late 1970s the breed was accepted in North American registries. Somalis made their appearance in Europe in the 1980s and were

WINTER COAT

Summer coat
The Somali's short summer coat gives it the look of an Abyssinian. Its coat grows much longer in winter before being shed during a spring moult.

RECESSIVES ARE FOREVER

The long hair of the Somali is a recessive gene. These genes can be carried without being seen because they are "masked" by a dominant gene. This can cause problems for breeders seeking to produce a consistent cat type, because two black cats carrying a masked dilute gene may produce some blue kittens when mated, or two shorthairs may produce longhaired kittens. However, they may not produce them in every litter, so recessives can be very hard to track and breed out. Over many generations, most are virtually eliminated, but "recessives are forever" remains a truism among breeders. In some cases, like with the Somali, this has been seized as the opportunity to create a new breed.

recognized worldwide by 1991. More colours are accepted in Europe than by some American registries.

FORM AND CHARACTER

The Somali's build is naturally similar to that of its parent breed, with long legs carrying a lithe, muscular body. The longer coat on a Somali can carry up to 12 alternating bands of darker-coloured ticking on each hair, which produces a striking shimmer when the cat is in full coat. Like all cats, the Somali will shed substantially in the spring, and can appear almost shorthaired in the warmer months of the year or if living in a hot climate. In their winter coat, they carry a full ruff and a brush of a tail, and together with their colouring and build this has earned them the nickname of "fox cats". The slightly wild looks are borne out in an active and independent personality, for Somalis make excellent hunters and will not take well to an indoor-only life unless it is all they ever know. They are gregarious, living happily in multi-cat households.

Moderately wedge-shaped head with smooth lines

Large almond-shaped eyes

SORREL

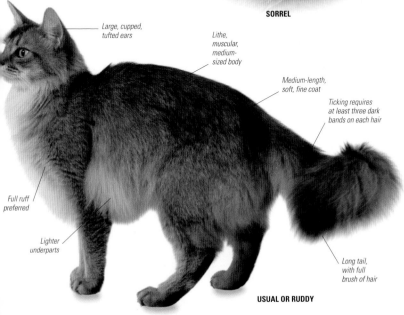

Large, cupped, tufted ears

Lithe, muscular, medium-sized body

Medium-length, soft, fine coat

Ticking requires at least three dark bands on each hair

Full ruff preferred

Lighter underparts

Long tail, with full brush of hair

USUAL OR RUDDY

ORIENTAL LONGHAIR (ANGORA)

DATE OF ORIGIN 1970s
PLACE OF ORIGIN Britain
ANCESTRY Siamese, Abyssinian
WEIGHT RANGE 2.5–5kg (6–11lb)
COLOURS All self and tortie colours in solid, smoke, shaded, and tipped, and all tabby patterns
BREED REGISTRIES GCCF

The name of this breed can cause some confusion. It is quite different from the Oriental Longhair (*see* pp.192–93) and the Turkish Angora (*see* pp.183–85), nor is it descended from the cats called Angoras in the 19th century. In fact, this breed came about by accident. In the 1960s, English breeder Maureen Silson mated a sorrel Abyssinian (*see* pp.112–15) and a seal-point Siamese (*see* pp.124–27) in an attempt to create a Siamese with ticked points. The descendants inherited the cinnamon trait (called sorrel in the Aby), producing cinnamon Oriental Shorthairs (*see* pp.128–29), and the gene for long hair, recessive in the Aby, which gave us this breed, known as the Angora until 2003. Oriental Longhair (Angora) is only recognized in Britain, although it was called the Oriental Longhair in North America until another breed of the same name developed separately there. To add to the muddle, this breed has been called the Javanese in mainland Europe (a name used for some pointed longhairs in North America) and was also known at one point as the Mandarin.

FORM AND CHARACTER

This British Oriental Longhair is svelte, but not extreme: its slim legs are well muscled, and the wedge-shaped head is not overlong. The fine, silky coat lacks an undercoat and lies sleekly against the body; for a longhaired cat, the Angora is relatively easy to look after. The eyes, green in all colours but white, have an Oriental slant, and the breed's personality reveals its Siamese parentage. These are playful, inquisitive, and gregarious individuals, happy in a multi-cat household, and moderately vocal.

Odd eye colours; eyes are green in all other colours of Angora

Long and slender neck

Medium-sized, svelte, and muscular body

BLUE-EYED WHITE

NAMING CAT BREEDS

The names cat breeders choose to give their creations provide an intriguing insight into the changing role of these pets. Early breed names tended to be tersely descriptive (there was a Black and White Cat Club in Britain for some years) or to state where the cat was from. In the 20th century, as new breeds emerged there was an increased tendency to prefer exotic place names over strict geographical truth – the Balinese is not from Bali, and the Angora is not from Ankara – with the aim, perhaps, of bestowing glamour. More recently, cuddly names like Ragdoll, LaPerm, and Munchkin have been used, a reflection of the North American trend of keeping cats as indoors-only pets.

Fine, silky coat with no woolly undercoat

Moderately triangular, wedge-shaped head

Long, slim, well-muscled legs

RED SILVER-SHADED

Eyes blue
in kittens

Nose leather
matches coat

FAWN KITTENS

Early days
The coat of this breed
is particularly slow to
reach its full potential.
Kittens and young cats,
such as this silver tabby,
often appear to be
shorthaired, but the
plumed tail gives away
their true nature.

BALINESE

DATE OF ORIGIN 1950s
PLACE OF ORIGIN United States
ANCESTRY Longhaired Siamese
WEIGHT RANGE 2.5–5kg (6–11lb)
COLOURS All self and tortie colours
and tabby patterns, in pointed pattern
BREED REGISTRIES GCCF, FIFé, CFA, TICA, TCA

Spotted whisker pads

Long, plumed tail

Medium-sized, lithe body

SEAL TORTIE TABBY POINT

It is not clear whether the longhaired gene has always been present in the Siamese (*see* pp.124–27), but a longhaired Siamese was registered in Britain in 1928, and as a recessive trait, it is not improbable that this gene was carried by the very first Siamese brought to the West. These Longhaired Siamese examples were usually sold as pets, but in the years following World War II, Marian Dorsey, a breeder in California, began to work with them. The resulting Longhair Siamese were shown in 1955 and recognized in American registries by 1961, arriving in Europe by the mid-1970s. Following objections by Siamese breeders, the name was changed to Balinese. The Traditional Balinese is promoted under the TCA by breeders who feel that the modern type has, like the Siamese, become overly etiolated.

FORM AND CHARACTER

A slightly confusing situation currently exists with regard to the colours of the Balinese. In Europe, the breed comes in a wide range of colours and even tabby patterns. In North America, however, the CFA and TCA recognize only the four "original" colours of seal, blue, chocolate, and lilac, just as in the Siamese. The CFA classes other colours and tabby points as a separate breed, the Javanese.

The medium-long coat of the Balinese lies sleekly against the body and its silky texture makes it relatively easy to care for, but in other respects the Balinese may be said to be high-maintenance. This is not a cat to sit back and watch the world go by, but a highly inquisitive breed that will investigate corners of your home you never knew existed. The Balinese is happiest at the heart of the action and commenting on everything, and potential owners should be prepared to provide plenty of entertainment for it, and preferably another feline companion.

COLOUR BARS

It is ironic that Siamese and Balinese were for a long time only recognized in seal (like the cat pictured below) and blue, traditionally regarded as Western colours, simply because those were the colours of the first Siamese imported into Europe. This distinction between Eastern and Western coat colours is to some extent artificial. In fact, black, blue, red, and cream, in solid and tabby, have been present for centuries in cats the world over. Chocolate, cinnamon, lilac, and fawn do seem to have first appeared in the East, travelling West with Oriental cats brought to Europe in the 19th century. As a result they are often not permitted in the older European breeds.

Soft shading of fawn on body

SEAL POINT BALINESE

Deep brown tail

Pointed ears and muzzle

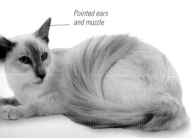

LILAC POINT

Deceptive appearance

Although it might look like an elegant pet, the intelligent and agile Balinese still has all the resources that sustained its more free-living ancestors. However, the pale, fine fur is not ideal protection against the sun, and a cream point like this may suffer sunburn on the ears and other areas.

ORIENTAL LONGHAIR

DATE OF ORIGIN 1985
PLACE OF ORIGIN North America
ANCESTRY Oriental Shorthair, Balinese
WEIGHT RANGE 4.5–6kg (10–13lb)
COLOURS All colours and patterns except pointed, sepia, and mink; many colours have special names
BREED REGISTRIES FIFé, CFA, TICA

In 1985, at Sholine Cattery, Houston, Texas, USA, an Oriental Shorthair (*see* pp.128–29) and a Balinese (*see* pp.190–91) escaped surveillance and mated. The result was a litter of silky, semi-longhaired kittens in solid Oriental colours. Wisely, cattery owner Sheryl Ann Boyle chose to develop the breed, and it was rapidly recognized by major registries across North America and Europe, with the exception of the GCCF in Britain, where it was felt to be too similar to the Angora, now known as the Oriental Longhair (Angora) (*see* pp.188–89).

In 1995, the CFA merged the Oriental Shorthair and Oriental Longhair into one breed with two coat lengths, a move that proved to be controversial with some breeders who would have preferred to keep the recessive longhaired trait out of the Oriental Shorthair breeding lines. Because of their pointed ancestry, all Orientals can produce pointed kittens from time-to-time, but these may not be shown in most associations, being confusingly similar to the separate Siamese and Balinese breeds.

The semi-longhaired Oriental Longhair completes what can be regarded as a quartet of

BROWN MACKEREL TABBY BICOLOUR

Long, flat profile

BLUE

Long, slim legs

THE ORIENTAL PERSONALITY

While the Oriental Longhair has elegant looks, its personality is generally described as anything but languid. All the Oriental breeds have a widely upheld reputation for being talkative, playful, highly inquisitive, and gregarious, needing either the company of other cats or the undivided attention of their owner for some time every day, and some surveys into cat character have backed up this picture. Much of a cat's personality is inherited, and over the decades breeders may have reinforced a naturally outgoing personality in the Oriental breeds. Owners report individuals that happily walk on a lead, and others that will play fetch just like dogs.

Oriental breeds; it is the longhaired counterpart of the Oriental Shorthair, just as the Balinese is the longhaired counterpart of the Siamese (see pp.124–27). While several decades separated the recognition of the Siamese and the longhaired Balinese, the Oriental Longhair followed the Shorthair fairly rapidly. This swiftness is perhaps a reflection on the changing nature of cat showing, which saw a great proliferation of breeds in the second half of the 20th century. The confusion between this breed and its British counterpart, the Oriental Longhair (Angora), is also an indication of how far feline fashions and breeding programmes have diverged internationally.

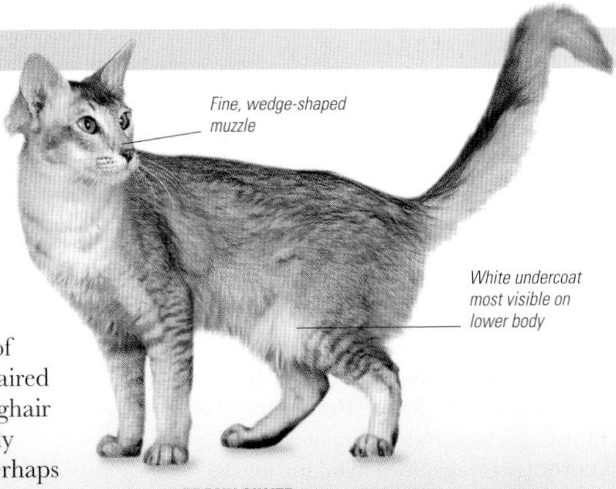

Fine, wedge-shaped muzzle

White undercoat most visible on lower body

EBONY SILVER

FORM AND CHARACTER

The coat of the Oriental Longhair is fine and sleek, which makes it as easy to care for as many shorthairs. Indeed, but for its gracefully plumed tail, this breed could be mistaken for a shorthair in summer. The svelte, tubular body can be surprisingly heavy, for this is an active breed with good muscle tone.

The Oriental Longhair possesses the typical Oriental personality, being an inquisitive, highly sociable, and vocal breed whose favourite place is at the centre of your attention.

CHOCOLATE MACKEREL TABBY

CHANTILLY/TIFFANY

DATE OF ORIGIN 1970s
PLACE OF ORIGIN Canada and United States
ANCESTRY Uncertain
WEIGHT RANGE 2.5–5.5kg (6–12lb)
COLOURS Traditional Eastern self colours in solid and mackerel, spotted, and ticked tabby patterns
BREED REGISTRIES None

This breed probably comes from the same crosses that produced the Oriental Longhair (Angora) (*see* pp.188–89). In 1967, in New York, Jennie Robinson bred from two golden-eyed, chocolate cats of unknown parentage; she called the kittens Foreign Longhairs. The name Tiffany was coined by Sigyn Lund in Florida. The breed languished and was all but extinct when in 1988 Tracy Oraas in Canada set about a rescue plan. The separate Tiffanie (*see* opposite) was by now recognized in

Britain, so the name was changed again to Chantilly/Tiffany. This affectionate, gentle cat has an endearing, chirping voice and is described by its breeders as "the chocoholic's delight".

Medium-length, slender, and elegant body

Triangular head, with gently curved profile

Plumed tail, equal in length to body

CHOCOLATE

NEBELUNG

DATE OF ORIGIN 1984
PLACE OF ORIGIN United States
ANCESTRY Russian Blue, household cats
WEIGHT RANGE 2.5–5kg (6–11lb)
COLOURS Blue
BREED REGISTRIES TICA, TCA

When blue cats from Russia were first shown elsewhere in the 19th century, both shorthaired and longhaired types were exhibited. The shorthairs went on to become the Russian Blue (*see* Russian Shorthairs, p.95), but the longhairs were largely forgotten. In Denver, Colorado, US, in 1986, matings of a shorthaired non-pedigree cat and a cat thought to be a Russian Blue produced two longhaired, blue kittens, Siegfried and Brunhilde. Cora Cobb, who owned these cats, used them and Russian Blues with the longhair gene to found the

Nebelung, a retiring breed that prefers a quiet life. Cobb took the name from the German word for mist, a reference to this elegant cat's semi-long hair, which is blue with silver tips that reflect the light.

Ears wide at base, with slightly rounded tips

Lithe and slender body

Long, fluffy tail tapers from thick base to fine tip

Small, round paws

TIFFANIE

DATE OF ORIGIN 1970s
PLACE OF ORIGIN Great Britain
ANCESTRY Burmese/Chinchilla crosses
WEIGHT RANGE 3.5–6.5kg (8–14lb)
COLOURS All self and tortie colours, in solid, shaded, and sepia pattern
BREED REGISTRIES GCCF

The only longhaired member of the Asian Group (*see* pp.140–41), this breed can be traced back to the same original mating of Baroness Miranda von Kirchberg's Chinchilla Persian and Burmese (*see* pp.132–35). The longer coat did not appear in the first generation, but resurfaced later.

The Tiffanie is recognized only in Britain; FIFé has the Burmilla, which is distinct from the Asian Group in Britain, and in North America there has been confusion with the Chantilly/Tiffany (*see* opposite). There is also a Tiffanie breeding programme in Australia.

The Tiffanie inherits its conformation from its Burmese ancestor, and a luxurious coat from the Chinchilla Persian. Its coat is not as long or as thick as that of a Persian, so is much easier to care for; the cat also has a silky ruff and a plumed tail. Being neither as demonstrative as a Burmese nor as sedate as a Persian, its owners and breeders find it the ideal, well-balanced longhair.

Fine, silky coat

Elegantly plumed tail

BLUE

Australian Tiffanie
The Tiffanie, long recognized in Britain, has not spread elsewhere. The Australian Tiffanie was founded in 1999, not from imports, but from new crosses.

Lilac Silver-Shaded
The coat of the Tiffanie is longest in the ruff and the plumed tail. On the body, it is just long enough to show off to perfection the shading of the silver colours.

LAPERM (LONGHAIR)

DATE OF ORIGIN 1982
PLACE OF ORIGIN United States
ANCESTRY Farm cats
WEIGHT RANGE 3.5–5.5kg (8–12lb)
COLOURS All colours, shades, and patterns
BREED REGISTRIES GCCF, CFA, TICA

CHOCOLATE TORTIE POINT

In 1982, Linda Koehl found a hairless, but otherwise apparently healthy kitten in the litter of a working farm cat in The Dalles, Oregon. The kitten survived and grew a soft, curled coat at about eight weeks old. Named Curly, this female produced a small colony of rexed kittens over the next five years, with numbers growing rapidly because the gene is dominant. This allowed a wide gene pool to be established for the breed, and outcrossing is still allowed to non-pedigree cats and, in Britain, a range of predominantly Oriental breeds. The LaPerm breed has, at least provisionally, gained recognition in registries worldwide. This relatively rapid international success may be due in part to the apparent health of the breed. There are no major medical problems associated with this distinctive gene, although LaPerms can be prone to some skin allergies.

Unlike the Cornish Rex (see pp.144–45) or Devon Rex (see pp.146–47), the LaPerm has an undercoat, and the longhaired version may appear "almost unkempt" according to the breed standards, a look named the Gipsy Shag. The coat is low maintenance, requiring minimal grooming because it doesn't mat easily. Although quiet, the LaPerm is an active and gregarious cat.

Curly hair at ear base

Large, expressive, slightly slanted eyes

Medium-sized body, with good musculature

Forelegs shorter than hindlegs

Long, tapering, plumed tail

BLUE MACKEREL TABBY

AMERICAN BOBTAIL (LONGHAIR)

DATE OF ORIGIN 1960s
PLACE OF ORIGIN United States
ANCESTRY Uncertain
WEIGHT RANGE 3–7kg (7–15lb)
COLOURS All colours and all patterns
BREED REGISTRIES CFA, TICA

The Longhaired American Bobtail has the same origins as the shorthaired type (*see* p.104). Although the early breeding programme concentrated on shorthairs, as the longhair trait is recessive it was never bred out, and the longhair is closest to the appearance of Yodie, the original Bobtail. Descriptions often suggest that this breed could be mistaken for a wild bobcat, and while this is poetic licence, Bobtails are large, muscular, and wild-looking cats. The longhairs have "mutton chops", a large ruff emulating that of the wild cat. In character the Bobtail is relaxed and generally tolerant, although it remains intelligent and an adept hunter.

BROWN MACKEREL TABBY

PIXIEBOB (LONGHAIR)

DATE OF ORIGIN 1980s
PLACE OF ORIGIN United States
ANCESTRY Farm cats
WEIGHT RANGE 4–8kg (9–18lb)
COLOURS Brown spotted tabby
BREED REGISTRIES TICA

The longhaired Pixiebob is the natural counterpart to the shorthaired version (*see* p.105), and is traceable back to the "legend cats", reputed to be hybrids of the domestic cat and bobcats. Testing has now disproved this theory, and breakaway breeders who attempted to cross the Pixiebob back to the bobcat to achieve a wilder look have not been conspicuously successful.

The coat of a longhaired Pixiebob is soft in texture and only semi-long; it lies closer to the body than that of the shorthair. Unusually, up to seven toes are allowed in this breed. Like the shorthair, the longhair Pixiebob is a quiet, affectionate pet, happy as the sole cat in a household.

Seasonal coat
In summer, the ground colour of the Pixiebob's coat becomes lighter, increasing the contrast in the pattern.

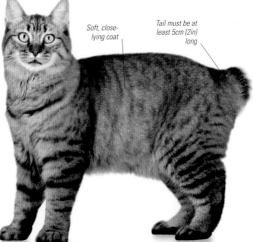

Soft, close-lying coat

Tail must be at least 5cm (2in) long

KURILEAN BOBTAIL (LONGHAIR)

DATE OF ORIGIN Before 1700s
PLACE OF ORIGIN Kuril Islands, Russian far east
ANCESTRY Domestic cats
WEIGHT RANGE 3–4.5kg (7–10lb)
COLOURS Traditional Western self and tortie colours and bicolours, in solid, smoke, shaded, and tipped, and with traditional tabby patterns.
BREED REGISTRIES FIFé

The mutation responsible for the short tail in this breed appears to be the same as that of the better known Japanese Bobtail (*see* opposite), and there is some rivalry as to which breed has the prior claim on the trait. The Japanese breed enjoyed a greater degree of popularity worldwide during the latter stages of the 20th century, in part because of the closed nature of the Soviet Union. In the wake of the Soviet Union's demise, the Kurilean Bobtail (or Kurilian or Kuril Bobtail) is now bred in North America and Europe, and is likely to be recognized by more major registries in the future.

A sturdier breed than the Japanese type, the Kurilean evolved in a freezing, harsher environment. Despite these cold conditions, there is a shorthaired version of the breed (*see* p.138). In character, these are sociable but independent cats who always seem to be about their own important business.

RUSSIAN BREEDS

Most of the world's cat breeds have been developed in Europe and North America, although the initial breeding stock of many originated elsewhere. Even the famous Russian Blue (*see* p.95) was more commonly bred in Britain and Sweden than in Russia. Although selective breeding programmes did exist under the Soviet Communist regime, they were aimed mostly at producing working dogs, not varieties of cat. With *glasnost* things changed, and unknown breeds began to appear beyond the old Soviet borders. These include the Urals Rex, known since World War II but only recognized in 1991, the Siberian (*see* p.176), and the Kurilean Bobtail.

Strong and muscular body

Short, curled tail carried high

Semi-long coat

Round paws

RED SELF

JAPANESE BOBTAIL (LONGHAIR)

DATE OF ORIGIN 1800s
PLACE OF ORIGIN Japan
ANCESTRY Household cats
WEIGHT RANGE 2.5–4kg (6–9kg)
COLOURS All self and tortie colours and bicolours in solid and traditional tabby patterns
BREED REGISTRIES FIFé, CFA, TICA

Semi-long, silky coat

TORTIE-AND-WHITE

The longhaired Japanese Bobtail shares the same historical path as the better-known shorthaired version (*see* p.138). Both types have been portrayed in Japanese art for centuries in a range of colours and patterns. The first Bobtails brought to the West carried the longhaired gene, but it was not noticed until the early 1970s, and remains much rarer than the shorthaired type. As a consequence of the recessive longhaired gene, matings to shorthairs produce some or all shorthaired kittens, and in a breed with such low numbers, mating only longhair-to-longhair would lead to dangerous levels of inbreeding.

The Japanese Bobtail is a sociable and inquisitive breed. The short tail, which makes a full, fluffy pompom, can be either straight or curled, and does not carry spinal or bone deformities with it.

With a well-muscled, athletic body, this is an action-loving cat that needs plenty of entertainment. Highly gregarious, it is easily bored and, when discontented, can be mischievously destructive.

MANEKI-NEKO

The most-prized Bobcat coat remains the tortie-and-white, especially in cats with odd eyes, reflecting the *Maneki-neko* (literally "Beckoning Cat"), a good-luck talisman throughout Japan (*see* p.50). The CFA recognizes only traditional Western colours in the Japanese Bobtail's semi-long, silky coat; other registries are more inclusive.

Curled pompom tail; can also be straight

Long, straight, slender body

Large ears, set wide apart and upright

Odd eyes, prized in this breed

Long, slender, but strong legs

TORTIE-AND-WHITE

NON-PEDIGREE LONGHAIRS

DATE OF ORIGIN Before AD 1000
PLACE OF ORIGIN Uncertain, possibly Turkey and Russia
ANCESTRY Domestic cat
WEIGHT RANGE 2.5–8kg (6–18lb)
COLOURS All colours and all patterns
BREED REGISTRIES Most registries have a household cat class for showing

The first domesticated cats were descended from the shorthaired African wildcat. A long coat would be a great disadvantage in the natural desert habitat of the wildcat, so any chance mutation would not survive. As the domestic cat spread northwards and eastwards, however, it moved into temperate climates where a long coat was not such a disadvantage, and eventually into regions with harsh winters, where such a coat was a necessity. Somewhere along the way, the mutation for long hair occurred and survived. This is thought to have happened in eastern Turkey, and possibly also in Russia. These longhaired cats spread to southern Europe and were probably also imported directly into Scandinavia by the Vikings, where they eventually gave rise to the Norwegian

Dominant patterns
In any random population, genetically dominant traits will be the most prevalent. The brown tabby pattern of this longhair is therefore one of the two most common coats seen in non-pedigree cats, the other being bicolour.

Forest Cat (*see* pp.172–75). It was also reported in the 16th century that the Portuguese had brought such cats from Persia to India as their trading empire expanded, and by the early 18th century they were recorded in China, where they may have arrived through trade or as a gift from Persia. From Europe, longhaired cats crossed the Atlantic to North America, where the longest, thickest coats naturally conveyed the greatest advantage in the cold continental winters.

FORM AND CHARACTER

Because the trait is recessive, only a minority of random-bred cats have long hair. This relative rarity of longhaired cats in the random-bred population may account for the fact that the most popular pedigree breeds tend to be longhaired. Nonetheless, the random-bred longhair remains more popular than any of the pedigree breeds, and is second in numbers only to the non-pedigree shorthairs (*see* pp.150–51). The coats of many of these will be what is called semi-long, similar to that of a Turkish Angora (*see* pp.183–85), perhaps closest to the original mutation. The thick coat of a Maine Coon (*see* pp.168–71)

Dramatic black eyeliner

Colouring similar to silver shaded Persian

SHADED SILVER

BLACK-AND-WHITE

may be found in colder environments, but the extraordinarily long coat of the Persian (*see* pp.154–57) is the result of many generations of selective breeding.

While feline character is strongly influenced by experiences in early kittenhood, personality traits are also inherited. There is evidence that pedigree cats tend to be more extrovert among strangers and in new situations, possibly due to many generations of breeding from cats that are happy in the show ring. A non-pedigree longhair may be more reserved than a pedigree cat.

Large, broad, rounded head

Dense, lustrous coat

TORTIE-AND-WHITE

KEEPING A CAT

FELINE BIOLOGY

The cat is a near-perfect predator, admirably designed to detect, capture, and kill small prey. Boasting the carnivore's physical prowess – a neat skeleton, sharp teeth, acute senses, powerful muscles, and first-rate balance – its internal organs and body functions are primed for superb flexibility and survival in the harshest of conditions.

A MODEL OF FORM AND FUNCTION

Simply by watching a cat stalking, it is easy to see that its design is that of the patient hunter. Its senses tell it of the presence of potential prey. Its hormones contain its excitement and keep it calm. Its brain integrates all the signals the body sends it, as well as controlling the spectacular bursts of energy of which its muscles are capable. A combination of flexible joints and superb balance give confidence on the ground or high up in trees.

The cat's organs are just as superbly designed. As with all mammals, the skin is the body's largest organ and a powerful component of the immune system. The feline heart and lungs are adapted for sudden flashes of speed. Cats are quick enough to escape larger predators in seconds, rather than suited to the endurance running of the dog. The digestive and excretory systems are those of the obligate carnivore – an animal that can survive only if it eats other animals.

Maternal bonding
Biologically prepared to care for her young, this new mum is responsible for their food, grooming, protection, and, eventually, teaching her kittens to defend themselves.

And to protect the cat from disease, its immune system defends the body against both external pathogens, such as viruses and bacteria, and internal dangers, such as cancer cells.

Complementing its supreme physical structure is the cat's great mental ability. Cats are intelligent animals that can find solutions to problems, apply them, and then adapt these solutions to different situations. Additionally, cats use their senses to communicate with each other: contented purrs and angry screeches (vocalization), facial expressions and postures (body signals), and nose-rubbing and grooming others (touch) make up part of the cat's communicative repertoire. These social behaviours also play an important part in the process of courtship and mating, thus ensuring the survival of the cat's genes.

Biology lesson
Thousands of years of domestication have done nothing to deter the cat from what it does best: stalk, pounce, and kill.

In full flight
Showing off its full feline splendour, this domestic cat harbours the same mental and physical traits as its wild ancestors.

Brain, hormones, and nerves

As befits a skilled hunter that depends upon its detection mechanisms, the parts of the cat's brain associated with the senses are well developed. The cat's nervous system allows the feline to react almost instantaneously to external stimuli, while hormones act as chemical messengers.

THE BODY'S CONTROL CENTRE

All the senses and the body's hormone-producing glands send information to the brain, which interprets it before instructing the body on how to respond via the nervous system. The brain also sends instructions to the master gland of the cat's hormonal system, the pituitary, in the base of the brain. Brain activity demands considerable energy and, although the brain accounts for less than one per cent of body weight, it receives 20 per cent of the blood pumped by the heart.

The cat's brain consists of billions of specialized cells (neurons), each with up to 10,000 connections to other cells. By seven weeks of age, messages move through a cat's brain at almost 390km/h (240mph). This rate of transmission tends to slow down with age.

Anatomically, the cat's brain is similar to that of other mammals. The cerebellum coordinates and balances the movement of muscles; the cerebrum – the largest part of the brain – governs learning, emotion, and behaviour; and the brain stem connects to the nervous system. A network of cells called the limbic system is believed to integrate instinct and learning.

THE ROLE OF HORMONES

Hormones produced in the brain control most of the body's daily functions, such as governing the metabolic rate and stimulating the adrenal gland to produce cortisol in response to stress or danger.

The anatomy of the brain
The brain receives a barrage of mostly chemical information from the senses. Information is analyzed, stored, or responded to according to the circumstances.

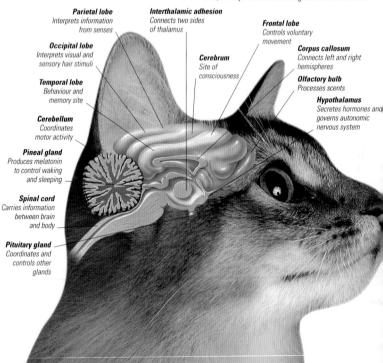

Parietal lobe
Interprets information from senses

Occipital lobe
Interprets visual and sensory hair stimuli

Temporal lobe
Behaviour and memory site

Cerebellum
Coordinates motor activity

Pineal gland
Produces melatonin to control waking and sleeping

Spinal cord
Carries information between brain and body

Pituitary gland
Coordinates and controls other glands

Interthalamic adhesion
Connects two sides of thalamus

Cerebrum
Site of consciousness

Frontal lobe
Controls voluntary movement

Corpus callosum
Connects left and right hemispheres

Olfactory bulb
Processes scents

Hypothalamus
Secretes hormones and governs autonomic nervous system

STRESS, HORMONES, AND BIOFEEDBACK

To stop hormonal reactions running out of control, hormones may regulate their own levels via a biofeedback loop. In the regulation of stress hormones, the balance of this biofeedback mechanism dictates the innate disposition, sociability, and tameability of the cat. The adrenal glands, which lie adjacent to each kidney, play a large part in releasing these stress hormones and orchestrating the fight-or-flight response. They produce epinephrine and norepinephrine, better known as adrenalin and noradrenalin, which control the heart rate and blood-vessel dilation. The adrenals also produce cortisol and other hormones instrumental in controlling metabolic rate. A calm cat quickly brings cortisol production under control, using the biofeedback loop pictured here.

Adrenal gland
ACTH stimulates adrenal gland to produce cortisol

Regulatory feedback
Cortisol suppresses CRH production to bring the fight-or-flight reaction under control

Scent stimulus
Unknown scent stimulus triggers hypothalamus to produce corticotropin-releasing hormone (CRH), starting the fight-or-flight reaction

Brain activity
CRH stimulates pituitary to release adrenocorticotrophic hormone (ACTH, or corticotropin), passing on the "danger" message

Hormone transport
ACTH is transmitted through blood to adrenal glands

Kidney

Production of sexual hormones, eggs, and sperm is controlled by follicle-stimulating hormone (FSH) in females and luteinizing hormone (LH) in males.

THE NERVOUS SYSTEM

The nervous system and hormonal system, which are linked through the brain and pituitary gland, coordinate all of the cat's natural functions. While hormones have slow but lasting effects, the nervous system, with its blindingly intricate circuitry, responds swiftly, accurately, and directly to both internal and external events. Some areas of the nervous system are under the cat's voluntary control: tensing its muscles before pouncing on prey, for example. Others function apparently on their own – the regulating of the heartbeat, for example – but they are in fact controlled at deeper, unconscious levels.

Information travels through the nervous system in two directions: sensory nerves inform the brain about how a cat feels, and motor nerves carry instructions for the body away from the brain.

Voluntary control
The peripheral nervous system consists of millions of nerve fibres that transmit information from the skin and muscles to the brain. The brain sends messages back, instructing muscles what to do. The entire structure looks, anatomically, like a sinewy root system.

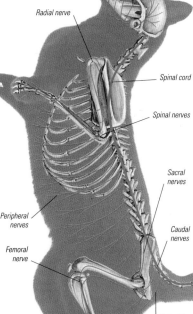

Facial nerve

Radial nerve

Spinal cord

Spinal nerves

Sacral nerves

Peripheral nerves

Caudal nerves

Femoral nerve

Pudendal nerve

The senses

The cat's sensory system is responsible for gathering information about the cat's world and then delivering it to the brain for analysis. In addition to the standard five senses, cats have incredibly refined balance and the sex-scenting sense of the vomeronasal organ.

VISION

A cat's eyes are dramatically large for its body size. The eyes are more sensitive to movement than ours are and, because cats are primarily nocturnal hunters, their colour vision is limited. What is most dramatic is the tapetum lucidum, a layer of reflective cells that bounces light back to the retina, heightening nocturnal vision.

HEARING AND BALANCE

Hearing is well adapted for hunting small rodents. The cat can detect the faintest high-pitched squeaks of a mouse or the rustle of tiny movements. The pinna – the external part of the cat's ear – can be rotated in an arc of 180° to help pinpoint the direction of a sound.

The vestibular apparatus, the organ of balance, is in the inner ear. Changes in direction or velocity register instantly in this organ, allowing the cat to compensate by changing its orientation.

SMELL AND TASTE

Cats have a good sense of smell, better than ours, but not as refined as a dog's. Cats use their sense of smell to scent prey or food, to detect danger, and to read chemical messages left in urine or faeces. Unlike us, but like many other mammals, cats have a vomeronasal (or Jacobson's) organ in the hard palate that forms the roof of the mouth. When a cat uses this organ, its mouth opens in a lip-curling grimace, called flehming. Assisted by the tongue, odours are "lapped" into the vomeronasal organ, which is connected to the hypothalamus area of the brain by a route separate to odours from the nose.

The cat's sense of taste lets it determine between palatable and unpalatable foods. Its tongue is covered with hook-like structures called papillae, on which the taste buds are located. An adult cat has about 250 papillae, each holding anything from 40 to 40,000 taste buds.

TOUCH-SENSITIVE WHISKERS

Touch-sensitive whiskers (vibrissae) on the chin and upper lip can be angled forwards in greeting or backwards out of the way when fighting or feeding. Whiskers above the eyes and on the cheeks warn of dangers to the eyes as the cat explores.

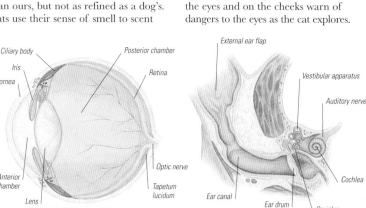

Cats' eyes
A protective, clear cornea covers the eye's anterior fluid-filled chamber. Behind this is the three-part uvea: the coloured iris, stabilizing ciliary body, and focusing lens. Behind the lens is the fluid-filled posterior chamber, the retina, and the reflective tapetum lucidum.

Funnel for sound
Sounds captured in the ear canal are accentuated by the ear drum. They are then refined by bones called the ossicles and the vibrations transferred via the inner ear, or cochlea, to the auditory nerve. The fluid-filled organ of balance, or vestibular apparatus, is located deep in the ears.

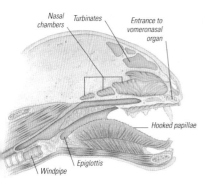

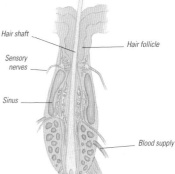

Chemical receptors

Each taste bud on a cat's tongue has a taste hair that detects the chemicals in foods. Inside the nasal chambers, odour molecules adhere to the sticky membranes that cover the turbinate bones. Other chemical odour molecules are captured in the vomeronasal organ in the roof of the mouth.

Sensitive roots

Beneath the skin, a whisker's follicle is about three times deeper than that of a normal hair. A special blood-filled capsule, the sinus, acts like hydraulic fluid and amplifies the signal sent to the web of sensory nerves around it. Information travels via nerves to the brain for processing.

Ears
A cat can hear frequencies as high as 65,000 cycles per second, a full octave and a half higher than our maximum of 20,000 cycles per second.

Eyes
Eyes directed a little sideways give cats a wider angle of vision than ours, and they also have superior peripheral vision.

Whiskers
Tip-to-tip, the facial whiskers indicate the smallest gap a cat can comfortably pass through.

Nose and mouth
Cats have twice as many smell-sensitive cells in their noses as we do. Their taste buds are specialized to detect the amino acids of meat, and are less able than ours to detect the carbohydrate constituents of vegetable matter.

The skin and coat

The skin is a cat's first and most important line of defence against environmental threats. Both the skin and hair have important life-preserving functions, and environmental changes are reflected by a cat's coat.

SKIN STRUCTURE

The skin is the feline body's largest organ. Skin contains cells vital to the immune system, keeping harmful micro-organisms from entering the body. Sensory functions are carried out by millions of nerve endings that detect heat, cold, and pain. A profusion of blood vessels helps the cat to regulate its body temperature.

A cat's skin has two strata. The surface, or epidermis, consists of about 40 layers of dead, flattened cells, embedded in fat-rich sebum, an oily skin secretion. Beneath this "cornified" layer is the living epidermis, or basal area, about four cells thick. And beneath the epidermis is the dermis, the major structural component of the skin. It consists of strong elastic connective tissue, and contains glands, blood vessels, nerves, and receptors.

COAT STRUCTURE

Hair consists mostly of keratin, the same tough protein that makes up the skin's outer layer (epidermis) and the claws (see p.213), which are technically skin. Because hair is made mostly of protein, normal hair growth consumes a good percentage of daily protein intake.

Coat communication
When cats are angry or afraid, the hackles – the hairs on the back – bristle to demonstrate the animal's obvious pain or discomfort.

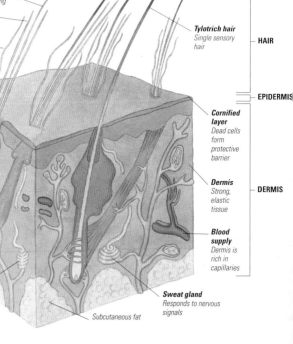

Guard hair
Carries the coat's colouring

Awn hair
Fine secondary hair

Down hair
Soft, wavy secondary hair

Tylotrich hair
Single sensory hair

HAIR

Basal layer
Supplies cells to cornified layer

EPIDERMIS

Cornified layer
Dead cells form protective barrier

Nerve
Carries signals from skin and hair

Dermis
Strong, elastic tissue

DERMIS

Follicle
Sheath containing multiple hairs

Blood supply
Dermis is rich in capillaries

Sebaceous gland
Secretes skin oil

Sweat gland
Responds to nervous signals

Subcutaneous fat

Built for warmth
With the protection of a dense, heavy coat and a layer of insulating down, cold-climate cats like this longhaired example are equipped for freezing conditions. They also have a layer of fat under the skin for extra insulation.

The surface of a cat's hair consists of overlapping cuticle cells, which point away from the body. These cuticle cells reflect light and give the coat its sheen. A dull coat may signify cuticle damage.

Humans have simple follicles: a single, large hair grows from each hair follicle. Cats have more efficient insulation, in the form of compound hair follicles: up to six primary (guard) hairs grow from each follicle, each surrounded by finer, secondary (down and awn) hairs. Each follicle has its own arrector muscle, which can make the primary hairs stand on end. Cats "raise their hackles" like this when alarmed or angry, but also to increase insulation and reduce heat loss.

Cats have two types of hair specialized for sensation. The whiskers, or vibrissae, are thick, stiff hairs found on the head, the throat, and the forelegs. Other large, single hairs, called tylotrichs, are scattered over the skin and act like short whiskers.

NATURAL FLORA AND FAUNA

As on all animals, the surface of the cat's skin is naturally colonized by a variety of microbes. These flora and fauna survive and proliferate without causing skin disease – in fact, they are vital to the skin's health. Different areas of the skin have different microclimates; those that are often moist or wet, or have dense hair and sweat glands, are most attractive to microbes. Conversely, as a cat's first line of defence, the coat and skin are prone to a variety of problems, from allergic or hormonal disorders to parasites, infections, or tumours. Coat problems are obvious because the hair becomes brittle, dry, and lustreless, or it falls out. A flea allergy is overwhelmingly the most common skin complaint.

SWEATING

Unlike humans, cats do not sweat to control their body temperature: they pant inefficiently or lick themselves. Instead, sweat-gland secretions maintain the skin's pliability, excrete waste, provide nutrients for the skin's microflora, and contain substances that protect the body from chemicals and dangerous microbes. They probably also secrete pheromones. Sweat glands associated with hair follicles are called epitrichial. Atrichial glands, such as those on the footpads, open onto the skin, rather than into hair follicles.

Cat licks paws to lose heat

The skeleton

The graceful cat, inspiration for the fashion models' gait, has a physique eminently adapted to its lifestyle. The basis of the cat's success is a perfectly proportioned, highly flexible skeleton, built for the bursts of speed and sinuous agility that a hunter requires.

CLIMBING FRAME

The cat's skeleton is a miniature version of that of the big cats. It is slight, but robust, enabling high-speed manoeuvring and efficient hunting. Slender legs support a narrow ribcage and an extremely supple spine, while the shoulder blades are not attached to the main skeleton. This combination of features provides the cat with an unrivalled flexibility at speed. Strong, fibrous ligaments, elastic tendons, and powerful muscles hold the skeletal elements together and allow for fluid movement. The skeleton also protects the vulnerable inner organs.

JOINTS AND LIGAMENTS

Cats have three different types of joints – fibrous, cartilaginous, and synovial – each with a different degree of articulation and a different function. Fibrous joints form at the suture lines between fused bones, and are not flexible. Cartilaginous joints, such as the thick discs between spinal vertebrae, are made from tough cartilage. These joints are more supple than similar joints in other species. Synovial joints provide the greatest degree of movement, for hip, leg, and jaw articulation. They are hinged or ball-and-socket joints, with contact surfaces of smooth, articulating cartilage surrounded by a joint capsule filled with lubricating synovial fluid.

The ligaments that hold all joints together are vital in keeping the inherently unstable synovial joints from dislocating.

SKELETAL VARIATIONS AND PROBLEMS

Cats boast skeletons that are remarkably consistent compared with the extreme variations in some other domestic animals, such as dogs. Environmental pressures create some natural variations in shape: hot-climate cats are smaller, with a higher surface-to-weight ratio to aid cooling, while cold-climate cats tend to have

THREE FUSED SACRAL VERTEBRAE

SEVEN LUMBAR VERTEBRAE

Pelvis
Ring made up of fused ilium, ischium, and pubis

Ilium

Pubis

Hip joint
Flexible ball-and-socket joint

Ischium

Tail
Each vertebra of the supple tail articulates

Caudal vertebrae
Eighteen to twenty in total

Femur

Tibia

Fibula

Tarsus
Cat's foot starts here

Metatarsals

Phalanges

larger, sturdier skeletons. Extreme skeletal anomalies are not normally perpetuated in the wild, as there are often survival drawbacks associated with them. However, isolated populations with limited gene pools have perpetuated traits such as taillessness or extra toes (polydactyly). More worrying is human intervention in the form of selective breeding, which has artificially changed the skeletons of some breeds. Today's Siamese and Orientals have much thinner leg bones than their predecessors, while the British Shorthair's skeleton is becoming heavier and more compact. Such exaggeration of natural shapes can increase the risk of painful inherited arthritis, and is ethically questionable.

Structure of the skeleton

The cat's skeleton is a masterpiece of engineering. When it walks or crouches, its shoulder blades rise above its spine; less visible is the variety of movement in the bones of its front paws, which produces exceptional dexterity.

RETRACTABLE CLAWS

A cat's claws are sheathed by protective ligaments. When needed for grip or defence, they are exposed by contracting digital flexor muscles in the legs and tautening flexor tendons under the paw.

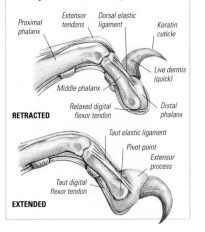

Extensor tendons

Proximal phalanx

Dorsal elastic ligament

Keratin cuticle

Live dermis (quick)

Middle phalanx

Relaxed digital flexor tendon

Distal phalanx

RETRACTED

Taut elastic ligament

Pivot point

Extensor process

Taut digital flexor tendon

EXTENDED

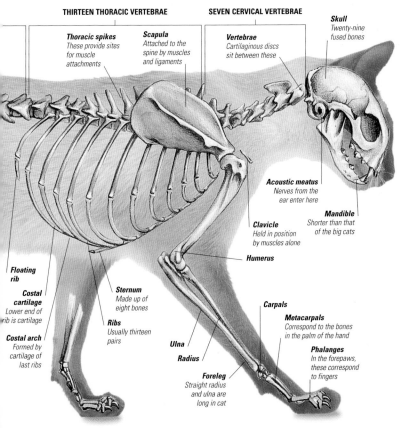

THIRTEEN THORACIC VERTEBRAE

SEVEN CERVICAL VERTEBRAE

Skull
Twenty-nine fused bones

Thoracic spikes
These provide sites for muscle attachments

Scapula
Attached to the spine by muscles and ligaments

Vertebrae
Cartilaginous discs sit between these

Acoustic meatus
Nerves from the ear enter here

Mandible
Shorter than that of the big cats

Clavicle
Held in position by muscles alone

Humerus

Floating rib

Costal cartilage
Lower end of rib is cartilage

Costal arch
Formed by cartilage of last ribs

Sternum
Made up of eight bones

Ribs
Usually thirteen pairs

Ulna

Radius

Foreleg
Straight radius and ulna are long in cat

Carpals

Metacarpals
Correspond to the bones in the palm of the hand

Phalanges
In the forepaws, these correspond to fingers

Muscles and movement

The cat's flexible skeleton allows an extraordinary range of movement, while its highly specialized muscular system gives the grace and control necessary for efficient hunting. Muscle combinations make the cat a superb small predator, capable of sprinting speed and controlled agility.

TYPES OF MUSCLE

Muscles are divided into three basic types. Cardiac muscle is found only in the heart (*see* pp.218–19). "Involuntary" muscle that controls the other organs without the cat's conscious control is called smooth, or non-striated, due to its appearance under a microscope. The other muscles in the body are known as striated or striped, and are controlled at will in all conscious or instinctive movement. Feline muscles are inherently more flexible than those of other mammals, allowing a greater range of movements. Muscles work in opposing pairs on either side of a joint; one contracts to bend a limb, the other contracts to flex it.

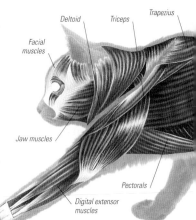

Facial muscles

Deltoid

Triceps

Trapezius

Jaw muscles

Pectorals

Digital extensor muscles

MUSCLE CELLS

Each muscle is made up of a bundle of muscle fibres held together with connective tissue. The muscle tissue consists of three types of cells. "Fast-twitch fatiguing" cells, which make up the majority of cat muscles, work quickly but tire quickly. They give the cat sprinting speed, and the ability to leap several body-lengths in a single bound, but they use up all their energy in an instant. "Fast-twitch fatigue-resistant" cells work quickly but tire more slowly. As cats have relatively few of these cells, they are poor endurance athletes. After less than a minute of sprinting a cat will have to stop and pant to release heat. "Slow-twitch cells" work and tire comparatively slowly, producing slow, sustainable contractions. These cells allow the cat to make the controlled, almost imperceptible movements involved in stalking, and to remain in a ready-to-spring position for long periods during hunting.

One giant leap
The cat's musculature is designed to complement its flexible skeleton, providing maximum power where it is most needed for the chase and capture of prey.

The striped muscles

The striped muscles are symmetrical across the body and under the control of the central and peripheral nervous system (*see* pp.206–207). These muscles act on joints, rather than individual muscles. Generally, they are arranged in opposing groups with opposite actions.

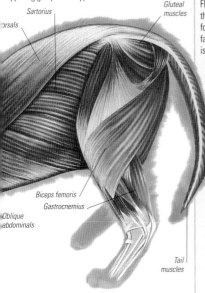

Sartorius

Dorsals

Gluteal muscles

Biceps femoris

Gastrocnemius

Oblique abdominals

Tail muscles

THE FELINE GAIT

Virtually all of the cat's forward propulsion when walking or trotting is provided by the hindlegs; its forelegs act as brakes, almost negating the forward push they generate. In a trot, the cat's legs move in contralateral fashion, the right front leg moving in tandem with the left back leg. When bounding, the cat pushes off with both back legs at the same time, and the whole body is airborne until the forelegs touch down.

POUNCES AND JUMPS

The cat's spine is so flexible, and its muscles so pliant, that it can curl into a circle, or rotate its body through 180° in mid-air. It has a floating shoulder, with a detached shoulder blade held in place by muscle that connects the forelimb to the rest of the body. This contributes to this great freedom of motion, effectively lengthening the stride and enhancing the range of manoeuvres. The cat's flexibility bestows a repertoire of graceful leaping, pouncing, arching, and springing movements, making it a master technician in the art of the hunt.

THE RIGHTING REFLEX

The amazing righting reflex that allows the cat to flip right-side-up in just 60cm (2ft) depends on keen sight, good hearing, a flexible spine, and resilient musculature. Flexible joints and soft paw pads absorb the shock as the cat lands. Cats generally survive falls of fewer than four floors, but falls from five to ten floors up are usually fatal: the acceleration involved means the impact force is too great to absorb. Curiously, falls from greater heights may cause little injury: once the falling cat has righted itself, it assumes the sky-diver's freefall position. Outstretched limbs effect deceleration, and muscular relaxation lessens impact and injury.

Organs of balance in ears register disorientation

Head starts to rotate to attain balance symmetry

Front limbs extend to help with orientation

Hindquarter rotation almost complete

Cat is righted, ready for landing

In the ascendant
Scaling the heights of a tree to conceal a catch from scavengers or simply climbing for fun? Wild or domestic, the cat's strong muscles and incredible physical agility are two of its greatest assets.

The heart and lungs

To enable sudden bursts of energy in its otherwise sedentary life, the cat's heart circulates blood to vital organs, distributing oxygen and nutrients and transporting waste and carbon dioxide to be expelled. Nerves and hormones respond to changing needs by regulating blood flow.

THE RESPIRATORY SYSTEM

With each breath a cat takes, air passes through the nose's scenting apparatus, which is surrounded by the frontal sinuses. Here, air is warmed, humidified, and filtered. It is then drawn down the trachea, or windpipe, and into the lungs through two bronchi, the major air passages. Each bronchus divides into many smaller bronchioles that end in tiny pockets called alveoli. It is within these alveoli that gas exchange takes place – the means by which the cat gets oxygen from the air into its blood and carbon dioxide out of its blood into the air.

THE CIRCULATORY SYSTEM

A typical 5kg (11lb) cat will have about 330ml (11fl oz) of blood in its system. The muscular, elastic walls of arteries expand and contract as the heart pumps the blood through, creating the pulse. The thinner walls of the veins are more easily damaged; they have no pulse, and contain valves to ensure that the blood in them moves only one way, to the heart. Different parts of the body need different amounts of blood. The brain makes up a small amount of body weight but requires 15 to 20 per cent of the blood flow. Resting muscles receive about 40 per cent of the blood, but during pursuits or escapes, up to 90 per cent of the blood can be diverted to them from the internal organs.

VEINS AND ARTERIES

Arteries carry bright-red blood from the heart to the body, oxygenated by the lungs and enriched by nutrients from the digestive system. Darker blood, carrying carbon dioxide, is returned in veins to the heart. Pulmonary arteries and veins have a slightly different function. Pulmonary arteries take oxygen-depleted blood to the alveoli, where the carbon dioxide is exchanged for oxygen from the inhaled air. Pulmonary veins then return the replenished blood to the heart, which

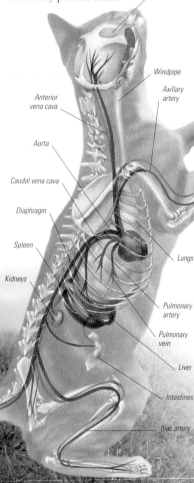

Frontal sinuses

Windpipe

Axillary artery

Anterior vena cava

Aorta

Caudal vena cava

Diaphragm

Spleen

Kidneys

Lungs

Pulmonary artery

Pulmonary vein

Liver

Intestines

Iliac artery

The heart and lungs
The cat's heart has a tremendous ability to suddenly increase its rate of contraction. Together with good lung capacity, this allows for sudden bursts of physical activity.

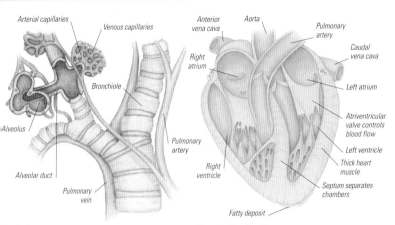

In the lungs
Carbon dioxide from used blood is exchanged for fresh oxygen inside the microscopic alveoli of the lungs. In a typical domestic cat, the total surface area of the alveoli is approximately 20sq m (215sq ft).

The heart's chamber
Blood from the body enters the right atrium, passes into the right ventricle, and is pumped to the lungs via the pulmonary artery. Blood from the lungs enters the left atrium, moves into the left ventricle, and is pumped to the body via the aorta.

is then pumped out to the body through the arteries. The oxygen diffuses into cells in exchange for carbon dioxide, which is brought back through veins to the heart to be pumped to the lungs again.

BLOOD COMPOSITION

The bulk of blood volume is pale-yellow plasma, the transport medium that carries nutrients from the digestive system and transports waste. Plasma levels are maintained by liquid absorbed along the

BLOOD TYPES

Cats have three blood types: A, B, and AB. Most are type A, but there is some geographical variation: the vast majority of Swiss random-bred cats are type A, but the incidence drops to 97 per cent in Britain, and 85 per cent in France. Many pedigree breeds are exclusively type A, but others show varying levels of type B, such as the Cornish Rex at up to 25 per cent, and the Devon Rex at almost 50 per cent. The AB blood type is very rare, and not breed-linked.

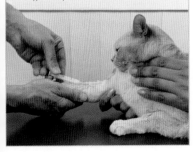

length of the large intestine. Another 30 to 45 per cent of blood is red blood cells, which carry oxygen to cells in the form of bright red oxyhaemoglobin molecules. After the oxygen is exchanged for carbon dioxide, the red blood cells return the blue-red methaemoglobin to the heart and lungs. The remainder of blood is made up of white blood cells and platelets. White blood cells defend the body against microbes and parasites, clear waste from injuries, detoxify substances released in allergic reactions, and fight infections with antibodies; platelets clot blood around wounds. All types of blood cells are produced by bone marrow in adult cats; in kittens, the liver and spleen make blood cells.

BLOOD PROBLEMS

Some circulation problems have external causes: if a cat does not eat, there is not enough water in the large intestine to maintain plasma levels, and so water is drawn from elsewhere in the body, causing dehydration. Anaemia, where the red blood cell count falls, may be caused by heavy flea infestation, injury, stomach ulcers, or tumours. It is corrected by bone marrow increasing the production of red blood cells. Heart disease, either of the heart muscle or valves, is compensated for either by the heart physically increasing in size (so that it holds more blood) or by beating faster.

Digestion and elimination

Like all living animals, cats need to eat to survive. Food is ingested and then the digestive tract helps to extract nutrients that supply the cat with energy and enable it to grow. After consumption, food is usually digested, utilized, dehydrated, and excreted within 24 hours.

BORN TO EAT MEAT

The feline digestive system breaks down food into molecules that can be absorbed into the bloodstream. It also acts as a barrier against harmful bacteria or other disease-causing agents that a cat may ingest. The cat's digestive system is similar to ours, but its carnivorous diet has led to some differences: it does not need a cecum to digest fibre, and its intestines are comparatively short in relation to those of herbivores, such as sheep, or omnivores, such as humans.

The cat's sharp teeth slice meat, and its barbed tongue scrapes flesh from bones. Saliva lubricates it for swallowing. Food passes down the oesophagus and into the stomach, where it is broken down by acid and enzymes. The stomach also secretes mucus to protect itself and the intestines against damage from these digestive juices. The duodenum receives fat-dissolving bile from the gall bladder in the liver, and enzymes from the pancreas. Along the length of the small intestine, digestion continues and nutrients are absorbed through the intestinal wall.

The blood carries these nutrients to the liver, which is the largest internal organ. The liver processes them into fatty acids and amino acids, which are the so-called "building blocks of life".

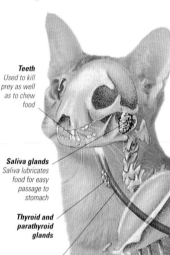

Teeth
Used to kill prey as well as to chew food

Saliva glands
Saliva lubricates food for easy passage to stomach

Thyroid and parathyroid glands

Oesophagus
Elastic wall stretches easily and peristaltic muscle contractions push food to stomach

From consumption to disposal
The feline digestive system is adapted to eating little and often. Once nutrients are absorbed, waste is eliminated via the large intestine and kidneys.

Natural meat eaters
Cats are obligate carnivores, which means they must eat meat to stay alive. A cat's liver requires this animal protein to guarantee the full complement of acids necessary to maintain good health. Eating a natural diet also ensures healthy teeth and gums.

WASTE DISPOSAL

After the nutrients are absorbed, waste enters the large intestine, or colon, where benign bacteria break it down and neutralize any hostile bacteria. Water is absorbed through the colon wall, and mucus is secreted to lubricate the now dry waste. It passes into the rectum for elimination. Waste from the liver is carried in the blood to the kidneys, where it is filtered and excreted in urine.

DIGESTIVE HORMONES

Hormones are important in digestion. Those produced by the thyroid glands control the metabolism. The parathyroid glands enable the extraction of calcium from bone, to be used by the muscles. Insulin, from the pancreas, allows cells to absorb vital glucose from the blood. Overactive pituitary or adrenal glands release hormones that increase blood sugar, mimicking the effects of diabetes.

THE CAT'S DENTITION

When kittens are born, 26 needle-sharp milk teeth are already in place. These are replaced by 30 permanent teeth during the first six months of life. The upper and lower incisors grasp the prey or food, the canines grip and kill, and the premolars and molars shear, cut, and chew meat. The cat has few molars, and the upper ones are almost vestigial because they are not vital in its mainly carnivorous natural diet.

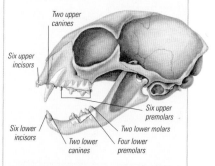

Two upper canines

Six upper incisors

Six upper premolars

Six lower incisors

Two lower canines

Two lower molars

Four lower premolars

The carnivore's mouth

The cat's teeth cut fresh meat like serrated blades. In a natural diet, they are cleaned as they scrape over bone; without this, the teeth are vulnerable to decay.

Stomach
Produces acids and enzymes that begin digesting food

Kidneys
Cleanse waste products from blood

Ureters
Pass liquid waste to bladder

Large intestine
Absorbs water from solid waste

Rectum
Stores solid waste before discharging through anus

Anal sphincter
Triggered by brain to relax and allow excretion

Pancreas
Secretes digestive enzymes and the hormone insulin

Liver
Processes nutrients and produces bile

Pyloric sphincter
Ring of muscle that releases food into duodenum

Duodenum
Nutrients absorbed from first part of small intestine

Urethra

Bladder
Holds up to 100ml (3½fl oz) of liquid and excretes 60ml (2fl oz) daily

The reproductive system

The cat has evolved a very efficient reproduction strategy, ideally suited to the lone hunter. Males are eternal opportunists, always ready to mate. Females come into season as daylight hours increase in spring, ensuring births during the spring and summer, when food is most plentiful.

THE MALE SYSTEM

Feline puberty usually occurs at five to nine months; from then on, a male cat's reproductive system is on stand-by, ready for use if the chance arises. Luteinizing hormone (LH) from the pituitary gland stimulates the testes to make both sperm and the male hormone testosterone. Sperm production is best at slightly less than body heat, so testes are held in the scrotal sac outside the body. Sperm is stored in the epididymis at the base of the testes until needed, when it travels through the two spermatic cords to the prostate and bulbourethral glands. Here, a sugar-rich transport medium, semen, is added.

The male shows sex-related behaviour, such as roaming, fighting, and spraying, all year round. His reproductive system is placed on high alert by scent. If his vomeronasal organ (see pp.208–209) captures female scent, he will disregard all else to seek out the female giving off the scent, and fight over her if necessary until she is ready and willing to mate.

FEMALE HORMONES

Like most other domestic animals, the female cat is polyoestrous, meaning she has many oestrous periods, or seasons, throughout the year. But, unlike many other animal species that have oestrous cycles all year round, cats are seasonally polyoestrous: the female's reproductive cycle is most active as daylight hours increase, and then winds down as daylight hours decrease.

At the end of winter, increasing daylight hours stimulate her pituitary gland to produce follicle stimulating hormone (FSH). The FSH induces her ovaries to manufacture eggs and the female hormone oestrogen. The oestrogen is released in the female's urine, acting as a calling card to any available males. At puberty, which occurs at the same time as male puberty, the necessary eggs are waiting in the ovaries. In contrast to the reproductive systems of virtually all other mammals, however, the ovaries will not release these eggs until after mating has taken place.

FSH sent to ovaries

Nerves carry information to brain

Ovary

Uterus
Split into two distinct "horns" in the cat

Bladder

Cervix
Opens during mating to admit sperm

Vagina

Vulva

Female reproductive system
The female's two ovaries, which manufacture eggs and the hormone oestrogen, are suspended from the roof of the abdomen. Females conserve their eggs, concentrating their reproductive activity into intense and well-advertised oestrous "heat" periods.

MALE SEXUAL BEHAVIOUR

For intact male cats, the presence of a female cat in season can have dramatic consequences. For example, a housetrained cat may start to spray pungent urine everywhere – against cars, fences, trees, and even in your home. If he goes outside, he is likely to fight with other males. He may even lose his appetite and stop eating for a while. Neutering (*see* p.272) is one way of preventing this behaviour.

FELINE MATING

The female cat does not permit a male to mate with her until she is completely ready. When the male is allowed to mount her, he grasps the skin on her neck and mates immediately. The male's penis is covered in hook-like barbs. As he withdraws, the barbs abrade the vulva, stimulating egg release. The female "screams" and turns to bite, but an experienced male will maintain his hold on the neck. He releases her and draws away when he feels it is safe to do so.

Cats only release eggs after mating, but two or more matings are usually needed. The pair mate repetitively, the male tiring first. The female retains her receptivity: other males are often then permitted to mate. When enough matings have occurred, production of FSH in the female's brain stimulates eggs to leave the ovaries and travel through the fallopian tubes to each horn of the uterus. If no matings occur when a female is in heat, no eggs are released. Once the eggs have left the ovaries, a period of calm ensues, lasting from two days to two weeks, followed by another heat cycle if she does not conceive. Under the influence of artificial indoor light, unspayed females can eventually come to be in permanent season.

PREGNANCY AND BIRTH

Fertilization takes place in the pencil-like uterine horns, and the foetuses are positioned in rows in each horn of the uterus. Pregnancy lasts about 63 days, during which progesterone, the hormone of pregnancy, brings behaviour changes and the swelling of the mammary glands.

Birth is usually an uncomplicated process, although some kittens may not live. Milk let-down occurs shortly after the birth, stimulated by suckling. The mother often leaves the birth nest a few days after the delivery, carrying her kittens one by one to a new, more odour-free and thus, to her mind, much safer den.

Male reproductive system
When a male picks up the scent or hears the distinctive call of a female in heat, the brain analyses the sensory information and sends a hormonal signal to the reproductive organs.

LH carried in blood to testes

Scent stimulus
Male picks up female's scent

Spermatic cords

Epididymis
Stores sperm

Testes
Respond to LH by producing sperm

Penis

Penile barbs
Abrade the vulva on withdrawal

Bladder

Prostate gland
Produces semen to carry sperm

Bulbourethral gland
Function is poorly understood in cats

The immune system

A cat's health depends on an efficient immune system. The immune system protects against internal dangers, such as cancer cells, and external pathogens, such as viruses and bacteria. As a cat ages, its immune system weakens, making it more prone to health concerns.

IMMUNITY FOR LIFE

Under normal conditions, the immune system turns on and off as necessary. White blood cells called neutrophils are its front line "attack soldiers". Their function is to guard and protect against bacteria and fungi. There are four other main types of white blood cells:

■ B-lymphocytes: these cells produce antibodies – proteins that "label" and neutralize harmful microbes.

■ T-cells: "helper" T-cells prompt the B-lymphocytes' production of antibodies, while "suppressor" T-cells turn them off when a job is finished.

■ Memory T-cells: these cells patrol the body, recognizing villains encountered in the past and mobilizing attack teams,

Protection against infection

A cat that spends time outdoors will have many chances to pick up infections from dirty surroundings or encounters with other cats. A strong immune system plays a vital role in protecting the cat from infection and keeping it healthy.

ASTHMA AND ALLERGIES

Feline allergic reactions to certain foods and chemicals are a relatively recent phenomenon. When a cat inhales, swallows, or is otherwise in contact with any "trigger" substance, the immune system produces an antibody called immunoglobin E (IgE). In allergic cats, IgE binds on to receptor sites on specialized immune cells, called mast cells, in the skin and the lining of the stomach, lungs, and upper airways. Mast cells are like primed mines, filled with irritating chemicals, and the IgE causes the mast cells to explode, scattering irritating and inflammatory substances, such as histamine. Anti-histamine drugs act to neutralize the released histamine.

Kitten inadvertently swallows "trigger" substance

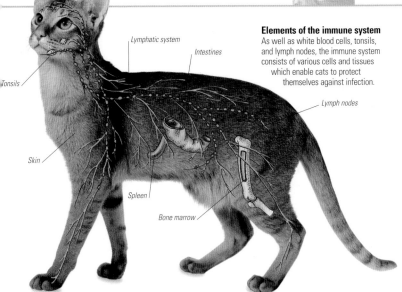

Elements of the immune system
As well as white blood cells, tonsils, and lymph nodes, the immune system consists of various cells and tissues which enable cats to protect themselves against infection.

Lymphatic system

Intestines

Tonsils

Lymph nodes

Skin

Spleen

Bone marrow

including "natural killer" cells that attack and destroy viruses or tumour cells.

■ Macrophages: these cells (literally "big eaters") are the final part of the system. They arrive and clean up the debris.

AN OVERACTIVE IMMUNE SYSTEM

Sometimes helper T-cells kick in when the cat's body is not under threat, but simply in contact with innocuous substances like flea saliva, house dust, or plant pollens. These can trigger an allergic reaction, which may appear as anything from itchy skin, watery eyes, sneezing, asthma, vomiting, or diarrhoea.

Problems can also arise if suppressor T-cells fail to turn off the helpers. The immune system remains in overdrive and may start attacking a specific part of the cat's own body – for example, the red blood cells. This self-destructive reaction is called auto-immune disease.

Many vets feel that both allergies and auto-immune diseases are on the increase. Corticosteroids are used to suppress an overactive immune system.

AN UNDERACTIVE IMMUNE SYSTEM

If the system does not turn on properly, a cat is "immune-suppressed". Feline immune deficiency virus (FIV) and feline leukemia virus (FeLV) are linked with immune suppression. A decline in the competence of a cat's immune system can be caused by old age or through

infection with conditions such as FIV or FeLV. Affected cats are susceptible to other problems, such as cancer. Cancer cells are renegades that trick the memory T-cells into regarding the cancer cells as "self" and not attacking and destroying them. Having eluded the immune system, cancer cells multiply and spread to other parts of the body.

PAIN AND STRESS

In the brain, chemicals called neuropeptides have a powerful effect on pain control, energy, and a sense of well-being. Pain is part of the cat's defence system, prompting it to avoid continuing dangers. During the emotional intensity of a fight, cats produce protective neuropeptides called endorphins that reduce the unpleasantness and intensity of pain. Chronic stress may trigger excesses or deficiencies in neuropeptides: pain and stress can therefore both affect susceptibility to, or speed of recovery from, illness. Use only feline painkillers: drugs that work in dogs or humans can be lethal to cats.

Stress is evident in this kitten's bristled fur

Cat intelligence

While it is easy to talk about feline intelligence, it can be frustratingly difficult to define what is meant by the term. Cognitive psychologists have varied theories about different forms of intelligence, and these can be modified for determining how smart cats really are.

WHAT IS INTELLIGENCE?

Scientists generally accept the idea that there are multiple forms of intelligence. For humans, intelligence manifests itself in eight different ways:

1 Linguistic
2 Logical-mathematical
3 Musical
4 Spatial
5 Bodily-kinesthetic
6 Naturalist
7 Interpersonal
8 Intrapersonal

This concept of human intelligence can be adapted to studying cats. The last five forms listed above may be used to describe feline intelligence. I believe cats have learning centres in their brains to facilitate these abilities. For example:

■ An excellent capacity to mentally map comparatively large territories = **4**
■ A natural knowledge of motion and forces: understanding mechanics = **5**

Mapping large territories

Tales about cats who have mistakenly climbed into vehicles and then been transported hundreds of miles away before somehow finding their way home are well-known. Exactly how cats achieve this feat of navigation remains unknown.

■ An ability to choose where to live, both for safety and for productivity = **6**
■ An acute understanding of danger, self-defence, and how to be cautious = **6**
■ An ability to know and remember what should and should not be eaten = **6**
■ An innate understanding of the behaviour of other animals, including a capacity to predict their likely behaviour from their initial actions = **7**
■ An intuitive inclination to patrol, investigate, and mark territory = **7**
■ A recognition of the role and importance of kinship, especially the maternal relationship = **7**
■ An understanding of the importance of personal hygiene = **8**

When it comes to spatial awareness, bodily-kinesthetic intelligence, and naturalist intelligence, cats are far more "intelligent" than both us and our other favourite animal companion, the dog.

HOW CATS THINK

Some behaviour experts believe that cats "think" by sensing through pictures and memories of smells and sounds. It has been shown that kittens learn best

Knowledge of motion and forces
Every day of their lives cats are tested in their understanding of concepts such as acceleration, force, and mass. Hunting for, or chasing, prey is a prime example.

through observation. For example, those that have the opportunity to see their mother capture and kill mice grow up to be better mousers than those that do not.

CATS DREAM

While it is asleep, your cat may flex its paws, twitch its whiskers, and give a flick of its tail; it may even mutter or growl. The cat is said to be in deep, "active", or REM (rapid eye movement) sleep. During deep sleep, electrical impulses in its brain are as active as when the cat is awake, so it is a reasonable conclusion that cats dream, just as we do, in this phase. Cats enjoy their sleep. On average, they rest for around 18 hours a day, and it has been suggested that this is when they rehearse potential body actions, such as the "fight-or-flight" response.

UNIQUE FORMS OF INTELLIGENCE

While cats (compared to dogs, pigs, or primates) are not particularly good at solving puzzles or escaping from mazes, many cat owners feel that their cats have a "psychic" form of

intelligence: that they have premonitions of events before they happen and see things we don't see. While most of the evidence for psychic abilities is anecdotal, there is sound scientific evidence that cats have a superb sense of direction. This may be associated with minute amounts of iron in the brain, allowing cats to orientate themselves according to the Earth's magnetic field. In addition, Professor Benjamin Hart at the University of California Veterinary School has reported increases in unusual behaviours in cats immediately before earthquakes.

Maternally minded
In cats, as with all mammals, the care and attention a mother affords her young is a form of instinctive behaviour. Feeding, licking, and carrying young are all linked to intelligence.

The emergence of personality

A cat's personality – how it behaves, feels, and thinks – is the result of a combination of factors, including genetics and its earliest interactions with its mother, litter mates, and people. Innovative research into feline personality is still taking place, and much remains to be discovered.

HOW PERSONALITY DEVELOPS

The cat has an amazingly adaptable and malleable personality. It evolved as a self-sufficient lone-operator, an independent hunter that made contact with its own kind only to mate. However, it has the ability to develop strong social bonds with other cats and with other species, such as dogs, and, of course, with humans.

The personality of a cat is defined by genetics (inherited behavioural characteristics) and environmental influences, particularly those that exist within the first two months of its life. Genetic behavioural traits are influenced by clusters of genes that affect hormone production, nerve-transmission times, and enzyme activity. This is a difficult science, since inheritance of behaviour is not as straightforward to observe as, for example, inheritance of eye colour or coat pattern. However, experiments carried out to examine the trait of

Handling your cat from an early age
Accustom your cat to handling by humans as soon as possible. Studies show that socialization, whereby an animal learns how to recognize and interact with the species with which it cohabits, helps shape personality.

"boldness" have revealed that certain aspects of personality are inherited. One study showed that fathers with a bold disposition – cats that were more likely to approach novel objects and people – tended to sire kittens with similar fearless personalities. Likewise, timid fathers tended to sire timid kittens. In another study, of British

Moulding a personality
A kitten shouldn't be separated from its mother too soon after being born because this period is crucial in terms of the development of personality. Physical and mental health in the adult cat will be shaped by these early experiences.

PHYSICAL AND EMOTIONAL DEVELOPMENT

Your kitten's personality is ultimately shaped by a combination of its mother's love and a variety of external stimuli. The first eight weeks are critical.

0–3 WEEKS
■ Totally dependent on mother.
■ Relatively immobile, responding only to smell, touch, and heat.
■ Eyes open at 7–10 days.
■ Teeth erupt at around 14 days.

3–4 WEEKS
■ Vision develops – learns by observing mother.
■ Can move a reasonable distance from the "nest".
■ Starts to eat solid food.
■ Quickly develops its interactions with rest of litter.

4–6 WEEKS
■ No longer needs mother to stimulate waste elimination.
■ Completely weaned by 6 weeks.
■ Will kill mice if given the opportunity.
■ Can run, and develops all adult gaits.
■ Play-fights with littermates and mother.

6–8 WEEKS
■ Continues to suckle, but mainly for social reasons.
■ Develops adult-like responses to visual threats or worrying smells.
■ Motor abilities continue to develop.
■ Fear-response matures.
■ Play activity becomes more physical and intense.
■ Ability to keep the body at a constant temperature (thermoregulation) matures.

0–3 WEEKS   **3–4 WEEKS**   **4–6 WEEKS**   **6–8 WEEKS**

Shorthairs, cats with the gene for a red coat colour experienced more difficulties than those with other coat colours when handled by unfamiliar people.

EARLY EXPERIENCE AND PERSONALITY

Indisputably, just as in humans, genes are partly responsible for the behaviour of cats. This explains why a litter of kittens that has shared early life experiences still contains a variety of personalities.

Nevertheless, early exposure to social and environmental stimuli, especially between two and seven weeks of age, is critical in personality development. To this end, virtually all cat behavioural studies reach the same two conclusions: that being handled by a number of different people increases a cat's sociability towards people, and that exposure to varied noises and experiences (dogs, children, car journeys) helps create a calmer and more confident personality.

DESCRIPTIONS OF PERSONALITY

For many years, cat character was described by the polar opposites of either excitable (reactive) or timid (quiet). In time, however, animal behaviourists became more interested in studying other dimensions of cat personality. Reflecting this development, the following diverse terms are now routinely used to describe cats:

■ Calm/excitable
■ Bold/timid
■ Alert/placid
■ Friendly/unfriendly
■ Outgoing/withdrawn
■ Active/passive
■ Vocal/quiet
■ Inquisitive/uninterested
■ Sensitive/insensitive
■ Affectionate/distant
■ Sociable/antisocial
■ Assertive/retiring

Each cat's personality is a combination of these elements, and particular breeds are often described using the same adjectives. For example, the Burmese is typically known as assertive, active, and outgoing, whereas the Siamese is regarded as vocal, sensitive, and sociable. Persians are generally described as being placid, quiet, and calm. The fact that particular breeds are described in this way affirms the concept that certain behavioural characteristics are inherited.

How cats communicate

Cats communicate both vocally and non-vocally. From early kittenhood, voice and touch are vital forms of communication, but by twelve weeks, kittens have also developed a range of body language. As they mature, cats begin to use scent and visible markers to advertise their presence.

THE MEANING OF TOUCH

Touch is one of the first senses that a kitten develops and it remains a potent form of communication throughout life. Cats that know each other use nose-to-nose touch in greeting. Some pet cats do the same with their owners. Too much touch, however, can occasionally lead to an aggressive response from cats to their owners in the form of petting aggression (*see* pp.284–87, *Common behaviour problems*).

VARIED VOCAL SOUNDS

Feral cats are remarkably quiet, while latchkey and house cats are far more vocal. It is thought that cats miaow and trill to us rather than to other cats because from early in life, we reward them when they do so. Respected animal behaviourists, such as Dr John Bradshaw, feel that cats miaow at us because they are trying to imitate human speech.

Kittens use their voice more than older cats; when cold or hungry, they emit a high-pitched distress call that even inexperienced mothers respond to. Mothers call their kittens using a chirrup sound. Maine Coons also use this noise when greeting their owners.

Purring can be performed from when a kitten is just a few days old and occurs during social greetings with other cats,

Kitten using its voice
Vocalization in cats takes many forms, from contented purrs to angry screeches to plaintive mews. Cat owners are able to discern their pets' moods from these oral outbursts.

while sitting on human laps, rubbing on objects, when nursing kittens, or even when dropping off to sleep.

Loud sounds (excluding the Siamese's strident, miaow) are used either during mating or when fighting or anticipating fights. Aggressive growls, yowls, and snarls are all made with the cat holding its mouth in a rigid position and tightly tensing its facial muscles. Hissing and spitting are defensive sounds, as

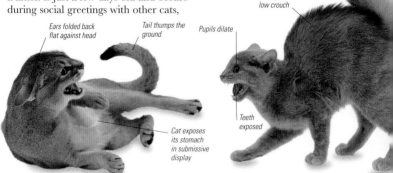

Tail bristles, exaggerating the cat's size

Cat adopts a low crouch

Ears folded back flat against head

Tail thumps the ground

Pupils dilate

Cat exposes its stomach in submissive display

Teeth exposed

Fearful aggression
Although its body remains low and off balance, this cat is not entirely ready to accept defeat. A show of pin-sharp claws and teeth tell its aggressor to beware.

Defensive posture
Faced with a display of aggression from another animal, this cat flattens its ears to protect them from attack and arches its back to make itself look bigger.

WHERE DOES THE PURR COME FROM?

Purring originates in the vocal chords. The sound is produced as the chords vibrate, as they are rapidly pulled to and fro by the muscles in the walls of the larynx (or voice box). These muscles are, in turn, controlled by nerves that set the rhythm of the purr. We associate purring with pleasure, but cats may also purr after being involved in traffic accidents or when frightened, such as when they are at the veterinary surgery.

faeces has a unique scent produced by a smelly secretion discharged from the adjacent anal sacs and deposited on it. Cats use unburied faeces as a visible and scented territorial marker.

Odours in urine are even more important scent markers. Unneutered males produce a sour and pungent urine that is sprayed intentionally on upright objects. Females in season leave a scented trail in their urine for local tomcats to follow. All cats also leave an odour trail from the sweat glands in their paws. Both males and females mark familiar objects, including humans, by rubbing glands on their cheeks, lips, and chin against them. Cats' cheek glands contain chemicals that seem to reassure them: samples of secretions from these glands have been synthesized and the results then used as a spray to calm frightened individuals.

Cat reaches for highest point

is the sudden shriek of pain, which may be intended to startle the attacker into loosening his grip.

REFINED BODY LANGUAGE

Body language is used in face-to-face communication. Aggressive cats try to look larger; submissive cats make themselves appear smaller. Nervous cats crouch, avert their eyes, and may yawn. A direct stare with body hair on end, the head and whiskers forward, the ears folded back, and a lashing tail, is a prelude to attack. Defensive cats make themselves look larger by arching the back and bristling the hair; this occurs most often with dogs and people than with other cats. The scared cat tucks its tail under its body.

SCENT MARKING

As with so many other animals, body waste – urine and faeces – is utilized by cats to help in communication. The

Clawing
As well as to sharpen their claws, cats scratch trees, posts, fences, or furniture as signs of ownership of a territory. Claw marks are made as high as possible for maximum visibility and are routinely freshened.

Claws retracted in non-aggressive posture

Line of vision relaxed and non-confrontational

Passive submission
We recognize this posture as being a playful one. At ease with itself and its surroundings, this cat gleefully rolls from one side to another, imploring someone to stroke its tummy.

The social cat

Although the African wildcat is solitary and territorial, its relatives, the domestic cats, are more sociable and readily adapt to living together. Where there is little need to defend territory or compete for food, two or more cats can peacefully cohabit, but always on their own terms.

SOCIAL DYNAMICS

There is nothing written into a domestic cat's genetic code that prevents it from living contentedly with other cats, if the conditions are suitable. Household cats willingly share a territory when food is plentiful, and in these circumstances they need to communicate, not just to defend territory but also to resolve differences of opinion and to maintain status within the group. Unlike a wolf pack, for example, a group of domestic cats has no distinct social hierarchy that all members adhere to. This makes it much more challenging for behaviourists to interpret the social dynamics within the group.

LIVING TOGETHER

Although relationships within any group of cats are fairly fluid, it is still possible to identify particular interactions. In a small cat colony, for example, every cat reacts differently towards each of the other members of the group.

MAKING NEW SOCIAL BONDS

Forging social bonds is easy for kittens under seven weeks old. It takes between two and five weeks for a mature cat to adapt to a new territory, and at least this long for a cat to accept a new feline in the human family. The ability to form new relationships varies with the breed: Persians appear to find it fairly easy, while Siamese find it most difficult. A short separation between cats that usually live together – such as a stay at the vets – can rupture their relationship.

In larger colonies, which are usually congregations of several families, a cat may know neighbours as individuals but recognize others only by their sex, age, and the family to which they belong.

Aggression is uncommon within a group or family and is reserved for cats outside the social group. Cats that are content in each other's company will

A chance encounter
These two cats are not related and do not live together. Even though it may not be the more dominant of the two, by moving to the highest point available, the cat in the foreground is elevating its social status.

Rubbing shoulders with good friends
It is part of normal greeting behaviour for cats to rub themselves against people and other cats. Rubbing the head and face is a form of scent marking – using the sebaceous glands – that extends to inanimate objects as well, such as furniture, garden fences, and trees.

"cringe" as a way of pacifying an aggressor, rubbing is never carried out as appeasement in response to a threat.

CATS IN YOUR HOME

Domestic cats behave in your home much as they would in an outdoor colony. For example, an individual may usually be affable towards other cats, but may aggressively defend its favourite sleeping area. When two cats meet on "neutral" territory, the cat on higher ground is temporarily in charge; if they meet on level ground, the "dominant" cat may take a symbolic swipe at the "inferior" individual. Body rubbing is much more common among domestic cats than it is in feral colonies. Neutered toms rub as much as neutered females, and both do so more frequently than unneutered females. This is an example of how human intervention in one area – the control of cat sexuality – has a dramatic effect in another, that of feline sociability.

sleep close together, or even in contact with each other, and they often groom each other. Mutual grooming – licking – cements feline relationships. In one study of a feral cat colony, 64 per cent of interactions between members involved licking, 29 per cent involved body rubbing, and only seven per cent involved forms of aggression.

THE BODY RUB

Cats frequently rub their bodies against each other, and which cat initiates this rubbing provides some clues about the hierarchical structure within a group. Kittens always start the process with their mothers, although once started mothers may rub their kittens in return. Females rub on tomcats, but toms virtually never return the compliment, unless they are neutered. All cats – male, female, and neutered – will initiate body rubbing with their owners, and even with strangers. It is not uncommon for cats visiting a veterinary clinic to rub against the vet's leg after they have had a medical examination. In each of these cases, rubbing is performed by the socially weaker on the socially stronger. However, unlike dogs, which sometimes

DO CATS MOURN?

In a study of a group of indoor cats living together, when one died, half of the survivors ate less than before, became more vocal, and demanded more affection from people in the household. Over 40 per cent of the surviving cats sought out the deceased cat's favoured resting place and spent more time there for a period of up to six months after the cat's death.

The perfect hunter

Every cat, feral or housebound, hungry or well-fed, is a hunter. Anything small and mobile is seen as prey, from insects and rabbits for outdoor cats, to moths and passing ankles for housebound cats. While hunger sharpens efficiency, well-fed cats are the most patient hunters.

HUNTING TACTICS

Cats prefer to hunt at dawn and again at dusk, although hunting activity varies with the weather. During hot, humid weather, some cats will hunt throughout the night while in cold weather, hunting is more likely to take place throughout the day. Most cats prefer simply to sit by the trail of potential prey and wait. This is the most favoured of all hunting strategies. When prey appears, the cat pounces. Hungry individuals, or those that specialize in birds, stalk, capture, and kill. A bird hunter uses ground cover, such as long grass, slinks forward, freezes, then slinks forward again until it is close enough to leap or pounce. Feral cats, especially nursing mothers, make the most successful hunters, catching prey every third or fourth pounce. It takes a nursing farm cat on average less than two hours to catch and kill a rodent to feed its kittens. Well-fed cats are more patient when hunting, waiting by a trail for hours until prey appears. Pet cats catch prey on average every twelfth pounce.

WHAT CATS HUNT

Although pet cats can be very demanding about what cat food they are willing to eat, they are in fact opportunist hunters, killing and often eating a wide variety of prey, from spiders to bumblebees, grasshoppers to birds, mice to rabbits.

THE CAT'S LARDER

While hungry feral cats like this one (below) eat their prey soon after capturing it, pet cats may eat some but store the rest in a "larder". Owners often find mouse corpses laid out in a specific location in the garden. The larder is more of a mortuary than a food reserve. As long as a pet cat remains well-fed it rarely returns to its food reserve for a meal.

In North America, cats eat chipmunks, ground and flying squirrels, gophers, mice, small rats, and birds, particularly robins. In Scandinavia, rabbits are common prey, while farther south in Europe, cats routinely take mice, voles, sparrows, and fledgling birds, although the voles are seldom consumed. In Australia, cats kill nuisance rabbits but also prey upon indigenous possums, reptiles, and ground-nesting birds. In tropical climates, both kittens and adults eat a variety of large insects. Frogs are

Playing with prey
The hunting instinct isn't tied to hunger, and trying to convert a natural mouser is a lost cause. The fruit of this cat's stalking, ambushing, and attacking is a helpless rodent, destined for a bout of batting before being administered a death bite.

routinely captured and killed, but they are rarely eaten. While pet cats naturally hunt, hungry cats – and that usually means feral cats – will also scavenge. If you find your rubbish bag has been slashed open overnight and the remains of the roast chicken strewn over the lawn, the perpetrator is more likely to be a hungry feral than a full-stomached pet.

Mother nature
Kittens learn hunting techniques by watching their mothers at work. This youngster has picked up the art of the ambush by his mother's example.

HOBBY HUNTERS

Feral cats hunt to eat, but latchkey and house cats hunt for the thrill of the chase, the capture, and the kill. Many cat owners will deny that their cats hunt, but there is a profound biological need to do so and it is not based on hunger. Hunger and hunting are controlled by different parts of the brain. If a cat, while eating even its favourite cat food, sees a rat or mouse, it will stop eating and chase the rodent and then go back to its food. In one European survey of pet cats killed in road traffic accidents, over half of the pet cats were found to have the remains of prey as well as cat food in their stomachs.

The hungry cat kills with a swift bite. Its canine teeth are perfectly shaped to slip between a rodent's neck vertebrae and sever the spinal cord. The rodent dies quickly from shock and is promptly eaten. Pet cats that hunt on full stomachs are inclined to capture, release, and capture again – a form of play activity.

Courtship and mating

Mating between cats is noisy and rough. Females may be labelled unfairly as being particularly promiscuous, but there is a sound biological reason for this zealous sexual activity: their heat cycles are infrequent, and it is necessary to take advantage of them when they occur.

FINDING A PARTNER

In contrast to cats, sociable species such as humans, dogs, or domesticated livestock have ideal mating circumstances: males are constantly available. Cats, however, evolved as lone hunters with individual territories, and when a female comes into season, it is possible that no males will be in the vicinity.

The female cat is sexually inactive for most of the year, but increasing daylight stimulates a hormonal cascade that leads to the onset of heat. Out of season, an unspayed female will behave much as neutered males or females, but at the onset of oestrus, dramatic changes occur. The first signs of heat are increased restlessness and a heightened desire to rub against objects or other animals. If allowed out, she will urinate more frequently and in new places, and she may also spray to announce her condition to local tom cats, leaving a scent trail indicating her receptivity. In her attempts to find a mate, she uses a distinctive, plaintive sexual voice, a provocative call

THE MATING PROCESS

Courtship is usually rather perfunctory, with a dominant tom invoking his rights over other males, and a receptive female eventually accepting his advances. The female controls the timing of mating activity, only permitting the male to mate when she is emotionally and biologically ready. Repeat matings occur throughout the day, a repetition that is necessary to induce eggs to be released from the female's ovaries.

2 Inexperienced males can be impetuous and a too-early approach may be physically rebuffed. The female will mate with a male of her choice when she is ready. When the chosen male grooms her behind her ears, she may show receptivity by stretching out and allowing him to sniff her.

Female's posture is not receptive

Prospective mate remains cautious

1 It is the female (left) who sets the pace for sexual encounters. This blue Burmese tom makes initial cautious overtures, and waits for signs of receptivity. If he is too forthright, he risks rejection, and even physical attack by the chocolate Burmese female.

to males within hearing distance. Ready for mating, she crouches down with her hindquarters raised and her tail turned to the side. Often she purrs, kneads with her front paws, and stretches her body.

THE MALE'S RESPONSE

The male cat is a sexual opportunist. If unneutered, he patrols his territory, spraying urine and responding to the scent posts and calls that tell him a female is receptive. He is invariably cautious in his initial overtures to her, which are usually met with a hiss and a slap. Often, however, he is not the only male who has been alerted by the female's activities. Soon, more males arrive and fighting may break out, although in most instances, one male dominates through intimidation rather than actual fighting. He earns the right to mate first with the female.

LITTERS WITH MULTIPLE FATHERS

Females do not release eggs until there have been repeated matings, which stimulate a flow of hormones. The hormones induce egg release, and fertilization occurs 24 hours later. Among feral cats, it is not unusual for a female in heat to mate with many of the queuing males. Genetic studies of subsequent litters have confirmed what breeders have long assumed, that a single litter may be sired by several fathers. Multiple partners tend to ensure a varied genetic mix within the litter, and may lead to strikingly dissimilar looking kittens.

Ejaculation is almost instantaneous

Male displays dominance by standing over female

Female rejects male advances

3 The female accepts the male and assumes a crouch. As the male mounts, he grasps the female's neck skin in his jaws to subdue her. When he withdraws after mating, his barbed penis irritates the vaginal lining, stimulating egg release.

Grooming begins with genitals

4 Post-coital grooming has a calming effect. Both individuals begin with cleansing their genitals, and grooming then extends to the whole body before mating resumes. Serial matings often continue all day, and the participants will groom themselves after each one.

LIVING WITH A CAT

It is a curious fact that the world's most successful feline has adapted so well to live with the world's most successful primate. "Owning" cats – playing with them, feeding them, grooming them, training them, even protecting them – gives us huge emotional rewards, but this life of reciprocated, consummate happiness takes a little work.

SATISFACTION FOR BOTH OF US

Since the 1990s, cats have surpassed dogs in popularity as pets both in North America and in Europe. The reason is not hard to find: there are documented physiological and psychological benefits to owning a cat. Contrary to previous assumptions, recent research indicates that children raised with a cat or dog in their early years have a lower than average incidence of hay fever and asthma. Australian studies revealed that cat owners visit their doctors less often, and are less likely to be prescribed medicines when they do, than people who do not own pets. A British survey also highlighted the emotional rewards of cat ownership, with 80 per cent of those aged over 50 surveyed crediting their cat with helping them to overcome feelings of stress. But with these benefits come certain responsibilities.

RESPONSIBLE OWNERSHIP

The essence of your relationship with your cat is that you take on the caring and teaching role of its mother. Your cat is neotenized, meaning it will retain its juvenile traits in adulthood: it is, in effect, a lifelong kitten. Caring

Start as you mean to go on
Getting your cat off to a good start in life is your priority. Cats have very specific nutritional needs, so ensure you serve food designed with a feline in mind.

well for your cat means choosing the best food, carrying out routine grooming and playing, and ensuring your cat is protected, not just from parasites and infections, but from any hazards associated with living in a human environment. In turn, we should be aware of the small dangers to us from sharing our homes with another species. At the core of a satisfying human–feline relationship is good training, which works both ways. Cats need very little training, and basic behavioural requirements, such as housetraining, are normally not an issue. We train them for their safety and to prevent behavioural problems. Conversely, cats are superb at training us; a miaow or touch of a paw and we respond.

The two of us
A cat provides company, tactile comfort, and an outlet for our inbuilt need to nurture.

The importance of exercise and play
Humans aren't the only ones who need exercise. Toys and other stimuli will get your cat moving, helping to ensure it stays healthy and happy.

Sourcing a cat

Kitten or adult, male or female, moggy or pedigree, longhair or shorthair: there are many decisions to make when choosing the cat that best suits you and your circumstances. Focus on what you can offer a cat as well as what its presence offers you, and choose your source carefully.

CHOOSE SENSIBLY

Think about your lifestyle before acquiring a cat. Are you house-proud? Does anyone in the family have hay fever, asthma, or other allergies? Is money tight and is it vital to watch your expenses? Do you travel or move house frequently? You may want a feline housemate but is your dwelling the right kind of home for a cat? If it is, your next decision is whether to get a pedigree cat or a moggy. The advantage of a pedigree is that, aside from it having looks that appeal to you, it is also likely to have a known temperament. For example, the Siamese and its close relatives are likely to be gregarious,

Make sure you see the mother
The mother cat's general health and appearance are the best indicators of your prospective kitten's well-being. Always make a careful study of the condition of both animals, and never choose a kitten that is sick.

Breed and temperament
Consider how your lifestyle will affect your choice of cat. For example, the Abyssinian (below) can be great with children and thrives on routine family activity, but it is not the most affectionate breed.

outgoing, and, as cat behaviourists describe them, "sensitive", while Persians are generally quiet, self-contained layabouts. Male cats commonly spray their pungent urine, and females can, with age, become aloof, almost spiteful. However, because most pet cats are

neutered or spayed, which eliminates behaviour differences, choosing which sex you prefer is not as vital as it is in other species, such as the dog.

AGE AND LOOKS MATTER

The pros and cons of acquiring either an adult cat or a kitten are pretty evenly balanced. Adults are usually litter-trained, often already neutered, and arrive with developed personalities – you have a fair idea of what its temperament will be. The advantages of a kitten are obvious. Aside from the pleasure you'll receive from simply watching its joyous antics, it arrives ready to be moulded to your lifestyle.

What type of cat to go for is also an important choice. Longhaired cats are stunning to look at, but are you willing and able to devote the time needed to care for a high-maintenance coat? Cats are brilliantly self-cleaning, but even the most fastidious longhaired cat needs your help with daily grooming. Whatever type you opt for, think about the cost of living with a cat. Some costs, such as food, essential accessories, annual health checks, and boarding, are fixed. Others, especially unexpected medical expenses, vary enormously. Pet-health insurance is one way to plan for unexpected costs. An alternative is to set up an interest-earning bank account and regularly deposit the equivalent of insurance premiums in it.

ASK QUESTIONS

If you are actively looking for a cat, a vet's notice board is an excellent source of "vetted" individuals. Beware of getting a cat from pet shops, as unhygienic establishments are notorious locations for cats to contract cat flu. Also avoid internet and newspaper ads, which are often placed by unscrupulous individuals in an effort to sell cats and kittens that aren't in the peak of health. Regrettably, some rescue centres should also be avoided. If you

RESCUING A FERAL CAT

Welcoming a feral cat into your home is a big challenge and should only be attempted by the most patient of would-be owners. At first, feral cats don't like physical contact and are generally frightened of all people. They are also more likely to harbour disease or infestation and are more difficult to both diagnose and treat. Once they have been checked over by a vet, however, feral cats can live happy, healthy lives, developing a greater feeling of ease in your company, and going on to make valued pets.

are acquiring a rescue cat, ask the people who run the rescue centre the following:
■ Has the cat been examined for good health by a vet?
■ Has the cat been neutered, inoculated, and wormed?
■ Has the cat been housed individually to reduce the transmission of infection?
■ Is it known whether the cat has been raised in a family environment or from a feral background?

Dog remains calm

Allow each pet to sniff the other

Kitten clambers over dog

Meeting the resident dog
Just because you have a pet dog doesn't mean introducing a cat to the household is a no-no. And acquiring a kitten makes the process even easier. A series of patient, gradual introductions mean cats and dogs can develop a harmonious cross-species relationship.

Indoors or outdoors?

Cats are exquisitely adaptable. A typical cat is capable of surviving outdoors, patrolling a territory of over a square kilometre, or living in a 50-square metre apartment. The choice of an inside or outside lifestyle for your cat is yours, but it can be a complicated issue.

LAWS AND MORES

The choice of whether or not to let your cat go outdoors is seemingly made for practical reasons, but there is also a strong cultural influence on your decisions. Until 50 years ago, virtually all cats spent part of each day outdoors. That lifestyle changed suddenly and dramatically and for a curiously simple reason: disposable cat litter was invented. With the advent of cheap, replaceable cat litter (instead of, up until then, using heavy sand) it became possible to keep cats permanently indoors.

In the US, the major purebred registries and cat rescue societies either recommend or instruct that cats acquired from these organizations be kept permanently indoors. In parts of Australia and New Zealand, there is legislation compelling cat owners to keep their cats restricted to the owner's property, while in some European countries, cats are not permitted to wander more than a specified distance from their owner's

Keeping your cat indoors
Housebound cats live longer, safer lives. With no outdoor dangers to contend with, life is simply a matter of improvising with anything that comes to paw.

home. In the UK, prevailing social attitudes are quite different. Owners are expected, where possible, to allow their cats to venture outdoors into a safe and secure environment. However, cats that are permitted outdoors should be kept indoors from dusk until dawn.

HABITAT AND "STRESS"

In choosing whether your cat lives indoors or has access to the outdoors, it's important to consider which type of lifestyle will be more chronically stressful to your cat. Stress is discussed in more detail on pp.284–85 (*Common behaviour problems*). It is natural for cats to experience short bouts of stress, but prolonged stress due to your pet's living conditions must be avoided. The decision is yours, but the following checklist shows the pros and cons of both indoor and outdoor lifestyles.

MOVING AN OUTDOOR CAT INDOORS

Each situation is unique, but it's up to you to balance the benefits of keeping your cat away from the potential dangers of living outdoors with the effects on your cat's behaviour of restricting it to the (from a cat's perception) tiny territory of your apartment or house. It's always easier to start with an indoor-only life than to convert an outdoor-living feline to an indoor-only lifestyle. Timid cats are often happy to avoid the added stresses of outdoor life, but others find moving indoors a disconcerting and stress-inducing experience. When for whatever reason an indoor life is unavoidable for a previously outdoor cat, increase play and activity time with him or her. A short course of anti-anxiety drugs may be suggested by your vet, but my experience is that this rarely helps.

ADVANTAGES OF OUTDOORS

■ A more natural existence, including direct exposure to sun, wind, and rain.
■ An outlet for necessary social behaviours, such as territory marking.
■ The maintenance of body tone by routine physical exercise.
■ Mental stimulation from challenges within the environment.
■ Social contact with other cats.
■ Vermin control in your garden.

DISADVANTAGES OF OUTDOORS

■ Road traffic injuries.
■ Cat fight injuries, especially those resulting in abscesses.
■ Risk of transmissible viral diseases from other cats.
■ Parasite infestation, especially fleas.
■ Poisoning from consuming garden chemicals or eating poisoned prey.
■ Getting lost.
■ After climbing into and resting in open vehicles, getting locked in or driven away.
■ Friction with neighbours because of feline activities.

ADVANTAGES OF INDOORS

■ Dramatically reduced physical risks from fighting and accidents.
■ Negligible risk of catching infectious diseases from other domestic cats.
■ Freedom from parasites, such as fleas.
■ Good relations with your neighbours.
■ Increased time for developing a closer relationship with your cat.
■ Few gifts of dead prey other than the possibility of house mice.

DISADVANTAGES OF INDOORS

■ Reduced exercise and consequent weight problems.
■ Unneutered toms may spray urine in the house.
■ Unspayed females may urinate more frequently when in oestrus, in addition to becoming restless and howling all day.
■ Fear of change, and trepidation when it is necessary to leave home.

■ Over-dependence on people.
■ Lack of social skills when meeting a new feline companion.
■ Boredom, frustration, aggression, and associated behaviour problems.
■ Greater risk of damage to household items, including scratching furniture, walls, and doors, and climbing curtains.
■ Risk of escape and loss if doors and windows are left open.
■ Owners having to keep doors and windows closed.
■ Owners having to clean or empty litter trays on a daily basis.

The outdoor life

Many cat owners believe their pets love the outdoors and that it is natural for them to be able to enjoy fresh air, sunshine, and contact with other outdoor creatures.

Preparing for your cat's arrival

All cats, whether they live inside or have access to the outdoors, have basic needs: food and water bowls, beds and bedding, and a secluded toileting area. Make your home cat-friendly if your cat lives permanently indoors, and ensure that it wears identification if it goes outdoors.

BEDS AND BEDDING

Cats feel most secure in soft, warm, enclosed spaces. A simple bed in a quiet location is perfectly adequate for most cats. Alternatively, you may like to buy a cat tent or igloo instead. Bean-bags are popular with many cats, providing warmth and allowing the cat to trample the beads to form a "nest". Whatever the style of bed, ensure it is hygienic and washable. Place it in a position your cat appreciates, such as in sunlight by a window.

Beds that can be suspended from radiators are also a firm favourite of most felines.

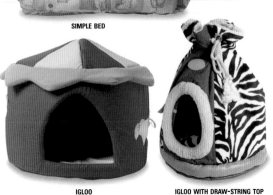

SIMPLE BED

IGLOO　　　　**IGLOO WITH DRAW-STRING TOP**

FOOD AND WATER BOWLS

Choose bowls that cater to your cat's needs, not just to your eye for fashion. Given a choice, cats prefer to eat from shallow, saucer-like bowls, shaped so that their whiskers don't touch the sides. They prefer a gentle contour to the interior, easier for licking clean. Many cats prefer to drink from dripping or gently running water. Some drinking bowls have battery-operated water fountains incorporated in them.

Wash all eating and drinking utensils daily. Use a separate can opener for your cat's tinned food. Cover any partly used can of food with a plastic lid and store it in the fridge for a maximum of two days.

Cat bowls

Choose shallow bowls with a wide eating surface. An inert material such as ceramic is excellent, but avoid cheap plastic as some cats find the odour from these bowls unpleasant. Stainless steel is hygienic, but it can be cold on the tongue!

KEEPING YOUR CAT CONTENTED

Whichever decision you make about whether to keep your cat indoors or to allow it outside, in kittenhood it will be an indoor cat until you decide otherwise. Choose basic accessories carefully, but also enhance the quality of life of an indoor cat by following these simple suggestions.
■ Get two kittens rather than one. This allows them outlets for natural activity, and reduces your guilt over keeping your cat(s) permanently indoors.
■ Offer mental activity by providing stimulating toys (*see* pp.254–55, *Playing with your cat*).
■ Keep things fresh. Routinely introduce new toys, games, and activities.
■ Don't be too house-proud. Place a scratching post in your home or concede that a piece of furniture will be scratched.

Two cats are better than one
Getting two kittens doubles your responsibility as an owner, but in the long-term it can make your life easier as your pets contentedly play, sleep, and eat together.

LITTER AND LITTER TRAYS

Litter trays vary from simple to the spectacular, and can even be disguised as house plants. Some are virtually self-cleaning while others eliminate odours. Cats are naturally clean and will use a "diggable" surface for toileting when provided with one. Some types of litter are designed to appeal to us – scented brands, for example – but what's most important to your cat is how it feels under the feet. Control odour with frequent cleaning and, as a general rule, provide a litter tray on each floor of your home.

Clay
The original and most common form of cat litter. Some varieties contain odour-absorbing granules while others form clumps when moistened, making litter disposal a much easier job.

Wood pellets
A by-product of the pulp and paper industry, these pellets expand when moistened and absorb liquid. Wood is completely biodegradable and can be composted or dried and burned.

Paper
Pellets formed from used newsprint are available and act much like wood pellets. This ecologically friendly form of litter can be safely burned. Waste coconut fibre is also used as cat litter.

Preparing for an outdoor cat

Allow your cat to go outdoors only after you have investigated and minimized the risks to its safety. Ensure the cat is clearly identified, the cat-flap is easy to use, and your garden is "cat-proofed". A compromise is to create safe access to a small, secured area of garden.

MINIMIZE OUTDOOR RISKS

Given a choice, most cats prefer to spend time outdoors, where they can patrol their territory and pounce on potential prey, be it falling leaves or scampering rodents. There are various ways you can reduce risks to your cats' safety.

- Train your cat to come when called (*see* pp.282–83, *Applied training*).
- Maintain inoculations against infectious feline diseases, and prevent both internal and external parasites (*see* pp.268–71, *Disease and parasite prevention*).
- Keep an ID tag on your cat's collar, and make sure the collar has an elastic section or a safety catch that will release it if it snags on an obstacle.
- Ensure your cat is microchip-identified.
- Neuter your cat. Neutered cats wander less (*see* pp.272–73, *Maintaining good health*).
- Night-time is more dangerous than the daylight hours. Cats are dazzled by headlights and may freeze in position.

Dense planting
As well as looking beautiful and providing your cat with a veritable forest to explore, tight positional planting helps ensure your garden doesn't become a cat toilet. Provide a sandpit toilet specifically for your cat to do its business in.

Allow your cat out during the day, but ensure it is indoors by dusk. For added safety, make sure its collar is reflective.

- Search your garden and remove toxic chemicals and any other possible dangers.

A CAT-FRIENDLY GARDEN

Plan your garden so that your cat enjoys spending time in it, rather than wanting to wander. Wooden posts are ideal for perching on and surveying the realm. Shrubs create

Provide shade
Although they love to be warm, cats also need shelter from the summer sun. Leafy shrubs and trees are one source of protection, but cats always seem able to improvise when a good spot is at stake.

CAT COLLARS

Cats enjoy climbing, so ensure yours won't get caught by branches entangling its collar. Use a collar with either a stretchy elasticized section or a snap that releases when a degree of tension is applied. Clearly, cats can lose these types of safety collars and their attached ID tags, which makes it imperative that outdoor cats are also identifiable by their microchip. Fitting a microchip is easy and painless for the cat. A transponder the size of a grain of rice is injected under the skin between the shoulder blades. Rescue agencies check strays for microchips; the unique number on the chip enables the cat to be reunited with its owner.

SAFETY SNAP FASTENING

SAFETY "BREAKABLE" FASTENING

FLUORESCENT COLLAR

NAME TAG

cover and provide shade in hot weather. Avoid bird feeders, and plant buddleia (*Buddleja davidii*) and other flowers that attract butterflies, instead. Keep planting dense so there is no visible soil that your cat could use as a toilet. If your cat digs, lay chicken wire or plastic mesh just under the soil. Prune trees near fences so that your cat cannot climb into the neighbour's garden, or try ringing tree trunks with "Elizabethan collars", which are 50cm (20in) wide, about 1.8m (6ft) above the ground. This prevents access to branches.

CAT-FLAPS

A cat-flap allows your cat to venture in and out at will. The most efficient are activated by a magnet on the cat's collar, which means only your cat can come in and out. Show your cat how the cat-flap works by holding the flap fully open and gently guiding it through. Graduate to holding it partially open so that the cat feels the flap on its back as it is in transit, and finally show it how it can operate the flap on its own simply by pressing its head against it. Using food rewards also helps.

OUTDOOR TOILET

Dig a sandpit toilet, away from where children may play, and scent it with litter from the cat's indoor litter tray. Sift the sand routinely, removing faeces, and dispose of it by either burying it or drying and burning it. Don't dispose of faeces on the compost heap as heat from the compost allows intestinal parasites to survive. Flush faeces down the toilet only if there is minimal sand adhering to it.

GARDEN FENCING

It is possible to erect fencing to keep a cat inside the garden, but this can be a major undertaking. Discuss plans with your neighbours and, if necessary, local planning officials. The fence must be 1.8m (6ft) high. The top is made cat-proof using an overhang that projects 50cm (20in) horizontally, then 30cm (12in) vertically, on the garden side. Secure fencing is usually erected on a wooden framework with welded wire mesh, chicken wire, or green or black polypropylene netting. Mesh should be no more than 2cm ($^3/_4$in) in diameter to prevent small heads getting caught in it.

Lookout spots
Cats love to sit in an elevated position to survey their territory. Fence posts, wall tops, windowsills, and garden furniture are all highly suitable locations to rest.

The arrival

While some cats settle into their new homes almost instantaneously, others take time to adjust to new surroundings. Prepare your house and family in advance. Start as you aim to continue. Check that your cat is healthy and give it a safe, personal space, and time to explore.

ARRIVING HOME

When you get your cat home, open the door to the car carrier and leave your new pet to wander about in its own time. Leaving a bowl of food or a few cat treats lying around for puss will help break the ice. As soon as you can, put your cat's collar and ID tag on, just in case someone leaves the door open and it bolts. Use the short, distinctive-sounding name you have chosen for your cat each time you call it.

Your cat needs time to adjust to its new surroundings. Remind children not to get too noisy or excited with the new arrival. Rather than playing "pass the parcel" with the newcomer, let your feline friend investigate the single room you will be keeping it in at first. Allow it to find the litter tray, in one corner of the room, and food and water, both well away from the litter tray. Leave a few toys dotted around to encourage play. Now is also a good

EARLY EXPERIENCE IS VITAL

Cats that have a greater number of chances to experience intermittent low-level stress when they are very young learn how to cope with it and manage stress far better when they are adults. Unfortunately, the stage of life when kittens are most adept at learning their coping strategies is between two and seven weeks of age. If it has been raised by a breeder in an unstimulating, unchallenging environment it will have developed few emotional defences to cope with stress. If you have the opportunity, contact your kitten's breeder long before you acquire your kitten and ensure it has a head start by experiencing as many low-level stress triggers as possible while it is still with its litter.

time to show your cat where its scratching post is; the post is a territory marker, so place it near to the cat's sleeping area.

PERSONAL SPACE

Where your cat sleeps is up to you, but its natural inclination is based upon its age and previous experience. Despite you providing comfortable bedding specially for your new acquisition, kittens will prefer to sleep with you, while older, independent cats are likely to try to find a comfy space of their own. If you don't want the cat in the bedroom – and if either you or anyone else suffers from allergies, the

Leave space to slip two fingers under the collar

Identity tag gives cat's details

Fitting a collar and ID tag

All cats should wear collars with an ID tag in case they go missing. Choose a collar that is partially elasticized so that your cat won't choke if the collar gets caught on something.

Time to adjust
Don't overwhelm your cat
with new experiences and people.
It may be nervous so remind children not to over-handle
the new arrival, and give it time and space to explore its
new surroundings on its own. Be patient while it settles in.

CHECKLIST FOR NEW ARRIVALS

Use this checklist to watch for any potential health
problems during your cat's first 24 hours in your home.
If there are any boxes in the "No" column that are
checked, schedule a visit to your vet.

	Yes	No
Eats normally.	☐	☐
Urinates and defecates in the litter tray without difficulty or distress.	☐	☐
Has not vomited or had diarrhoea.	☐	☐
Breathes easily with no noise or effort.	☐	☐
Has bright eyes and clean ears.	☐	☐
Has white teeth, pink gums, and not unpleasant smell to the breath.	☐	☐
Has a glossy coat without shiny black speckles of dirt (flea droppings).	☐	☐
Moves and stretches without difficulty.	☐	☐
Active and alert, although may be frightened.	☐	☐

cat should never be permitted there (*see*
p.266) – ensure it has a soft, comfortable,
warm, and safe place it can call its own.

THE FIRST MEAL

Moving home is stressful for cats and it's
best to continue feeding them whatever
they have been eating previously, at least
for a few days, before making any changes
to their diet. The choice of food depends
on both your and your cat's preferences
(*see* pp.256–59), but start the mealtime
ritual as you aim to continue: always
feed your cat in the same location and at
the same times. Feeding time is ideal for
teaching your cat to miaow on command
or to come when called (*see* pp.282–83).

Meeting the rest of the family

Introducing a new cat or kitten to your other pets can be a tense affair. Ensure your new cat is comfortable with you and your family before doing so, and don't expect them to hit it off from the start. It's likely you'll need to control the situation rather than let nature take its course.

MEETING YOUR RESIDENT DOG

It is generally easier to introduce a new cat to a dog than to another cat. Barring the odd exception, cats rule dogs, and dogs don't mind being bossed around by animals usually much smaller than they are. Dogs are so gregarious, most simply enjoy the companionship of cats.

Keep your newcomer separated from your dog by a closed door until the cat has settled in and gained its confidence. A glass door is ideal, as this allows sights and sounds to flow between the two, and smells can creep under. When the first meeting takes place, hold your dog firmly by the collar, especially if it is a terrier. Kittens usually take immediate charge –

a simple bat with a paw on the dog's inquisitive nose is often enough to create the basis for their future relationship. Older cats are likely to be fearful (unless they have lived with dogs previously), but an unequivocal hiss will put most dogs in their place. Never leave the dog and cat together unattended until you are happy they are a safe pairing.

HOUSE RULES

Create rules for all members of the family to follow and post them in your kitchen. For example:

- Keep all windows and doors closed [for indoor cats].
- Lock the cat flap in the evening when Smokey is inside [for outdoor cats].
- Mum [or whoever] is responsible for feeding Smokey.
- In mum's [or whoever's] absence ...... [specify whom] is responsible for feeding Smokey.
- Smokey is not allowed ...... [specify where].
- Smokey's bed stays ...... [specify where].
- Do not give Smokey treats.
- Use Smokey's name when calling him.
- Don't forget about Smokey when you're making any plans that will result in him being left alone.

MEETING YOUR RESIDENT CAT

Your home belongs to its first occupier. It is bound to be unhappy to now be sharing its turf. Don't force meetings. Let relationships develop gradually. Let your resident cat make all the overtures. Let it into the kitten's room for an investigative sniff only after the kitten is deeply asleep. If the newcomer is older, keep the two separated for several days but feed them on opposite sides of the closed door.

Afford all of your pets equal protection

A goldfish in a bowl may provide endless fascination for your cat, but make sure that aquatic pets are placed high up and out of reach of prying paws.

Don't be surprised if your resident stares, growls, and hisses. Luckily, most residents restrict themselves to these theatrical displays and don't actually attack.

Start feeding both cats in the same room, initially at opposite ends and then, day by day, move the bowls closer until the cats are separated only by a chair. Chances are, after a tasty meal, they will sniff each other then walk off in separate directions.

MEETING OTHER ANIMALS

Ensure that all small mammal pets such as gerbils, hamsters, mice, or rats are out of harm's way. If you introduce kittens at an early age – between three and seven weeks – to small mammals, they are unlikely to chase them when they are mature. Keep caged birds where your cat cannot reach them. While unneutered big buck rabbits can be fierce, they are still at risk and, as with guinea pigs, should be protected from your cat.

Cat's twitching tail indicates curiosity

Eye contact establishes dominance

Confident stance makes kitten appear larger than it really is

Youthful meetings

The young are most adept at successful introductions. This four-month-old Siamese, already familiar with dogs, stands his ground while the pup performs a playful inspection.

Getting to know one another
It's important to have realistic expectations when introducing a new pet to a resident pet. The whole process could take weeks or months, and the net result may be only tolerating each other's presence.

Playing with your cat

All cats, but especially indoor individuals, thrive on play activity. Provide opportunities for your cat to play with you or other cats, or with inanimate toys. Cat furniture, such as climbing frames or cat gyms, makes excellent alternatives to fences and trees.

THE IMPORTANCE OF PLAY

Play is as important for adult cats as it is for kittens. For the young cat, games serve as practice for independent adult life. Offensive and defensive roles, attack, pursuit, ambush, and killing techniques are all rehearsed with great gusto. Play is also an integral part of developing social awareness among cats: kittens that aren't able to, or have difficulty, playing with other cats as they develop often turn out to be retiring, anti-social individuals.

For the older cat, especially an indoor cat, play doesn't just provide physical activity: it provides mental stimulation as well. Play is easy, and you can motivate your cat with the simplest of games: most felines will enjoy patting and pushing a small ball around with their paws.

THE SCIENCE OF PLAY

Technically, play activity increases the level of the brain chemical serotonin. Low serotonin levels, both in cats and in humans, are associated with increased

WHY DOES CATNIP CAPTIVATE MY CAT?

Catnip (*Nepeta cataria*) contains an essential oil called nepetalactone that most, but not all, cats find alluring. One whiff of this herb can reduce a cat to a crumpled heap – purring, rubbing, rolling about, and chewing the bruised leaves. Nepetalactone's chemical structure is similar to that of the hallucinogen LSD, and a cat's ecstatic reaction to it is caused by the aroma of catnip reaching the vomeronasal organ (*see* pp.208–209). The effects last, on average, around 15 minutes. You should ration your offerings of catnip to ensure your pet remains stimulated by it. Interestingly, some cats simply don't succumb to catnip's charms; these pusses may warm to honeysuckle (*Lonicera periclymenum*) instead, which has similar properties to catnip.

Encourage your cat to play
Cats are naturally drawn to sources of amusement that we, as owners, might not give a second thought. This curious individual is both stimulating his mind while physically playing.

irritability, depression, even aggression. Higher serotonin levels are associated with a greater feeling of well-being and self-confidence. By providing an enriched environment for your cat, you allow it to release pent-up physical and emotional energy. If you don't provide these outlets, your cat will create its own games, such as stalking your ankles and climbing curtains. These are acts stemming from feline frustration, but the risk the unwitting owner runs is that he or she may wrongly assume their cat has behaviour problems (*see* pp.284–85). Spending time playing with your cat is essential.

PLAYING WITH YOUR CAT

For cats, the most exciting forms of play involve your interaction. Wands and rods are superb, especially for children to use to play safely. These consist of a rod with a long string to which an item such as a feather is attached. With you manipulating the toy, your cat has an opportunity to stalk, chase, and pounce. Some "teasers" (as they are also known) come in the form of fishing rods, so you can cast off and see what bites! Take special care with toys containing wool, thread, or string. Cat's love the feeling of these items in the mouth, but if they are swallowed there can be devastating consequences.

String your cat along
Guaranteed to get even the laziest cat up and "dancing", string toys, wands, and rods provide a great opportunity to get closer to your cat while simultaneously exercising it.

PLAYING WITH TOYS

When it comes to toys, cats have never had it so good. A bewildering range of products includes interactive toys that offer intermittent food rewards, such as food dropping out of holes when a ball is batted across the floor. Clockwork toys, with a small ball trapped inside a circular track, move enticingly as a cat tries to catch the mobile object. Cat trees and gymnasiums allow your cat to safely climb and gaze down on its domain. Some models contain hiding places while others incorporate scratching posts. But you don't have to spend money to entertain your cat: large paper bags make superb toys, especially with food treats left in them. And plastic water bottles with a few drops of water inside are lightweight enough to be batted around.

GLOVE TOY

Getting physical
He's not just enjoying himself: this cat is also controlling his weight, as well as developing muscle tone, agility, and stamina.

Eye/paw coordination encouraged

SOFT MOUSE

Feather lure on string provides cat with moving target to bat

Physical exercise induced as cat stands

LIGHTWEIGHT BALL

Good nutrition

Cats are what nutritionists call "obligate carnivores" – they must eat other animals to obtain the right balance of nutrients for survival. Manufacturers of quality cat food carry out feeding trials to ensure their range of products contain the vital ingredients for a healthy diet.

A SENSIBLE EATER

Cats are generally fussy eaters, and there's logic behind this fastidiousness: a cat existing in the wild depends entirely upon the nutrients it consumes by eating natural prey. Unlike the dog, cats cannot manufacture certain essential amino and fatty acids, and if it is fed solely on a vegetarian diet, a cat will eventually die.

Animal fat contains essential fatty acids such as arachidonic acid and linoleic acid. The former is vital for efficient reproduction, blood clotting, and coat condition, while the latter is necessary for body growth, wound healing, and liver function. Vitamin A, responsible for maintaining

Kittens
Young cats will start to eat solid foods from about the age of seven or eight weeks. What type of food you decide to feed them on at this stage is crucial in their development.

good eye health, is another natural substance that cats cannot manufacture; instead they must eat parts of animals high in natural vitamin A, such as fish oil and liver. A fresh mouse or bird offers a cat not only balanced nutrition – amino acids in the form of protein, fatty acids

As nature intended
Natural prey provides all of the cat's essential nutrients, but this isn't a diet you are expected to provide. Instead, you should feed your cat easily obtainable foods that fulfil its daily nutritional quota of protein, fat, carbohydrates, vitamins, and minerals.

VARYING NUTRITIONAL NEEDS

Kittens and outdoor cats have the highest energy demands while older cats benefit from higher levels of vitamins and minerals (especially antioxidants) and more easily digested protein in their diets. Special kitten and "senior" cat foods are readily available, as are products for longhaired cats (to help them pass hairballs) and foods that reduce tartar build-up in cats.

BALANCED NUTRITION

To remain healthy, cats require a range of nutrients. Some, such as proteins and fats, are needed in large quantities while others, such as vitamins, minerals, fruits, and vegetables (also known as "micro-ingredients"), are consumed in smaller quantities. In commercial cat food, protein, fat, and bone are usually derived from what is left after the human food industry has taken what it wants from an animal carcass. The remnants include trimmings, organs, bone marrow, and bones. These are mixed with carbohydrates, which are either "raw" or "processed". Raw carbohydrates may contain more nutrients, but are almost invariably tougher to digest. Processed carbohydrates may contain artificial processing ingredients. An oil/water combination is added to the mix before the micro-ingredients are added.

NUTRIENTS	SOURCES	FUNCTIONS
■ Amino acids	■ Meat or manufactured by cat from other sources.	■ Building blocks for body tissues and enzymes that support body's chemical reactions.
■ Essential amino acids ■ Taurine	■ Meat only. Cannot be manufactured.	■ Vital for heart function. Absence leads to heart disease.
■ Fatty acids	■ Animal fat or manufactured by cat from other sources.	■ Energy and carriers of fat-soluble vitamins.
■ Essential fatty acids ■ Linoleic and arachidonic acids	■ Animal fat only, cannot be manufactured.	■ Body growth. ■ Wound healing. ■ Blood clotting.
■ Fibre	■ Fur, feather, viscera.	■ Influences blood sugar. ■ Influences bowel function.
■ Vitamin A	■ Liver. ■ Cannot be manufactured.	■ Healthy eyes.
■ Vitamins D, E, K	■ Plant/animal sources. ■ Fat-soluble vitamins.	■ Bone development. ■ Free-radical scavenging. ■ Blood clotting.
■ Vitamin C	■ Unlike humans, cats manufacture their own vitamin C.	■ Helps fight infection. Dangerous in excess – leads to bladder stones.
■ B-group vitamins	■ Plant/animal sources.	■ Heart health and metabolic functions.
■ Calcium ■ Phosphorus	■ Bone.	■ Cell membrane and nerve function. ■ Bone growth and maintenance.
■ Zinc ■ Selenium	■ Plant/animal sources.	■ Free-radical scavenging. ■ Maintains healthy immune system.
■ Iron	■ Plant/animal sources.	■ Red blood-cell production.

from fat, fibre from beaks, nails, feathers, and fur, and vitamins and minerals from viscera and intestinal content – it also supplies a satisfying variety of textures to chew on. Texture is very important to cats, which is why dry cat foods come in such a dramatic variety of shapes and densities, and wet foods are sold in the form of solid loaves or have extra jelly.

FEEDING COMMERCIAL CAT FOOD

Dry cat foods are prepared by cooking food under pressure, drying it, then spraying it with fat to add palatability. Preservatives are added to prevent the fat from spoiling. Wet foods are cooked, heat sterilized, then sealed in tins or sachets. Because they are vacuum-sealed, preservatives are not necessary. The choice between wet or dry foods is based on convenience and palatability. Nutritionally, one type is no better than another. Dry foods exercise the teeth and gums more and may slow down the development of dental problems.

All cat food must, by law, be safe for human consumption. For this reason, reputable cat-food manufacturers only use surplus nutrients from foods produced for the human sector. Other manufacturers may use products that have been deemed unfit for human consumption, so source your cat food carefully.

Whatever the texture of commercial food, the recipes follow either a fixed or variable formula. Fixed formulas remain constant and form the "premium" or "super-premium"

end of the market. These are the most expensive foods, because in them the manufacturers always use the same ingredients, making no substitutions. A variable formula product is not necessarily inferior, as long as the varying ingredients

COMPARING NUTRIENTS

To compare accurately the nutrients of one food with another it's necessary to convert the label information to a "dry matter" basis. This is how you do it:

A wet food label may say:

Crude protein	8%
Crude fat	7%
Ash	2%
Fibre	1%
Moisture	82%

This food is 82% moisture and 18% dry matter.

Once you have calculated the percentage of dry matter, you can compare percentages of nutrients on a like-for-like basis between foods. To calculate the dry matter percentages of protein and fat, use this formula:

$$\text{Dry matter} = \frac{\text{The label's nutrient percentage} \times 100}{\text{Content's dry matter percentage}}$$

For example:

$$\text{Protein dry matter} = \frac{8 \times 100}{18} = 44.4\%$$

Texture of wet food closer to natural diet

The importance of drinking fresh water

Water is essential for life, so always provide some for your pet. This cat is drinking from a specially designed fountain, which helps keeps the water oxygenated.

Wet or dry food?

The only significant difference between wet and dry foods is the level of moisture. Dry foods are usually around 10–15 per cent moisture, while wet foods are around 80 per cent. Dry and wet food may both be made to identical nutritional standards, but the information on package labels will vary enormously because of the different moisture levels.

remain of high quality and nutritional value. Variable formula foods maintain the same energy value.

Advances in the understanding of the benefits of controlled diets as part of the treatment of medical conditions, such as diabetes, have led to the development of an ever-expanding range of veterinary diets, invariably made to a fixed formula. However, fixed formula foods that use the same ingredients all the time may still periodically alter certain characteristics, such as size of the kibble (pellet size), or flavouring components.

HOME COOKING

Home cooking is excellent if you have the time, inclination, and knowledge of what's good for your cat. Because of modern abattoir methods, it's best to avoid raw meat, particularly poultry, as it may be contaminated by bacteria. Raw meat can also harbour the protozoan parasite that causes toxoplasmosis. Vary the diet. Muscle meat alone, low in calcium, will lead to serious medical problems. A tuna-only diet will lead to severe liver problems. A vegetarian diet is, of course, impossible. Bone-rich foods, such as cooked chicken necks, are an excellent source of nutrients and also exercise teeth and gums. Bones can be dangerous for cats

Special light diet
A proliferation of pet foods in recent years means greater choice for your cat. This bowl contains food formulated for adult cats that have a tendency to be overweight.

that, dog-like, wolf down their food, but in most cases, just as cats cope with mouse and bird bone, they can deal with well-cooked chicken bone.

COMMON DIET-RELATED PROBLEMS

Two of the most common reasons cats are taken to the vet are diet related: obesity (*see* pp.292–93), and tooth and gum disease (*see* pp.298–99). Both problems can be prevented, by controlling calorie intake, and by ensuring that the teeth and gums are given good exercise. Watch your cat's weight, and if it's increasing, either cut back on the quantity of food you are feeding or switch to a low-calorie diet. Watch for urinary problems: your cat might visit the litter tray more often than normal or have difficulty urinating. Almost invariably, these cats benefit from consuming more liquid. This usually means feeding a wet, rather than dry, diet, and you should still provide your cat with clean, fresh water. There are many reasons for vomiting or diarrhoea, but one of these is an intolerance to a component in the diet. Switching to another type of food may be necessary.

MILK AND CREAM

Most cats love drinking milk, particularly creamy milk. Unfortunately, in older cats that don't have enough bacteria in their intestines to break down the lactose it contains, milk sometimes upsets digestion and causes diarrhoea. Lactose-free milk is available at all supermarkets, either as "cat milk" or as a UHT (ultra heat-treated) milk for lactose-sensitive people.

Grooming and hygiene

We willingly share our homes with cats because they are fastidiously tidy. Cats are superb self-groomers, instinctively and routinely keeping their coats in pristine condition. Even so, our help with grooming and maintaining is beneficial, and enhances the bond between pet and owner.

HOW CATS GROOM THEMSELVES

A typical cat spends on average over 10 per cent of its waking hours grooming itself. This is done in a ritualized manner, first licking the coat all over and removing tangles and debris, then licking the paws and applying cleansing saliva over the head and face – regions that can't be reached by licking. Efficient grooming removes food from the most recent meal, dirt, and debris, but just as importantly it removes odours that might attract larger predators.

THE VALUES OF HELPING WITH GROOMING

Regularly grooming your cat – brushing it, checking its skin, eyes, ears, teeth, nails, and anal region – does more than keep your cat in tip-top physical condition. Carried out sensibly and sensitively, simple grooming is a superb way to form and maintain a fruitful relationship with your cat, one in which your cat understands and accepts that you are the "parent" and it is the dependant.

GROOMING UTENSILS

Your basic grooming kit should include brushes and combs suitable for your cat's coat type, talcum powder to aid the removal of tangles, and suitable shampoo for washing. A child's toothbrush will fit a cat's mouth, while "guillotine" nail clippers cut nails without crushing.

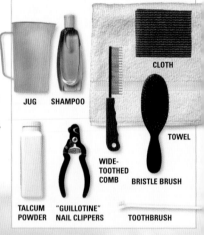

JUG   SHAMPOO

CLOTH

TOWEL

WIDE-TOOTHED COMB   BRISTLE BRUSH

TALCUM POWDER   "GUILLOTINE" NAIL CLIPPERS   TOOTHBRUSH

Pride and groom
Cats are renowned for their cleanliness, washing themselves daily to keep their coats soft, glossy, and free of dirt. All cats, however long their coats, require additional grooming from their owners. Older cats especially benefit from human intervention.

BASIC GROOMING

A smooth, short coat is simple to care for. Use a rubber or bristle brush, or even a chamois or hound glove, over the body once a week.

A semi-long coat requires more frequent attention, at least twice weekly with a slicker or bristle brush, followed by combing the longer hair with a wide-toothed comb. Longhaired coats need daily attention.

Needless to say, routine grooming is also the ideal way for you to spot potential medical problems, such as unexpected lumps, odours, or any changes from the norm. Accustom your cat to this routine grooming and examination from an early age, preferably while it is still with its mother. Give rewards for good behaviour: food treats are a powerful incentive.

1 Use a slicker or bristle brush all over to remove dead hair and debris. Mats are likely to develop behind the ears, behind the elbows, on the belly, and between the hindlegs. Tease these loose using talcum powder, then brush through. If your cat resents you teasing the knots, either very carefully cut them off using scissors (it's surprisingly easy to accidentally cut the skin) or arrange for them to be removed by a professional groomer.

2 Starting at the front and working back, comb the hair with a wide-toothed comb, removing the small tangles that can build into mats. Part the hair as you comb, moving from the roots out. Using a bristle brush, part the hair on the tail and brush from the roots sideways. Many cats dislike their tails being brushed along the length. Finish by combing and brushing the undercarriage, another sensitive area.

HELPFUL HINTS

■ Keep initial grooming sessions brief and learn your cat's limitations.
■ Watch your cat's body language.
■ A lashing tail means it's time to stop.
■ Once your cat is used to short sessions, gradually extend them but without ever exceeding your individual's limitations. Try to groom as economically as possible.

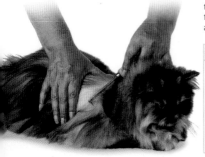

WASHING A CAT

Cats naturally clean themselves by rolling in dust. Dry shampoos mimic the benefits of a dust bath but there are occasions when your vet may ask you to wet-wash your cat, or when your cat has been investigating something particularly pungent. It is a rare cat that willingly accepts washing. Follow these suggestions to make it as simple as possible for both of you. Always reward compliant behaviour.

1 Brush your cat before bathing to remove any tangles and debris from the coat. Use a non-slip rubber mat in the bathing area to prevent accidents. Use a restraint bag if you have one, or alternatively suspend a rope above the bathing area, which your cat will instinctively grasp on to. Always check the water temperature before applying it to ensure that it is not too hot for your cat.

2 Use shampoo recommended by your vet and apply it following the instructions on the bottle. Take care to avoid getting shampoo in your cat's eyes. Lather the coat before rinsing off the shampoo using a hand-held shower. Towel dry or, if your cat is not frightened by the sound, gently blow-dry with a hand-held dryer set on cool to warm, not hot. Congratulate yourself and your cat on a job well done.

EYE AND NOSE CHECKS

A cat's large, bright, alluring eyes can be its most stunning feature. Check your cat's eyes regularly for debris or changes in appearance. In cases of chronic redness, discharge, tear overflow, or nasal discharge, contact your vet. Long-faced breeds tend to collect mucus in the corners of their eyes. This can be removed with damp cotton wool. Flatter-faced breeds are prone to tear overflow. When exposed to air, tears soon turn a mahogany colour, staining the hair below the eyes. Cleanse the eyes and associated nasal skin fold daily with cotton wool dampened either with water, saline, or proprietary eye wash. Discharge and crust can develop around the nostrils, especially in longhaired cats. Clean this using dampened cotton wool.

COTTON WOOL BALLS

Cleansing the eyes
Flat-faced breeds, such as this longhaired Persian, are prone to tear overflow and crusty build-up around the eyes and nostrils. Check and cleanse your cat's eyes regularly.

EAR INSPECTION

The inside of the ears should be odourless and free from wax or debris. An excess of oily but normal, clear, colourless wax is not uncommon, especially in indoor cats. Use damp cotton wool or a proprietary product recommended by your vet to remove this wax. Ear mites are common in kittens (*see* p.271) and create dark, gritty, sandy debris. Take special care when cleaning the ears, especially when using cotton buds. Used incorrectly a cotton bud acts like a plunger, pushing wax deep into the ear, turning a minor condition into a potentially serious medical problem.

Cleaning the ears
To remove excess wax build-up in your cat's ear, swab the ear canal with dampened cotton wool, or an ear-cleaning solution recommended by your vet, to loosen the wax. The excess can then be carefully removed with cotton wool. If there is a moist discharge, contact your vet.

Brushing the teeth
Use a child's toothbrush or a special toothbrush designed for cats. At first, brush up and down for only a few seconds then give a food reward. Gradually increase the length of time you spend on brushing. Gently massage the gums and brush the back teeth, where most dental problems occur.

TEETH INSPECTION

Bad breath usually means oral problems. Lift the lips and check the gums and teeth. Gums should be uniformly pink with no redness near the teeth. Teeth should be white, free from tartar, and firmly rooted. Train your cat from kittenhood to accept that your brushing its teeth is simply part of life. Meat-flavoured cat toothpaste can be a reward on its own. An alternative for cats that resent brushing is to apply an oral antiseptic, which your vet can provide, once a day to the gums.

PET TOOTHPASTE

Trim to here

TOO LONG

CORRECT LENGTH

Claw clipping
Press gently behind the claw to extend the nail. Position the guillotine-type clippers over the nail, just in front of the "quick". Squeeze firmly, cutting straight across the claw. Reward your cat to finish.

TRIMMING THE NAILS

Cats trim their nails by biting them and scratching off the longest, oldest bits of keratin, the nail's primary constituent. Check the nails at least weekly by pressing the bone immediately behind the nail. This extends the nail, which should be clean and white although possibly frayed from the previous day's activities. Remove any foreign debris that is wrapped around the base of the nail. Check older cats' nails more frequently. They are self-groomed less frequently and as a result grow longer, sometimes so long that they curve around and penetrate the paw pads. This is most common with the dewclaws. Outdoor cats use their sharp claws as part of their natural defences, and to assist in climbing. Housebound cats' claws will require trimming more regularly to keep them blunt. As with all grooming, accustom your cat from an early age to having its paws handled and nails extended.

Nail trimming causes no pain. Extend the nail by pressing on the bone behind and, using a guillotine-type clipper, clip off the thin, sharp point. Avoid clipping into the pink region inside the nail. This is the "quick", living tissue which is painful and bleeds when cut. Reward your cat with treats both during and after a nail-cutting session. Nails need trimming every two weeks to keep them blunt. If your cat will not allow you to trim its nails, try doing so in a completely different location in your home so that it does not learn to associate a particular site with the process. Veterinary staff routinely clip the nails of some cats.

ANAL SACS

The anal sacs, under the skin on both sides of the anus, are territory-marking glands that produce a distinctive smelling substance cats use to anoint their faeces with "the daily news". Outdoor cats are likely to empty their anal sacs naturally, but indoor cats more commonly suffer from anal sac irritation caused by the liquid becoming dried out and difficult to pass. Check the anal region for redness or inflammation, and the hair around the anus and between the hindlegs for signs of excessive licking, an indicator that the anal sacs are bothering the cat. To empty the sacs, wear disposable gloves. Place your thumb and forefinger at 4 and 8 o'clock positions on either side of the anus and gently squeeze slightly up and out so that your fingers end up at 3 and 9 o'clock.

Cat shows

Cat shows are a contest of beauty, health, and temperament. Through these shows, breeders have produced many new kinds of cat and had them recognized. Depending on which organization is running it, rules, classifications, and what happens at a cat show can vary considerably.

THE FORMATION OF BREED REGISTRIES

The first formal cat show was held in 1871 at the Crystal Palace in Hyde Park, London, UK. It was organized by cat lover Harrison Weir, who wrote the standards – descriptions of the ideal cat of a particular breed – for all the breeds shown and acted as one of the three judges. This show, and others across mainland Europe and in the US, was the main impetus for modern selective breeding, encouraging the vogue in pure-bred cats.

The rules of cat shows are positively Byzantine in their complexity, chiefly because each registering body has written its own unique set of regulations.

To this end, some registries will not permit cats registered with them to be shown at shows organized by other registries. In the UK, however, the Governing Council of the Cat Fancy (GCCF) now permits its registered cats to be shown at shows under the auspices of Felis Britannica (FB), a federation of UK cat clubs affiliated with the international cat association Fédération Internationale Féline (FIFé). Permission is granted as long as owners inform the GCCF in writing and, for health reasons, do not take their cats to GCCF shows for 13 days before or after the non-GCCF show. In North America,

Jolly good show
A winning entrant and proud owner at the 2005 International Cat Show in Warsaw, Poland. For some people, breeding and showing pedigree cats is a full-time business. If you want to take part in a show, you must decide whether your cat is a suitable competitor.

Brush with stardom
At the very early shows, cats such as these four Blue Persians – being groomed at a London event – ran a high risk of catching fatal infections. Fortunately today, vaccinations will guard against this danger.

and show presence" while others simply look for "uniqueness" in entrants.

Only the strongest, most robust personalities thrive on the travel, activity, contact with people, and presence of other cats that are associated with cat shows. Cats win cat shows not just because they are closest to breed perfection, but also because as individuals they are relaxed, have a presence, and boast a flair for the spotlight. If you plan to show your cat, start training as early as possible. Familiarize your cat with travelling in the car, unexpected noises and commotion, and remaining quiet in its cage. Accustom it to routine nail clipping, frequent grooming, and occasional bathing. Train it to allow you to clean its eyes, ears, and teeth regularly.

the Cat Fanciers' Association (CFA) does not permit the showing of declawed cats, while from an opposite standpoint, The International Cat Association (TICA) states in its rules that "Cats that have been declawed shall not be penalized".

SHOW CLASSIFICATIONS

Each registry has its own unique list of show classes or categories. In general, cats compete against other cats of the same breed, sex, and colour. Individual cat shows are categorized as either all-breed or speciality. In an all-breed show, all cats, regardless of coat length, compete for various honours. In a speciality show, only cats of similar coat length compete for awards.

While all cat shows have a "Kitten" category, the definition of a kitten varies considerably: three to six months of age in some shows, and four to eight months of age in others. Cats that are new to the concept of shows are also welcome. The GCCF, for example, has a "Debutante" class for cats that have never been shown under GCCF rules. More mature entrants are also catered for – the CFA has a "Veteran" class for individuals over seven years old. Every show organization also has a category for non-pedigree cats, variously called "Household Pets" or "Domestic Cats". While often there are classes for unneutered pure-bred cats, household cats must invariably be neutered before showing. Reflecting this abstruse means of classification, some registries judge household cats by "condition, beauty,

---

WHAT HAPPENS AT A CAT SHOW?

Many shows begin with a "vetting-in", during which a vet checks your cat's inoculation certificate is up to date before examining your cat for signs of infectious or contagious disease. You will then take your cat to its designated pen. After cleaning the cage with disinfectant, let your cat have a drink of water and use the litter tray. Dress the cage with bedding and curtains. Depending on which body is supervising the show you may then be asked to leave the judging area to hide your identity. After the judges have picked the best of each breed, it is time for the finals. The judges then present the top cats in each class. From these top cats, Best Cat in Show is awarded to the overall winner. Remember to bring the following with you:

■ Up-to-date vaccination records.
■ Disinfectant.
■ Litter tray and litter.
■ Bedding for the cage.
■ Curtains and clips for three sides of the cage.
■ Grooming equipment.
■ Nail clippers.

VACCINATION CERTIFICATE

Dangers to us from cats

Cats are renowned for their cleanliness, but some of the diseases and parasites that live on or in cats can, in certain conditions, infect humans. Ranging from allergies to toxoplasmosis, these conditions are rare, but knowing how to control or treat them is important.

ALLERGY TO CATS

The frequency of allergy, particularly in children, has increased enormously over the last 30 years. While we can be allergic to many things, a protein found in cat skin and saliva, Fel d1, provokes a particularly intense allergic response.
■ To control the build-up of irritating, allergy-inducing protein on your cat's fur, damp-sponge the coat daily. Keep cats out of the bedroom and ensure your house is cleaned regularly. Good ventilation is essential.

A classic sign of cat allergy
It is estimated that as many as 15 per cent of people may be allergic to a specific protein found in cats' skin and saliva. As yet, science has been unable to find a solution.

CAT BITES

Cat bites are surprisingly common. Most cause only minor inconvenience, but some, particularly those contaminated by a bacteria called *Pasteurella multocida*, cause painful, swollen reactions, and in some cases even abscesses.
■ If you have been bitten by a cat, thoroughly wash the wound immediately using antibacterial soap. Seek medical attention if swelling, pain, or obvious infection occurs. Routine protection against tetanus is vital, and advice should be sought from your doctor.

Once bitten
This cat may simply be playing with its owner, but all scratches or bites from a cat should be treated with caution. Seek medical advice if pain or swelling develop.

CAT SCRATCHES

Cat scratches are more common than cat bites, but only rarely does a scratch transmit bacteria. Occasionally, however, the bacterium *Bartonella henselae* causes cat scratch disease – a systemic illness whose hallmarks include enlarged lymph nodes – particularly in people with impaired immune systems.
■ If you have been scratched by a cat, wash the cut with antibacterial soap. While antibiotics are effective at treating people with cat scratch disease, they are not efficient at ridding carrier cats of the *Bartonella* bacteria. If swelling or pain develop, consult your doctor.

RINGWORM

Ringworm is a fungal infection that affects all mammals including cats and humans. Ringworm spores get caught in cat hair and, if they infect the cat's skin, cause circular skin lesions, hence the name ringworm. Spores can be transmitted to humans without actually infecting cats. Among pets, Persians are the most common carriers.
■ Cats and humans are treated with topical antifungal medication and antibiotics, but ringworm may take several months to clear completely.

FLEAS

One of the most common parasites of cats are fleas. Fleas need warm temperatures to reproduce, and our preference for using central heating means they are becoming a year-round problem even in cool-temperate regions. Cats may become allergic to flea bites; the anti-coagulant saliva left in a flea-bite wound causes itching. Scratching can lead to a number of skin problems, including scaling and hair loss. Fleas enjoy taking meals from us too, often snacking on blood from our ankles, causing itches that look and feel like mosquito bites.

■ To make sure of controlling fleas effectively, all animals in the house must be treated regularly with an anti-flea product. These kill the fleas on your cat or prevent them from breeding by making the eggs sterile. Check your cat's coat regularly for flea dirt. Vacuum and wash bedding, and spray carpets and furniture if necessary.

FLEA SPRAY

Stopping the spread of fleas
De-fleaing your cat by using a spray or spot-on treatment won't rid your home of fleas. You also need to use a household biological spray on carpets and furniture to prevent flea eggs from hatching in the future.

TOXOPLASMOSIS (TOXO)

Toxoplasmosis is an infectious disease whose effects are not apparent until considerable damage has occurred. The parasite can cause developmental problems in unborn babies, including blindness and increased risk of developing allergies and asthma. Immune-compromised individuals are also high risk. A single-celled parasite called *Toxoplasma gondii* causes the condition, which is most commonly contracted from eating undercooked meat, but it can also be caught by coming into contact with cat faeces after the cat has consumed contaminated prey. Soil or litter trays are common sources of contamination. To prevent contracting toxo, pregnant women should wear rubber gloves when cleaning a cat's litter tray, when gardening, and especially when handling raw meat. Eating undercooked meat should be avoided. There is currently no simple treatment for toxo.

Disease and parasite prevention

The development of effective vaccines to protect cats from potentially lethal infectious diseases is one of the great success stories of 20th century veterinary medicine. Safe and simple parasite treatments also enable cats to live longer, more comfortable lives.

VACCINATION

Preventing disease through inoculation is a technique that harnesses the body's natural ability to fight infection. The concept has been around since ancient times. Soldiers in the Persian army were intentionally exposed to scratches containing material from sores on people with smallpox in order to protect them from the disease. However, it was not until the late 1700s, when Edward Jenner showed that a mild cowpox infection provided protection against smallpox, that the modern era of vaccination began. An infectious agent such as a virus or bacterium is modified so that it is no longer pathogenic. However, it is still similar enough to its unmodified form that when an immune system is exposed to it, the immune system creates antibodies – proteins that attach to and help destroy the agent. Vaccines are created either by killing infectious agents, modifying them so they are still alive but no longer infectious, or by taking vital components of them and, through genetic engineering, enslaving bacteria to produce replicas of these parts.

A variety of vaccines is available for use in cats, but very few of these should be routinely used in all cats. Talk to your

> ### VACCINATION AND PET PASSPORTS
>
> Breeders usually have their kittens vaccinated against feline enteritis and cat flu at least one week before sale and will provide you with a vaccination certificate signed by a veterinarian as proof of inoculation. Up-to-date vaccination certificates are also required to be seen by all reliable catteries. In many countries, proof of rabies vaccination, in the form of a vaccination record signed by a veterinarian, is a legal obligation. In EU countries, the blue Pet Passport has a separate section for recording all inoculations as well as rabies jabs.
>
> **EU PASSPORT**

vet and develop a vaccination timetable appropriate to your cat's lifestyle and where you live. Not all serious infectious diseases and viruses can be vaccinated against, but a range of conditions that *may* be prevented through vaccination is listed in the chart opposite.

SUSPECTED ADVERSE REACTIONS

Although rare, adverse reactions to any form of injection can occur. In Britain, the Veterinary Medicines Directorate supervises a Suspected Adverse Reactions (SAR) Surveillance Scheme. In recent years, the most commonly reported feline SAR in Britain was lameness or polyarthritis, followed in second place by a simple temporary injection-site reaction, such as redness or swelling. In the United States in the 1990s, however, one in 10,000 cats developed injection-site tumours, almost always sarcomas (often malignant tumours of connective tissue), usually after rabies or leukaemia vaccines. The British SAR Surveillance Scheme reported a much lower incidence of tumours during the same period (1995–1999), at only one in half a million cases. At that time, while leukaemia vaccine was used routinely,

A cat protection plan
Vaccinating your cat against infectious diseases as well as protecting it against infection from common parasites will help to ensure both its health and comfort. Make sure you keep a record of what jabs your cat has received and when.

INFECTIOUS DISEASES

An infectious disease is caused by a biological organism such as a virus, bacterium, fungus, or parasite. These can be passed from one cat to another, which is why they are sometimes called communicable diseases. The biological agent invades and uses the cat's body to duplicate itself, and by doing so causes illness. The list below includes all the viruses and bacteria that cats can be inoculated against.

VIRUS	PREVENTATIVE ADVICE
Rabies Rabies is a potentially fatal virus transmitted in the saliva of infected animals. Symptoms of rabies include lameness and seizures. Once the disease develops, there is no cure.	Vaccination is recommended and in some regions, where rabies exists in wildlife or stray animals, is compulsory. Most rabies vaccines are effective for three years. Your vet will vaccinate according to the manufacturer's guidelines or legal requirements. In North America this vaccine is commonly given under the skin in the right hindleg. In Britain it is only given to cats travelling abroad under the Pet Travel Scheme (PETS).
Feline infectious enteritis (FIE) Highly contagious yet preventable, FIE is also known as feline parvovirus or feline panleukopenia. Symptoms include vomiting and diarrhoea.	FIE can be fatal if not treated, so vaccination is advised for all cats. While most manufacturers recommend yearly booster inoculations, independent research suggests that primary inoculation followed by a booster a year later provides prolonged immunity of at least three years to most cats.
Cat flu "Cat flu" is a term used to describe two different viruses, feline herpesvirus 1 (FHV-1) and feline calicivirus (FCV), both of which cause eye, nose, and throat disease.	Vaccination is advised for all cats. Vaccines protect only against the strains of these viruses incorporated into the vaccines. Other strains exist in the wild and vaccination offers only limited protection against them. Inoculation lessens the severity of these infections rather than offering full immunity. A booster should be given a year after primary inoculation and then every three years or as recommended by your vet.
Feline leukaemia virus (FeLV) FeLV has a long incubation period – often years – and usually leads to serious, and eventually fatal, disease. Signs include contracting lymphoma.	Vaccination is recommended for all cats at risk of exposure to potentially contaminated saliva from cats carrying this infection. Outdoor cats at risk of exposure to FeLV should receive primary inoculation followed by annual treatments. In North America, this vaccine is often given under the skin in the left hindleg.
Feline chlamydophilosis *Chlamydophila felis* (formerly called *Chlamydia psittaci*) is spread by direct contact between cats and causes severe conjunctivitis. It is most common in kittens living in multiple-cat households. *Chlamydia* are bacteria so small, they were once considered viruses. Other members of this group of bacteria cause sexually transmitted disease in humans.	The condition responds to antibiotic treatment and because of this, together with an adverse reaction level to the vaccine of approximately 3 per cent, leading veterinary authorities do not recommend routine use of this vaccine. **MULTIPLE-KITTEN HOUSEHOLD**
Feline *Bordetella bronchiseptica* The most severe form of canine cough, it can cause clinical infection in cats.	An intranasal vaccine is licensed for use in cats but because this infection responds well to antibiotics, respected experts do not recommend its routine use.
Feline immunodeficiency virus (FIV) With its long incubation period, FIV is a disease that suppresses the immune system and can be an eventual killer.	A vaccine to protect against FIV was released in the United States in 2002. However, leading veterinary schools question whether it offers sufficient protection against the variety of FIV subtypes and strains that exist. At present its use in "at risk" cats remains controversial.
Feline infectious peritonitis (FIP) Young kittens are most susceptible to FIP, which is a mutation of feline coronavirus. Clinical disease is usually lethal. FIP is divided into "wet" and "dry" forms.	An intranasal vaccine against this almost invariably lethal form of feline coronavirus has been available in the United States for many years. However, the fact that it cannot be given until a cat is 16 weeks old – to protect against a disease almost always contracted around the time of birth – makes many experts question its value. Its manufacturers also acknowledge that the duration of immunity is relatively short.

rabies vaccine was seldom given to
British cats. In the United States, the
high rate of tumours led vets to give
leukaemia and rabies vaccines in
separate hind legs. It also encouraged
vaccine manufacturers to produce
adjuvant-free vaccines. Adjuvant,
often made with aluminium, is added
to vaccines to increase their potency,
and could be a cause of the sarcomas.

FELINE PARASITES
A parasite is an organism that lives
on or in another organism and gets
its nourishment from its "host". The
most sophisticated parasites feed off
their hosts without causing so much
damage that they kill off their source of
nourishment. Parasites can occur inside
or on the outside of cats. External
parasites are particularly common,
especially in warm climates where
they survive year-round. Ear mites and
fleas are spread either by direct contact
between cats or indirectly by dropping
off one cat and then hitching a ride and
a meal on another. Internal parasites
have evolved increasingly elaborate
methods of transmission. For example,
the most common feline tapeworm can
only be transmitted when a cat eats

Spot-on treatments
There are numerous spot-on treatments available that
provide a simple and convenient way to treat and prevent
flea and tick infestation. These are applied to the back of
the neck where the cat is unable to lick them off.

a flea that has been parasitized by
the tapeworm and is carrying its egg.
Parasites are most dangerous in the most
susceptible individuals, namely the very
young and the very old.

SINGLE-CELLED PARASITES
Single-celled parasites live mostly
in the gastrointestinal tract, although
there is one that lives in red blood cells
(*see* below, *Haemobartonella felis*).
 Giardia is a single-celled parasite that
lives in the small intestine of cats. *Giardia*
cysts (their dormant, infective stage) are
found in water and now occur worldwide.
The parasite causes smelly, loose bowel
movements and sometimes lethargy and
reduced appetite. A laboratory test to
identify this parasite can be performed.
 Cryptosporidium felis causes diarrhoea
in cats. Cysts are identified using high-
power microscopic examination of
diluted faeces. The cysts are resistant
to cold and heat and can survive for
months outside of cats. There is no
really effective treatment for this parasite.
 Isospora felis is a parasite that causes
watery, sometimes bloody, chronic
diarrhoea, often in large amounts.
Some cats carry the parasite for many
years and periodically shed cysts but
experience no obvious illness.
 Haemobartonella felis is a red-blood-
cell parasite that causes anaemia. It is
diagnosed through faecal and blood tests.

THE TROUBLE WITH TICKS
Ticks are small, nasty relatives of spiders, and they
feast on blood. A tick waits, often in long grass, for a
meal to pass by, which it senses in the carbon dioxide
given off in the mammal's breath. Ticks are capable
of carrying a variety of lethal diseases that can be
transmitted to cats. Remove ticks using tweezers by
grasping them close to their attachment to the skin and
removing with a twisting movement to ensure the head
does not remain embedded in the skin.

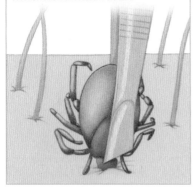

PARASITE PREVENTION

A variety of both internal and external parasites has evolved to live with cats, often in peaceful harmony. A few are potentially transmissible to us, or are certainly happy to live on or in us. Fortunately, advances in parasite control mean that it is relatively simple to prevent, or treat, almost any infestation. Outdoor cats should have routine preventative treatment for a variety of parasites. Indoor cats are less susceptible to infestation.

INTERNAL PARASITES	CONTRACTED	SYMPTOMS	TREATMENT
Roundworms	■ Often inherited by kittens either via the placenta or in the first milk.	■ May be vomited or passed in faeces.	■ Use oral or topical products such as fenbendazole, milbemycin, or selemectin.
Tapeworms	■ Most commonly contracted by eating an infected flea. ■ Can also be contracted by consuming livestock viscera containing tapeworm eggs.	■ Rice-grain sized worm segments are passed from the cat's anus. These segments move like inchworms. They are seen in the hair around the anus or in the faeces.	■ Praziquantel and milbemycin are virtually 100-per-cent efficient. ■ The most common tapeworm can be prevented through routine flea prevention.
Hookworms	■ Spread through skin penetration.	■ Can cause watery to bloody diarrhoea.	■ Fenbendazole or milbemycin.
Giardia	■ Contracted by drinking contaminated water.	■ Causes chronically loose stools.	■ Fenbendazole or metronidazole.
Heartworms	■ Transmitted by mosquito bites. ■ Worms more likely to mature in dogs than cats.	■ If worms mature, they clog the heart and major blood vessels, thus reducing the capacity to exercise.	■ Selamectin topically, and Ivermectin or Milbemycin orally, all prevent heartworm infestation.

EXTERNAL PARASITES	CONTRACTED	SYMPTOMS	TREATMENT
Fleas	■ Eggs fall off a cat and remain in the carpet, bedding, or soil. Eggs develop into white larvae. ■ Larvae develop into cocoons. These remain viable for a year before pupating. Five days later, an adult flea emerges.	■ Scratching – from a mild itch to dramatic scabbing or hair loss – can be caused by a single flea bite. ■ Fleas leave black shiny specks of dirt in the coat. ■ Fleas lay eggs, which can sometimes be seen in the cat's coat.	■ Treat all contact animals with a flea killer such as fipronyl, selamectin, or imidocloprid. Use the same products preventatively. ■ Alternatively, use lufenuron as a spot-on or injection as a form of flea birth-control.
Ear mites	■ Often inherited from mothers or contracted from neighbouring cats. ■ Most common in kittens and outdoor cats. ■ Ear mites are just large enough to be seen without magnification.	■ Produce gritty, sandy debris in ears. ■ Cats are likely to scratch or rub their ears. ■ Ears may be inflamed if infestation causes allergic reaction.	■ Treat all contact animals. Selamectin on the skin by the ears kills most mites. Mineral oil in the ears smothers mites but some may temporarily be outside the ear canal. Continue topical treatment for at least 2 weeks to eliminate stragglers.
Ticks	■ Drop off other animals and rest in grass or carpet. ■ Ticks sense movement, heat and carbon dioxide and attach to passing cats.	■ When hungry, ticks gorge on blood for several days before dropping off. ■ Ticks carry a variety of potentially serious diseases.	■ Fipronyl spot-on prevents as well as kills. Diazinon collars are licensed in the United States. Only use products safe for cats.

Maintaining good health

Your cat's enduring health depends upon more than simply the control of parasites and infectious diseases: you need to make decisions based on your cat's physical health and well-being. Neutering reduces the risk of infection or cancer and prolongs life, while modern drugs save cats' lives.

NATURE AND NURTURE

Each individual cat inherits a health and longevity potential, which is embedded in the cat's genes. For example, Siamese and Burmese cats inherit the potential to live longer than other breeds. On top of this potential we need to add the influences of living with us. From the food we feed our cats to the environment we keep them in to both the preventative and emergency veterinary care we provide them with, we influence how healthy they are and how long they live. Additionally, there are a couple more surprisingly simple ways to help your cat maintain its good health.

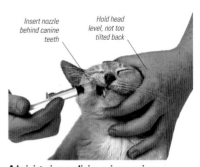

Insert nozzle behind canine teeth

Hold head level, not too tilted back

Administering medicine using a syringe
Giving your cat medicine in liquid form is an alternative to foisting tablets on it. Holding your cat's head, bend it back on the neck until the mouth automatically opens a little. Using a syringe, drop the liquid slowly into the mouth. Be patient, and do not flood your cat's mouth with fluid.

THE EFFECTS OF NEUTERING

The obvious benefits of neutering cats are that it is an effective method of birth control and that it helps to eliminate the more unpleasant aspects (at least to us) of reproductive behaviours. As if further incentive to neuter was needed, the practice also has a dramatically positive effect on the health of cats, especially in females. Neutering before the first season eliminates the risk of breast cancer, the most common form of feline cancer. Less common ovarian, uterine, and

cervical cancers are also cancelled out, and the risk of pyometra, a potentially life-threatening infection in the womb, is similarly eradicated. The net effect is that neutered female cats live considerably longer than unneutered individuals.

Neutering in male cats is not as life-enhancing as it is in females in that their existence is not as significantly prolonged. Neutered males, however, fight less and the consequence is less risk of contracting

---

NEUTERING

Neutering a male cat is a minor operation. Under general anaesthesia, the testicles are removed through a small incision in the scrotum. The spermatic cords and associated blood vessels are tied. This is usually done at about six months. Neutering a female, or

spaying as the procedure is more commonly known, is more major abdominal surgery. It involves the removal of both ovaries and much of the uterus down to the cervix under general anaesthetic. Spaying can be carried out before sexual maturity.

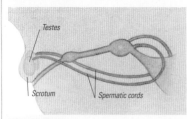

Testes

Scrotum   Spermatic cords

MALE NEUTERING

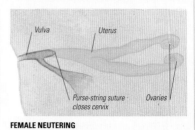

Vulva   Uterus

Purse-string suture closes cervix   Ovaries

FEMALE NEUTERING

The epitome of good health
Your cat is dependent on you for its well-being. The food you feed it and the care you provide are the determining factors for a long and contented life.

life-threatening viral conditions (*see* p.269) such as feline immunodeficiency virus (FIV) and feline leukaemia virus (FeLV), as well as fewer infections from bites and the complications these can cause.

USING MEDICINES PROPERLY

Cat owners often worry about treating their pets with modern medicines. Many feel uneasy about the steroid cortisone in particular, preferring to use "natural" means to overcome ailments. Drugs seldom actually cure a disease or illness. In most instances, drugs simply but crucially help the body repair itself. For example, antibiotics may kill bacteria, but a return to "homeostasis" – the natural equilibrium in which internal body conditions are kept constant – really depends upon the antibiotics giving the immune system time to carry out its function. This function is to counterattack by sending in scavenging macrophage cells and "natural killer cells". Medicines used efficiently and appropriately not only maintain good health – they can dramatically prolong life.

DECLAWING IS NOT NECESSARY

Surgically removing the claws holds no benefits for a cat. It is done for us, not for them, to save furniture, curtains, carpets, or us from being scratched. In countries where declawing is not performed, cat owners have learned there are humane alternatives, from simply cutting the nails routinely to applying soft caps to them to ensuring your cat has cat furniture placed specifically for it to carry out its natural need to scratch (*see* pp.284–87, *Common behaviour problems*).

The elderly cat

Cats are living longer than ever before and it's now common for individuals to reach 20 years or more. Gerontology, the study of ageing, is one of the growth areas in veterinary medicine, and studies show that elderly cats naturally experience a wide variety of behaviour changes.

AGEING IS NATURAL

Ageing is not an illness. On the contrary, examples of feline golden oldies should be celebrated. In North America, Britain, Germany, and Japan, cats over ten years of age now account for one-third of the entire cat population. Ageing is a natural process, controlled by a biological clock set deep within an evolutionarily ancient part of the brain called the hypothalamus. Losing the old grey matter isn't simply the preserve of humans; a number of studies have suggested the normal ageing process in mammals causes a loss of brain cells that produce a key chemical called dopamine, in a part of

Old-timer
Along with Orientals and Burmese, Siamese cats enjoy a longer lifespan than your average domestic cat. Scientists are trying to unlock the secrets behind this longevity.

the brain known as the substantia nigra. Not all cats are affected in the same way though: Siamese, Orientals, and Burmese live on average 10 to 15 per cent longer than other breeds.

NATURAL BEHAVIOUR CHANGES

Ageing can bring with it an increasing rigidity in some cat behaviours. Mentally and physically, a 16-year-old cat is roughly equivalent to an 80-year-old person (*see* chart opposite) and, just as with humans, while some cats remain responsive and lucid, others become forgetful or irritable. In one major study, over 70 per cent of 16-year-old cats were seen to have become disorientated in some way. Many forgot how to use their cat-flaps while others walked into corners or tight spaces and forgot how to get out

Eyesight starts to degenerate

Coat loses its sheen, often thinning in places

Weight loss apparent in cat's slender frame

Aching joints, often caused by feline arthritis

Know the signs of old age
Advanced ageing in cats is most evident in their deteriorating physical appearance. Arrange a check-up with your vet before any ailment becomes serious.

The secret of sleep
It isn't just older cats that spend a surprisingly large proportion of their time asleep. Without the revitalizing results gained from engaging in this high degree of rest, it's highly unlikely that cats would live to the age they do.

of them. Some simply stared into space while others increased their miaowing, especially of the plaintive and apparently pointless kind. Over 60 per cent of the owners of these more senior cats said that their pets were more irritable, often hissing and spitting with no provocation. One-quarter reported that their elderly cats slept more during the day, but were increasingly awake, restless, and demanding of their owners at night.

Studies of cats in California, US, revealed that one in four medically-fit, 16-year-old indoor pets has developed toileting problems, either urinating or defecating outside its litter tray. It seems that, with ageing, some cats become less fastidious; hygiene and grooming are no longer as important to these individuals as they once were.

NUTRITIONAL CONCERNS

In some older cats, eating becomes the most satisfying event of the day. They become obsessed, bullying their owners into feeding them much more than they need. Obesity is the most common nutritional problem in cats (*see* pp.292–93,

The overweight cat) and, especially in elderly cats, it can lead to joint pain, diabetes, and cardiovascular disease. An even greater reason not to give in to your demanding puss is that by feeding it only enough food to maintain a normal body weight, you may increase its longevity.

STIMULATE BODY AND BRAIN

Routine mental and physical stimulation may help to maintain dopamine levels and so slow down a cat's natural ageing process. Help your cat stay young by doing the following:

■ Change toys frequently to stimulate new interest in playing.

■ Groom often to enhance the circulation of blood.

■ Provide warmth and comfort for resting and sleeping.

■ Include high levels of antioxidants (free-radical scavengers) in your cat's diet, such as selenium and zinc.

■ Feed small meals frequently, turning each mealtime into an "event".

■ Keep your cat's litter trays clean and tidy. Provide two trays – one upstairs, one down – for ease of access.

Dangers to cats

Even in the most secure environment, cats can be exposed to unexpected dangers. Licking contaminants from their coats can poison cats, for example, as can harmful products we unwittingly give them. Getting trapped or straying from home are also common dangers.

POISONING

Cats are most likely to consume poisons indirectly, either by eating poisoned rodents or by accidentally consuming toxic substances while grooming contaminated hair. Some poisons are absorbed through the skin on the paws. All too frequently, we accidentally poison our cats by mistakenly giving them human medicines such as paracetamol or aspirin. Cats can be poisoned by flea-control products licensed only for dogs, or by dabbing cats with potentially toxic essential oils. And keeping decorative house plants is always risky, because some are toxic if chewed.

The perils of poisons
Our homes are filled with chemicals that can cause suffering or even death to cats. The excessive salivation, or drooling, in this cat is a reaction to poisonous toxins. If you think your cat has ingested a poisonous substance, the most important thing to do is shut your cat in and call the vet.

If your cat has swallowed acid, alkali, or petroleum products:
■ Do not induce vomiting.
■ If acid is swallowed, give bicarbonate of soda and vegetable oil by mouth.
■ If alkali is swallowed, give milk and vinegar mixed in equal proportions.
■ If petroleum is swallowed, try to ensure that your cat drinks plenty of water.
■ Seek veterinary attention, taking the product packaging to the vet.

If your cat has swallowed other potentially poisonous substances, such as human medicines:
■ Induce vomiting by giving your cat a crystal of washing soda or a 3 per cent solution of hydrogen peroxide. Repeat every 15 minutes until vomiting occurs.
■ Seek veterinary attention, taking the product packaging to the vet.

If your cat's coat is contaminated by chemicals:
■ Put on rubber gloves. Wrap cat in a towel to prevent it from licking its coat.
■ Remove flea collars and contaminated identity collars.
■ Snip off as much of the contaminated coat as possible. It will grow back.
■ For coats contaminated by alkali, such as caustic soda, flush the skin with fresh water for at least 15 minutes.
■ Placing your cat in a nylon mesh string bag will help to restrain it as you remove as

On the tip of its tongue
It's an unfortunate truth that because cats are such sticklers for cleanliness, they are more likely to poison themselves by inadvertently ingesting toxic chemicals while washing. Clean up any spillages as soon as they happen.

much contaminant as possible. Then wash the cat in warm soapy water.

■ Remove oily material by dabbing it with warm cooking oil. Then rub it off and cleanse with washing-up detergent.

■ Dry the coat well to prevent chilling.

Keep cats away from poisonous plants

No responsible cat owner keeps poisonous plants, such as those listed below, if they can help it,

CHERRY LAUREL

AZALEA

■ Azalea
■ Bulbs of flowering plants
■ Castor-oil plant
■ Cherry laurel
■ Dieffenbachia
■ Laburnum
■ Laurel
■ Foxglove
■ Hemlock

■ Ivy
■ Jasmine
■ Lily of the Valley
■ Oleander
■ Mistletoe
■ Philodendron
■ Poppy
■ Rhubarb
■ Rhododendron

WHAT TO DO IF YOUR CAT GOES MISSING

No cat owner is likely to go through life without their pet going missing at some point – even in the case of indoor cats. Curiosity often leads to cats becoming locked in sheds or garages, while a spooked or injured cat may seek solace somewhere private. Don't panic, instead:

■ Be pragmatic. Think about where your cat might hide if separated from you. In the airing cupboard perhaps?

■ Search locally and ask neighbours if they have seen your cat. Leave your telephone number with each person you speak to so they can contact you.

■ Contact the local police, vets, and cat shelters, giving them a brief description and your cat's microchip number if it has one.

■ Photocopy and post fliers locally, with a photo of your cat, your contact details, and the word "MISSING" printed on them in bold lettering.

■ Fingers crossed, your cat will make a safe return. Be sure to contact everyone on your telephone list to give the good news and thank them for their help.

but knowing which plants in your home and garden are safe to have around takes a bit of research. So choose carefully next time you're at the garden centre. While adult cats are usually sensible about their eating habits, kittens and young cats are more likely to make reckless and sometimes potentially lethal decisions about what to chew on. If your cat tends to nibble on plants, find out which plants in your area are dangerous to small animals, and remove them from your garden. And if your cat hasn't access to a garden, provide it with a small seedbox planted with herbs and weeds.

Plants and your cat

Just because some plants are poisonous doesn't mean you should deny your cat access to the outside world. Instead, rid your garden of any botanical species you know to be toxic, and then plant some safe feline favourites to chew on, such as catmint, sage, and parsley.

Travelling with your cat

Cats don't enjoy enforced journeys, but travel is inevitable if only for the annual visit to the vet. Accustom your cat to its carrier and consider the practicalities of how best to transport your cat. In some cases, a stay in a cattery is the more sensible option.

CAT CARRIERS

For every vehicular journey you make with your cat, you should guarantee the safety of both you and your cat by transporting your pet in a travel basket or carrier. This protects it from roaming freely and prevents it from running off. Two cats may be the best of friends at home, but when travelling together you should always provide each cat with its own personal cat carrier. Don't wait until you travel to introduce the carrier to your cat. Leave it open at home and fill it with comfortable bedding. The likelihood is that your cat will use it as a secure den and will feel more relaxed when the den becomes a method of transport at a later stage.

TYPES OF CARRIERS
■ Soft nylon Sherpa bags: come in varying sizes and are very comfortable. Airline approved for use in passenger cabin.
■ Plastic carrier: rigid and easy to store by inverting the top into the bottom. Airline approved for travel in the hold.
■ Wicker carrier: attractive but very difficult to clean or disinfect when soiled.

■ Wire carrier: provides your cat with excellent visibility and allows for increased air circulation.
■ Cardboard carrier: cheap, but cat urine and cardboard don't mix well.

Cat and carry
This plastic carrier is a fine example of how your cat can travel in comfort. Sturdy, lightweight, easy to clean, with good visibilty and excellent air circulation, it can also be disassembled for storage.

CAN I SEDATE MY CAT?

Using drugs to make travelling easier for your cat can be a hit-and-miss affair. Sedative and anti-anxiety drugs prescribed by a vet should be tested out at home first. Some cats fight the feeling of sedation and become more agitated under its influence. Many airlines will not accept drugged cats as some medications can affect cats' normal methods of temperature control during the flight. Anti-nausea drugs can reduce motion sickness and associated frothing of saliva during travel, but again, these should first be tested on your cat at home.

Cat being given sedative to calm it

TRAVELLING BY CAR

When travelling by car, ensure your cat carrier is stowed safely in case you brake suddenly. Generally speaking, it is best to secure it using the seat belts on the back seat. This also provides good air circulation, which your cat won't benefit from if its carrier is placed on the floor or in the rear of a hatchback. Never place the carrier in the boot of a car: your cat will stress and is liable to overheat.

Securing your cat carrier
Your cat carrier must be properly fastened in your car, either by a seat belt or by placing it on the floor so that it will not slide around.

On long journeys, stop frequently and ensure your cat has water to drink.

If there is room, place a small litter tray inside the carrier. Never leave your cat in a car in hot weather as animals can die of hyperthermia. If you stop for a break, take the carrier from the car and place it in the shade.

LEAVING YOUR CAT BEHIND

Sometimes, taking your cat with you on your travels just isn't viable or wise. Fortunately, there are some excellent catteries and "cat hotels" available that can accommodate your cat while you are away. Given the choice, however, most cats prefer to stay in their own home with a reliable person visiting once or twice a day to clean the litter tray, play with them a little, and feed them. An expensive alternative is to employ someone from an agency to move into your home and care for your cat. Leaving your cat with friends or relatives isn't advisable – just because you know them well doesn't mean your cat will take to living with them.

Stay-at-home cat
Leaving your cat at home while you're away is often the best decision for both of you. Owners often feel that their cats will "resent" them upon their return, but having the run of the house far outweighs the stress of having to travel.

THE CATTERY OPTION

Catteries vary from basic to luxurious, but regardless of their cost you should choose only from those where you receive positive answers to the following questions.

	Yes	No		Yes	No
Are you made to feel welcome?	☐	☐	Are the cat units odour-free?	☐	☐
Do the premises look tidy?	☐	☐	Are you asked about your cat's vaccination record, health, and diet?	☐	☐
Is there a shelf to lie on or under?	☐	☐			
Is there access to personal outdoor areas?	☐	☐	Is there a kitchen area where the cats' meals are prepared?	☐	☐
Is there a scratching post?	☐	☐			
Do cats have an interesting view?	☐	☐	Are there solid barriers between the cat-accommodation units?	☐	☐
Is there a vet on call?	☐	☐	Do the cat units have the cats' names on them?	☐	☐
Do cats have individual sleeping accommodations and runs?	☐	☐	Do litter trays and food bowls look clean?	☐	☐
Is there heating for each cat?	☐	☐	Do the cats in residence look contented?	☐	☐

If you answer all these questions in the affirmative, the chances are you are visiting an excellent cattery. You can leave your cat behind safe in the knowledge that it will be well looked after.

Training concepts

Why train a cat? Because a trained cat is easy to groom, easy to manage, and easier for your vet to examine. Training a cat is simpler than you might think. Clicker training and teaching a cat to sit form the basis for more advanced commands.

CATS ARE KEEN TO LEARN

Contrary to popular belief, cats are amenable to training, as long as you remember your cat is not a dog in disguise. Cat training is based on reward – never discipline – because cats never respond to punishment. Cats really respond well only to food rewards. You might not realize it, but your cat already responds to your unplanned training. Running to the kitchen after hearing the sound of the tin opener is trained behaviour. This means your cat has learned that the sound is usually followed by a reward: food.

THE POWER OF FOOD

Cats that hunt in an outdoor environment know that patience while stalking prey earns them a food reward. This observation mirrors cat training, where persistence is key, and food treats are invariably the most powerful of rewards. Provide treats your cat truly loves – treats with strong odours, such as dehydrated prawns or small pieces of chicken. Break them into tiny portions so you can use several in each training session. Use food treats sparingly; they are tools for training, not a means of feeding your cat titbits between meals.

FOOD TREATS

A RECIPE FOR GOOD TRAINING

Active shorthaired cats tend to learn a little faster than more reserved longhairs. Young kittens do not have the necessary concentration, and older cats are seldom interested. Cats from the age of four months onwards that are used to handling are the most responsive to training. A one- or two-minute lesson is perfect for most cats. Five minutes is too long.

Cat focuses on
teaser toy

Feathers attract
cat's attention

Touch training
Using a teaser toy, like the one above, it is possible to teach your cat to exchange a high five with you. Each time your cat raises its paw to touch the toy, say "Good cat, high five" and give it a food reward. Gradually replace the toy with the palm of your hand, and encourage your cat verbally instead of giving food treats.

Paw raised in
anticipation

HELPFUL TRAINING HINTS

A cat will only "perform" if it wants to, and no amount of training will make it do something that it doesn't want to do. Follow these guidelines to make training easier.

■ Have realistic expectations and clear goals about what your cat can do. Don't attempt the impossible.

■ Train your cat while it is hungry, otherwise your food treats will generate little interest.

■ Practise in a quiet place with no distractions.

■ If you sense that your cat is restless or unhappy with the training, stop the session and try again later.

TRAINING YOUR CAT TO SIT

Teaching your cat to sit after it has come to you in response to its name or the sound of a clicker (*see* box, right) is the first part of training your cat to do pretty much any other sequence of behaviours. Hungry cats will usually respond to this training within ten attempts. Finish the session with "Okay", which indicates to your cat that training is over, and then feed it breakfast or dinner. Try another session just before the next meal.

Food treat catches cat's attention

Cat stands in upright pose

1 Place your hungry cat on the middle of a table. If it naturally sits down, stroke its rump to trigger its instinctive "rump-in-the-air" response. Hold a tasty food treat 2.5–5cm (1–2in) in front of your cat's nose to gain its attention. (If using a clicker, hold it in your other hand.)

Owner strokes cat as part of reward

Cat is given food treat

Food treat kept at same distance from cat's head

Cat concentrates on food treat

Cat begins to sit

2 Make sure the treat is never more than a hand's length away from your cat's head, otherwise it is likely to stand up on its hindlegs in an attempt to get at it. As the cat follows the path of the treat, it will start to sit. When this happens, say your cat's name, followed by "Sit".

3 At the exact moment your cat sits, say "Good sit" and give the food reward. If using a clicker, click fractionally before you give the treat. As you practise this trick, raising your right hand up above the cat's head becomes the hand signal for "Sit", and you can phase out the food treats.

Applied training

Training your cat makes life easier for you and safer for your pet. Coming to you and miaowing on cue are useful commands to teach your cat. Training to walk on a harness can also enhance your cat's quality of life, and make for a more satisfying relationship with you.

COMING TO YOU

Training your cat to come to you on command is critical, for example, to attract your outdoor cat indoors when you are going out. Train your kitten to come to you as soon as it arrives in your home.

■ With your cat hungry, hold a favourite food treat in your hand and call your cat by its name. As it moves forwards, take a step backwards, say the word "Come", and then offer the treat. If you are using a clicker (*see* pp.280–81, *Training concepts*), remember to click it as the cat comes for its food reward.

■ Keep repeating this exercise, increasing the distance until your cat comes to you from another room. Eventually, the food reward can be phased out, and a click or the verbal cue "Come" will be enough to induce your cat to come running.

Food treat tempts cat forwards

Cat walks towards owner

MIAOWING ON CUE

This training is particularly useful if your cat goes outdoors and disappears. Cats recognize human voices, and it's easier to find a lost or frightened cat that responds to you by miaowing.

■ Once your cat is trained to come to you, let it see and smell the food treat but don't give the reward. It may try to bat the food from your hand in frustration.

■ Wait until your cat miaows, and as it does so, say its name and give the treat. Reinforce the miaow response by giving the food reward only intermittently during subsequent training.

■ Gradually eliminate the food reward until your cat miaows each time you say its name. It is relatively simple to combine miaowing on cue with coming to you.

Catcalling

Sometimes a cat's curiosity can lead it into situations that it finds frightening, or mean that it ends up getting lost. This cat is miaowing in response to its owner's calls.

WALKING ON A HARNESS AND LEAD

Training a cat to walk on a harness and lead is a good way to get an indoor cat outside without subjecting it to the dangers of cars, other cats, or infectious diseases. Make sure you purchase a harness and not a collar, as most cats are able to slip out of collars. Some cats, especially kittens, are easy to graduate from training to come on command to walking on a lead and harness. If you have an older cat, training is still possible, but it could take a little longer. Cats won't "heel" like dogs do, but they will follow your lead if you train them properly. Assume that training will take several weeks.

HARNESSING YOUR CAT

A cat harness is usually made of sturdy nylon cord. Part of it fits around the cat's midsection, while another part goes around the cat's neck. A third piece connects these two sections on top of the cat's back, on which is attached a metal ring to clip the lead onto.

Harness sits comfortably around cat's neck and back

Attach lead only when cat is comfortable wearing harness

1 Fit the soft, lightweight harness properly, not so tight that it compresses your cat's chest. Leave it on over short periods of time for a couple of days to enable your cat to get used to it. Praise your cat with food and verbal rewards.

2 Once your cat is accustomed to the harness, clip on the lightweight lead and allow your cat to drag it around for a few minutes each day, again praising calm behaviour. When your cat is comfortable doing this, hold the lead and let your cat take you for a walk indoors.

3 Soon you'll be ready to graduate to the outdoors, and early morning is a good time to wander out. Starting in a quiet location, allow your cat to take you in its chosen direction. Cats need lots of time to stop, stare, sniff, and decide when to move a paw forward. When your cat is content taking you for a walk, take a few steps in front of it and gently encourage it to follow you, using food rewards combined with the encouraging word "Come".

Common behaviour problems

Scratching furniture and carpets, attacking ankles, being downright aggressive – these are just some of the activities that cats find exhilarating and we find annoying. With the right approach, however, almost all feline behaviour problems can be corrected.

MEDICAL OR BEHAVIOURAL?

Always check with your vet to eliminate the possibility that an unwelcome behavioural change in your cat is caused by a medical problem. For example, pain can trigger aggression, while urinary tract disorders can cause a cat to seek out a new place to urinate. Once your cat is given a clean bill of health, you can tackle the problem safe in the knowledge that it's a behavioural concern.

Before attempting to overcome any behaviour problem it is vital to determine whether stress is involved and, if it is, to find a way of reducing it. This could be as simple as investing in climbing and scratching posts, and toys that can be chased and caught, which will allow your cat to express its natural predatory behaviour without being a nuisance to

COMMON CAUSES OF STRESS

Changes in a cat's environment can cause stress. Significant levels of anxiety can result in behavioural changes, some of which may be undesirable. The most common stresses that cause behaviour problems in cats are those that threaten their "resources". Resources include a cat's territory (specifically your home) and the attention it gets from you. A new cat, a new baby, a puppy, or the presence of strangers are sufficient enough stresses to trigger emotional conflict. Unlike humans, who show their feelings through facial expressions, cats can appear inscrutable, but convey their feelings by increasing their marking activity: scratching, urine spraying, and defecating.

you. If problems persist and you feel stress is a contributing factor, your vet can provide you with a synthetic facial pheromone treatment that reassures and pacifies cats, helping to reduce stress-related behaviour, such as urinating in places they shouldn't. Another type of synthetically produced feline pheromone can help in reducing aggression, both towards other cats and towards people.

CAT BULLIES

Aggression is a normal behaviour in cats, and just like in other species, cats have different forms of aggression. Pain, of course, triggers aggression. So does getting over-excited when playing too vigorously. Some cats become aggressive when they are being petted or stroked, while others redirect aggressive activity because of boredom. Aggression towards other cats or dogs can develop after a break in relationships, for example after another cat has been at the vet's or in kennels. After checking there are no medical, pain-producing reasons for heightened irritability and bullying, follow these suggestions to reduce aggressive behaviour.

■ Have your cat neutered before six months of age. Leaving it unneutered will only encourage territorial disputes.
■ Socialize your cat as early as possible. Exposure to a variety of different stimuli early in your cat's life makes for a more relaxed and well-rounded pet.
■ Supervise your cat with other animals. If you have a dog, train it not to provoke your cat, and keep them apart if necessary when you are not present.
■ Keep your cat's home environment as calm as possible. Avoid traumatic experiences, such as loud music or letting groups of children chase your cat.
■ Play with your cat. Exercise it more to release pent-up energy.
■ Don't play games that encourage grabbing or biting.

ANKLE AMBUSHING

A cat attacking your ankles can be painful. This is natural play activity, although sometimes there's a sexual component involved, even in neutered cats. Male cats ambush ankles more than females do. If your cat has maintained a juvenile mindset into adulthood, it may still exhibit this playful pouncing behaviour. There are several ways to redirect this kind of stalking.

■ Avoid over-stimulating your cat, especially with rough play.

■ Increase play activity with interactive toys such as ping-pong balls, empty water bottles, wands with feathers attached, or cat-friendly laser lights.

■ Anticipate problems. Where possible, equip yourself with a catnip toy mouse and toss it ahead of you to induce your cat to chase it rather than targeting your ankles.

LOVE BITES

What behaviourists call "petting aggression" is surprisingly common. A cat is seemingly enjoying your petting it when, suddenly, it lashes out and bites. Sometimes the grab and bite is inhibited – the cat only mouths you – but in other instances it is a full bite. Cats do so because they have mixed emotions. On one hand, they enjoy your contact as it may remind them of their mother licking them. On the other hand, unrelated adult cats only make contact with each other when fighting or mating. With these mixed signals, most cats eventually feel uneasy. There are ways to prevent petting aggression.

Cat bite
The simplest ideas are often the most effective in preventing behaviour problems. For example, your cat can't chew anything you keep up high, out of reach.

■ Let your cat initiate your petting sessions.

■ Most cats dislike having their stomach touched, so take care to avoid this area.

■ Watch your cat's whiskers. If they rotate forward, that's a clue to stop petting at once.

■ If your cat mouths your hand while you are stroking it, stop immediately.

Fighting with other pets
Early socialization with other pets is crucial to prevent your cat from fighting with them. If you plan to own a dog and a cat, for example, get them when they are both young. This way, they should grow up to accept each other.

SCRATCHING AND CLAWING FURNITURE

Scratching is as normal for a cat as urinating and defecating. It exercises the claws, sharpens the nails, and stretches the muscles. Scratching is also marking behaviour, to demarcate the boundaries of a cat's territory, leaving scent and visible marks for other cats. You can't eliminate this normal behaviour, but it is relatively easy to redirect it.

■ A scratching post may stop the cat from using the furniture to sharpen its claws.

■ Most cats like to use vertical scratching posts, but some like scratching on a horizontal plane. Learn which your cat prefers, and provide for it accordingly.

■ Provide scratching posts in all the locations you know your cat likes to scratch, such as by the sofa or on the patch of carpet at the top of the stairs.

■ If your cat is at first reluctant to use the scratching post, rub a little catnip against the post or attach a favourite batting toy to it.

■ Scratching at more than three or four sites indoors is unusual behaviour and may be your cat's way of attention-getting or a sign of stress. Consult your vet.

If a scratching post doesn't solve the problem, you need to introduce deterrents to prevent your cat causing damage.

■ Put double-sided sticky tape on surfaces you don't want scratched – cats don't like the tacky sensation under their paws.

■ Use palm-sized portable infrared alarms that shriek when the beam is crossed.

■ Glue purpose-made plastic caps onto your cat's nails.

Sisal covering

Toy mouse attached

REGULAR SCRATCHING POST

PYRAMID SCRATCHING POST

Carpet covering

Ping-pong ball attached

DISCOURAGING UNSOCIABLE BEHAVIOUR

Sometimes, passive, non-confrontational methods of preventing behaviour problems don't work. Instead, gentle forms of discouragement may be called for. Using a water pistol, for example, to stop a cat from jumping onto the table while you are eating can help stop the behaviour. Aim for the cat's rump – not its face – and it should soon get the message to stop.

WATER PISTOL

■ A plastic rug cover with the gripping pointy side up will make cats think twice about scratching.

■ A shot from a water pistol discharged as your cat starts to scratch delivers a curt reminder to puss to stop right there.

■ Scrub areas scratched previously by your cat with biological detergent, then with surgical spirit – cats hate the smell.

SPRAYING URINE

A cat marks its home territory by spraying urine. While males are more inclined to spray urine, both sexes do so, some even after they are neutered. Spraying is a normal activity, but it can be triggered suddenly by stress, for example when a cat feels threatened by a new cat in the family. Seeing another cat in the garden can also encourage spraying. Until you can identify the cause, try the following.

■ When you leave your cat alone at home, try keeping it in a large pen, with enough room for a litter tray, blanket, food, and water bowls.

■ Clean sprayed areas with an enzyme-containing product that will get rid of smells, not just mask them. Special deodorizing sprays are available from pet stores and your vet.

■ If you see your cat back up to a wall and raise its quivering tail,

Up to scratch
Scratching helps cats shed the outer sheath of their claws, and is an essential part of their daily grooming ritual. Providing your cat with a scratching post can help you redirect this behaviour away from your sofa, ensuring cat and owner live in perfect harmony.

gently push the tail down and distract your cat with some play activity.

■ Leave a bowl of food in the locations that have been sprayed. Cats are less likely to spray on or near food.

LITTER TRAY PROBLEMS

Any feline that fails to use the litter tray makes life miserable for everyone. A dirty litter tray, or one in which another cat has left urine or faeces, is the most common reason a cat loses its naturally perfect toileting hygiene. The definition of "dirty" varies from cat to cat. Some are content if you clean the tray daily. Others want the tray cleaned after each use! The following tips will help your cat retain its instinctive toilet-training habits.

■ Choose a litter tray that appeals to your cat, rather than only to you. While we like covered trays because they control odour, some cats find them offensive *because* they retain odour.

■ Finding the ideal variety of litter for your cat is a process of trial and error. For some cats, for example, the feel of the litter under paw is particularly important.

■ Once you find a variety your cat likes, stick with it, as changing brands of litter can trigger a reluctance to use the tray.

■ Cats like privacy when doing their business. Ensure the tray is not too far away from activities yet is sufficiently secluded. Keep as many trays as you have cats, and in houses with several floors, keep a tray on each level.

Plant pests
Some house plants are poisonous to cats. If your cat is attracted to your house plants, put them out of reach and either grow or buy your cat its own kitty grass.

THE OVER-ATTACHED CAT

Around 10 per cent of problems referred to animal behaviourists involve over-attachment. Behaviour problems involving either learned helplessness or exaggerated attention-seeking are particularly difficult to overcome because they are intimately associated with the owner's psychological needs. Cats may urine spray, attack feet, defecate in unusual places, refuse to eat unless hand-fed, or miaow constantly to gain attention. Treatment invariably involves convincing the owner of the cat to alter his or her own behaviour. This can be difficult and may need the help of a family counsellor.

■ After a cat has soiled outside its tray, keep the cat in a small room, such as the bathroom, with its favoured litter and litter tray. Keep it in there until normal service has been resumed.

JUMPING ON WORK COUNTERS

Cats like to survey their manors from a good height. Kitchen work counters and tables are also ideal for hunting for food.

■ Eliminate reasons for counter walking by not leaving food lying around.

■ Make the work surface inhospitable by applying double-sided sticky tape, which acts as a form of aversion therapy.

■ If your cat jumps up while you're preparing food, bait its food bowl with tasty scraps to act as a distraction.

■ Food isn't always the problem: satisfying your cat's need for a high viewing location might be the answer, so set aside an elevated location especially for this purpose.

EATING HOUSE PLANTS

Check out all your house plants to ensure you do not have any that are potentially dangerous if chewed (*see* pp.276–77).

■ Keep plants out of reach, for example by suspending them in hanging baskets.

■ Decorate your home with plants that cats don't like, such as cacti.

■ Use a commercial deterrent spray on plant leaves within your cat's reach.

FELINE HEALTH

Designed for a solitary existence, many of the domestic cat's health problems are associated with living with humans and being in close proximity to other cats. Learn from the beginning to observe your cat's weight, appearance, mobility, and behaviour. You need to be aware of which changes may indicate a potential health concern.

YOUR CAT DEPENDS ON YOU

While it may be a natural born killer, the domestic cat is a relatively small animal, meaning it was historically at risk from larger predators. To compensate, it evolved the ability to suffer silently in order to hide signs of vulnerability. As a result, cats taken to the vets are often in more advanced states of illness and disease than dogs. Concealing injury or infection may be a matter of survival in the wild, but it is certainly not good for a domestic cat's (or its owner's) health or well-being.

A healthy cat is one in which all body functions are in balance. Changes in what is technically called "homeostasis" – the natural equilibrium in which internal body conditions are kept constant – suggest probable health concerns. For example, a deterioration in coat quality, weight fluctuations, and hindered mobility are overt signs that all is not well with your cat. Stress or poor condition can also

Checking teeth
Regular inspections of your cat's teeth can pick up the early signs of tartar build-up and gum disease, which can lead to pain and poor health for your cat if left untreated.

lower your cat's resistance to illness, giving disease a chance to attack. Other common maladies include eye and mouth diseases, urinary and kidney failure, and skin conditions. Fortunately, there is almost always an effective treatment available to bring your cat back to good health, many of which are listed in the following pages. You are your cat's best defence against illness though. You can take precautions to keep your cat healthy by arranging an annual check-up, for example, or by learning how to administer first aid, but if your cat does succumb to illness, you should consult a vet as soon as possible.

Glowing with health
A strong, healthy cat, such as this handsome Bengal, shows its vitality in its glossy, well-conditioned coat, bright, clear eyes, and alert demeanour.

Self-medicating
Eating grass is good for cats. Grass is an emetic, helping the cat to regurgitate unwanted matter such as furballs.

Signs of ill health

For the healthy cat, one day is much like the next. Routines and rhythms are invariably maintained. Even the slightest alteration from their routine may be an important indicator of ill health. Cats pretend nothing is wrong, so it's up to you to recognize when help is needed.

APPETITE AND THIRST CHANGES

A reduced appetite is always cause for concern, but so too is increased eating, which could signal an over-active thyroid gland or diabetes. Reduced drinking is invariably a worry, while increased drinking suggests a wide variety of metabolic diseases.

■ **IMPORTANT** Cats are relatively small. If your bathroom scales are accurate, routinely weigh yourself holding your cat then subtract your weight from the total. A gain or loss of 200g (½lb) is a significant amount and should be reported to your vet. An increased appetite and weight loss in older cats may indicate thyroid problems. An increased appetite and thirst with weight loss are the symptoms of diabetes.

QUICK TIPS

SIGNS
■ Pestering for food.
■ Raiding the rubbish.
■ Water bowl is continually emptied.

WHAT TO DO
■ Measure the amount of water given daily.
■ Record the amount drunk over several days.
■ Report results to your vet.
■ Measure, record, and report on food consumption.

A reduced appetite
Reluctance to eat may be associated either with pain or illness. Pain can be caused by mouth or internal conditions while an extensive range of diseases are accompanied by loss of appetite.

BREATHING CHANGES

Normal breathing is so light and relaxed it is virtually indiscernible. When breathing gets laboured, the belly often becomes active before the chest does. The mouth gapes open only with severe conditions.

■ **IMPORTANT** Chest and upper respiratory tract infections may cause breathing difficulties. So too does asthma, a serious, even life-threatening problem. Trauma to the chest or diaphragm seriously affects breathing. Do not mistake natural panting for laboured breathing. Cats normally pant when hot, nervous, excited, or exhausted. Contact your vet if there is inexplicable panting. Sudden breathing changes can be associated with life-threatening conditions.

QUICK TIPS

SIGNS
■ Reduced appetite.
■ Hiding.
■ Lying outstretched.
■ Intense expression on face.

WHAT TO DO
■ Avoid putting pressure on the chest or abdomen.
■ Ensure access to fresh air.
■ Seek immediate veterinary advice.

CHANGES IN GUM AND LIP COLOUR

A healthy cat's gums and lips are pink. Gum colour indicates what is happening to the circulation and how much oxygen there is in red blood cells in the cat's bloodstream. Seek veterinary advice for any gum colouring other than pink (*see* box, right). Examine the chin and lips. There should be no inflammation, swelling, or unpleasant odour.

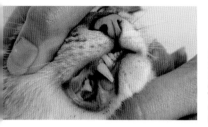

SIGNS

■ Yellow gums – your cat may have jaundice, associated with liver disease; blood parasites; or FIP (*see* p.269).
■ Blue gums – your cat may be in shock (due to oxygen deficiency).
■ Red gums – your cat may be bleeding in the mouth or suffering from carbon monoxide poisoning, fever, or infection.
■ White gums – your cat may be in shock or it could have anaemia or blood loss.
■ Pale pink gums – your cat may be in shock or it could have anaemia or blood loss.

Gum inspection
Checking the colour of your cat's gums provides valuable information about its state of health. Lift a lip and look at the colour of the gums. Disregard any black pigmented areas. When blood is circulating normally, slight finger pressure on your cat's gums blanches the area under pressure. When pressure is relieved, the area instantly refills with blood.

DEHYDRATION

Dehydration can be caused by diarrhoea, vomiting, excessive urination, severe sweating, or by not drinking enough fluids because of nausea. A vet can help rehydrate your cat with intravenous or subcutaneous fluids.

■ **IMPORTANT** The elasticity of the skin on your cat's neck is usually a good indication of its state of hydration (*see* box, right). This lifting procedure is known as "tenting". For elderly or excessively fat cats, check hydration by feeling the gums. Dehydrated individuals have dry, sticky gums.

WHAT TO DO

■ Gently pull up the skin on the top of the cat's neck.
■ An immediate snap back indicates good hydration.
■ The slower the snap back the more severe and dangerous the condition.

LETHARGY

While some cats are downright lazy, sleeping through life, most are active and alert for up to eight hours a day. Increased lassitude, even in sofa-hogs, suggests that a medical condition has developed and veterinary intervention is needed.

■ **IMPORTANT** Obesity is perhaps the most common medical condition suffered by indoor cats. Obesity and lethargy are twin problems. After overcoming obesity, lethargy often spontaneously resolves itself.

SIGNS

■ Reduced mental activity.
■ Reduced physical activity.
■ A reluctance to jump.

Going nowhere
Until proven otherwise, assume that any unwillingness to undertake normal physical activity is associated with discomfort. Cats rarely complain about pain, but joint pain in particular is common in older cats.

The overweight cat

According to veterinary surveys, between 25 and 30 per cent of cats are overweight. Some of these individuals are genuinely obese. Carrying excess weight is not just an aesthetic concern; being overweight or obese leads to a variety of medical conditions and may shorten life expectancy.

WEIGHT GAIN

Weight gain in cats can be insidious, often going unnoticed for some time. With the trend towards cats living permanently indoors, it is likely that the number of overweight cats will increase in the future. Already, obesity is the most common dietary problem seen in cats. It is most frequently diagnosed when cats are seen for annual health check-ups. While owners often believe there is a medical explanation for their cat's weight gain, the truth is often much more easily identified: on a daily basis, the cat has consumed more calories than it has expended. The net result is that excess calories are converted to fat and stored both under the skin and in the abdominal cavity.

Weight watching
Persistent overfeeding of cats will result in gross obesity (like in this individual), which will put strain on the heart, liver, and joints.

ASSESSING YOUR CAT'S WEIGHT

Use this chart to assess whether your cat is overweight or obese, comparing top and side views with the pictures below. If your cat appears larger than "ideal", contact your vet for nutrition advice. This chart is only a rough guideline, however, and you shouldn't rely on a visual inspection alone. Routinely weigh your cat. If your cat is on a calorie controlled diet, there should always be weight loss within three weeks of starting.

IDEAL	OVERWEIGHT	OBESE
■ Slight fat cover over ribs.	■ Ribs not easily felt, with moderate fat cover.	■ Ribs cannot be felt because of thick fat over chest wall.
■ Hip bones at base of tail smooth, covered in thin layer of fat.	■ Hip bones at base of tail felt through moderate layer of fat.	■ Hip bones at base of tail difficult to feel because of fat layer.
■ Minimal abdominal fat.	■ Moderate abdominal fat.	■ Extensive abdominal fat.
■ Waist can be seen behind ribs.	■ Waist hardly discernible.	■ No waist, abdomen distended.
■ Walking and grooming easy.	■ Walking and grooming hindered.	■ Walking and grooming difficult.

AT A GLANCE	AT A GLANCE	AT A GLANCE

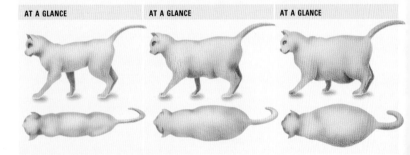

QUICK TIPS

PREVENTION
■ Avoid overfeeding during kittenhood.
■ After neutering, assume there will be weight gain and reduce food consumption by between 10 and 20 per cent.
■ Provide activity toys for your cat to play with in your absence.

WHAT TO DO
■ At the first sign of weight gain, increase activity or decrease the amount of food offered.
■ Switch to a low-calorie diet.
■ Don't give snacks or treats.
■ Monitor your cat's weight every other day.

PROBLEMS ASSOCIATED WITH OBESITY

Age-related lameness is a common consequence of obesity. Joints built to carry a normal weight load become overburdened, leading to painful arthritis. Affected cats become tentative when jumping up or down. Sugar diabetes is more common in fat cats. Urinary conditions are more frequently reported in overweight, sedentary, indoor male cats. Fatty liver disease is also a rare but serious complication of obesity.

■ **IMPORTANT** Obesity is really a condition created by owners. Cats have a natural instinct to pester for food, and cats get obese only when owners give in to their pets' constant demands. The hardest part of overcoming feline obesity is for an owner to acknowledge that there may be a short period in a cat's life when mealtimes are not as rewarding as the cat would want them to be. Once the cat's weight has dropped to a reasonable level, a cat is invariably more active and can then be given slightly larger portions of food.

Fat cat
This cat may look perfectly healthy, but it is carrying a little more weight than it should be. Even weighing only 10 per cent more than its optimum weight increases a cat's risk of joint pain and sugar diabetes.

THE THIN CAT

There is substantial evidence that thin cats live much longer than even mildly overweight cats. This figure could be as much as 18 months longer. Weight gain in cats with cobby body types, such as Persians, is more difficult to detect than in breeds with lithe body types, such as the Oriental Shorthair (pictured right).

Lameness and limping

Physical injuries, rather than disease, are the most common reasons for lameness and limping in cats. Bone is living tissue with a superb ability to repair itself but, just as with us, joints eventually suffer from wear and tear, commonly leading to age-related lameness.

SPRAINS AND STRAINS

A strain damages muscle fibres and tendons, whereas a sprain overstretches ligaments. These injuries are invisible, but the affected region is tender and sensitive to touch. Symptoms include pain, swelling, and bruising. The greater the damage, the more likely there will be lameness and difficulty moving.

Apply bag of frozen peas to affected site for 10 to 15 minutes

Applying a cold pack

The body's natural reaction to injury almost invariably involves inflammation and associated swelling. The amount of swelling associated with strains and sprains can be reduced by applying a cold pack as soon as possible to the injured site. A frozen bag of peas is ideal.

QUICK TIPS

CAUSES
- Falling.
- Road traffic accidents.
- Animal attacks.
- Abuse by people.

WHAT TO DO
- Part the hair and look for redness.
- Apply a cold pack for up to 15 minutes.
- Ensure prolonged and enforced rest for three weeks.

CUTS AND BITES

Cuts and abrasions to the paw pads are not uncommon in outdoor cats. Depending upon their severity, these cuts may cause limping or force the cat to hold up the affected foot. Bites are a natural part of cat life. Bites to the hindquarters may cause hind limb sensitivity and limping. Puncture wounds are small, and bite wounds are seldom obvious. Bites to the head and neck – common injuries from head-to-head combat with other cats – cause puncture wounds that commonly abscess. These require antibiotic treatment.

Reluctant fighters

Cats naturally avoid fights, but battles are sometimes unavoidable. The consequences aren't always apparent until infection sets in.

- **IMPORTANT** Serious viral diseases, such as feline leukaemia (FeLV) and feline immune deficiency virus (FIV), are transmitted in saliva. A bite wound may be minor, but the consequences far more damaging. All cats at risk from cat bites should be vaccinated against FeLV.

QUICK TIPS

SIGNS
- Cat flinches when you touch a specific area.
- Matted hair.

WHAT TO DO
- Clean wound with disinfectant.
- Tears may need stitching.

SIGNS
- Increased irritability.
- Walking stiffly.
- Tentative or reluctant to jump up or down.

WHAT TO DO
- Control your cat's weight.
- Add natural anti-inflammatories, such as fish oil, to your cat's diet.
- Control pain with prescription medicines and antibiotics.
- Always see your vet if your cat shows signs of lameness.

OSTEOARTHRITIS (ARTHRITIS)

This painful condition often goes unrecognized until it is well advanced. The first indication of a problem is the cat's reluctance to jump up or down. Maine Coons (*see* pp.168–71) and Himalayans (*see* pp.158–59) are more prone than other breeds to hip dysplasia, an inherited joint disorder. Most cats over 12 years old experience arthritic changes to some joints.

■ **IMPORTANT** Make sure the diagnosis is correct. There are many causes of lameness, and arthritis is only one. Once you are certain the symptoms are arthritis-related, take great care giving pain killers to cats. Only use drugs licensed for safe use in cats. Drugs such as paracetamol and aspirin that are safe for us and for dogs are potentially lethal for cats.

DISLOCATIONS AND FRACTURES

While an open fracture is obvious, a closed fracture or dislocation is not visible, but immediately affects weight bearing. These injuries are most frequently caused by falling or road traffic accidents. It is vital to treat associated shock first before attending to broken bones. Hips are frequently dislocated in falls of over 10m (33ft). Jaws may be fractured too, but this is one of a rare type of fracture that does not lead to lameness.

■ **IMPORTANT** Splinting a fracture can be difficult, time-consuming, and needless. Never try to straighten a break. Wrapping a blanket or towel under and around the cat provides whole-body support, including the fractured bone, and is a safe way to take the cat to the vet.

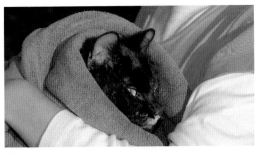

Wrapping in a blanket
Moving an injured animal is potentially dangerous because of the risk of causing further injury. Reduce its anxiety and its ability to move by wrapping it firmly in relatively thick, insulating material. A fleece blanket is ideal.

SIGNS
- Sudden lameness, often accompanied by swelling.
- Inability to bear weight on one or more paws.
- Cat looks in extreme pain.
- Cat emits unexpected hissing or spitting when either approached or touched.
- Inexplicable hiding, cowering, or "shrinking".
- Vocalizing: either distress sounds or unexpected purring.

CAUSES
- Road traffic accidents.
- Falling.
- Gunshot wounds.

SIGNS
- Loss of touch and pain sensations.
- Loss of voluntary muscle movement.
- Changes in spinal reflexes and muscle tone.

SPINAL CORD DAMAGE

Spinal cord damage can occur anywhere, from the top of the neck to the base of the tail. The higher up the spinal cord the more devastating the consequences. Neck damage can cause complete paralysis, while damage near the hips may paralyse the hindlegs. This type of injury is often irreparable.

■ **IMPORTANT** If a back injury is suspected, keep the spine as straight as possible. Use something with a flat surface, such as a piece of plywood, as a makeshift stretcher. Gently secure the cat to the stretcher using a firmly wrapped towel. Transport the cat to the vet as quickly as possible.

Skin and coat problems

Skin and coat problems are the most common medical problems vets see in cats. Two out of five visits are made because owners notice scratching, hair loss, pimples, lumps, or inflamed skin. The state of the skin and the sleekness of a cat's coat are among the best indicators of good health.

LUMPS AND SWELLINGS

A swelling or lump can be as trivial as a crusty pimple or as serious as a life-threatening skin tumour. All such conditions should be reported to your vet who can decide whether an immediate examination is warranted.

■ **IMPORTANT** A vet's diagnosis is based on your cat's age, sex, and breed as well as its veterinary history, the location and texture of the lump, and the speed at which it is growing. Rapidly growing swellings usually contain liquid. To yield a definite diagnosis, a biopsy sample of the swelling can be studied under a microscope by a pathologist.

QUICK TIPS

CAUSES
■ Abscesses, often the result of a cat fight.
■ Tumours.
■ Feeding ticks.
■ Injection reactions.
■ Burst blood vessels (haematomas).
■ Allergic conditions, such as eosinophilic granuloma complex.

QUICK TIPS

CAUSES
■ Parasites, including fleas, ear and skin mites, mosquito bites, lice, and ticks.
■ Infections, especially fungal infections such as ringworm, but also pox virus and bacterial infections.
■ Allergies to parasites, food, drugs, plants, pollen, and mould spores.

WHAT TO DO
■ Cut your cat's claws to prevent further damage.
■ Try to eliminate the trigger from your cat's environment.
■ Feeding oily fish may diminish any itchiness.

SCRATCHING

Scratching is easy to observe, but the cause of the itchiness that induces scratching can be frustratingly difficult to determine. It is not uncommon to treat the itch rather than the cause of the itch.

■ **IMPORTANT** Some cats need cortisone to control their intense itchiness. This is highly effective on a short-term basis, giving time for a diagnosis of the cause of itchiness to be made. A single flea bite is perhaps the most common cause of scratching in cats.

Cat scratching
Scratching is the consequence of a condition. Finding the cause of skin irritation can often be frustratingly difficult.

HAIR LOSS

Licking and scratching are the most common causes of hair loss. Allergy, especially allergy to flea saliva, is a common and treatable cause. So too is ringworm, especially in longhaired cats.

■ **IMPORTANT** Incidence of allergy is increasingly diagnosed in cats, although epidemiologists don't know whether this is a true increase in incidence or just better diagnoses.

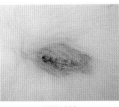

HAIR LOSS

Regardless of the cause, avoiding the trigger to allergy is the best treatment. When this is not possible, some cats can be desensitized to specific allergens using vaccines.

■ **IMPORTANT** Cat bites are the most common skin injuries. Leaving scant skin damage, these often develop into local abscesses. A burst abscess often causes more skin damage than the original bite. Treat all bites immediately with appropriate antibiotics.

SKIN INJURIES

Small, penetrating injuries, for example bite wounds, rarely cause bleeding. Skin tears are remarkably free from blood. Even deep, penetrating gunshot wounds can be hidden under the cat's dense coat of hair. Bleeding usually means significant injuries to muscles or blood vessels. Cats rarely complain about their injuries, which is why it is important to groom your cat routinely and check the skin.

Trimming hair
Serum, blood, and hair can form a matt over a wound, increasing the risk of infection. It is best to clip away the hair to facilitate cleaning and let air get to the wound. Apply water-soluble jelly to the scissor blades to prevent cut hair from contaminating the wound.

Cut away the hair surrounding a wound

DEBRIS AND MATTING

Cats are superbly adept at cleaning their coats. There are never matts or debris in a healthy cat's hair. Long hair matts easily and the consequent tangles increase risk of localized skin infection. External parasites exacerbate itchiness and additional matting due to skin scratching. Look for evidence of fleas, the most common skin parasites. Always check the cat's mouth because oral pain will prevent a cat from carrying out routine grooming.

COMBING OUT MATTS

Face and mouth problems

Medical conditions can and do affect any of the senses. The cat's prominent eyes are prone to physical injury as well as being susceptible to viral infections. Ears are frequently damaged during fights. Tooth and gum problems are very common, especially in indoor cats.

EYES

Eye changes that outwardly appear slight may well indicate serious conditions. If you see even minor alterations to your cat's eyes, it is always best to contact your vet, who is equipped to make immediate diagnoses. The eyes are often a vital clue to changes elsewhere in the body, especially in the cardiovascular system.

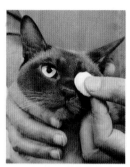

Removing tear overflow
Normal tear overflow can be removed using cotton wool dampened with either eye wash or tepid water.

QUICK TIPS

SIGNS
- Eyes produce mucus for protection from infection or external irritant, such as pollen.
- A green-yellow discharge indicates possible infection.
- A mahogany discolouration around the eyes indicates tear overflow.
- Eyelids swell during an allergic reaction.
- Inflammation is caused by infection or allergy.
- A blue-grey surface to the eye means corneal problems.
- An enlarged eye suggests increased ocular pressure (glaucoma).
- Squinting indicates injury or pain.
- Unequal pupil size means a serious problem needing immediate attention.

WHAT TO DO
- Eye disorders in cats are among the easiest to recognize. Almost invariably, it is important to seek immediate veterinary advice if you notice cloudiness, a bulging or sunken eye, yellow-green discharge, sudden loss of vision, severe redness, swelling, or obvious pain.

- **IMPORTANT** A cataract is a loss of transparency to the lens of the eye. Physical injuries and sugar diabetes are the most common causes of feline cataracts. Cats over eight years old are more prone to cataracts.

EARS

The ears tips are most commonly injured during cat fights, while ear mites are a common cause of scratching at the ears. So too is allergy. Allergic skin conditions often start with itchy ears. Chronic ear infection may lead to damaged ear drums and middle ear infection.

- **IMPORTANT** Impaired hearing is common in elderly cats. If your cat is, or has become, deaf, be patient with it. If you have to wake your cat, do so with a gentle touch. If your deaf cat is a kitten, think about getting it a feline companion to act as its ears.

Deafness in cats
White cats with blue eyes are prone to congenital deafness, inherited from birth. These animals cope well, but should be kept indoors at all times.

QUICK TIPS

CAUSES
- Scratching to the ears can be caused by mites.
- Green-yellow discharge from ears suggests infection.
- Crusty ear tips may indicate insect bites or allergy.
- A swollen ear is caused by an abscess or blood blister.
- Tilting of the head indicates middle ear infection.
- Thickening of ears may be caused by an allergic reaction.

WHAT TO DO
- Use insect repellent in summer to prevent insect bites. In most instances, ear conditions should be treated by a vet within 24 hours. Chronic ear infection can lead to the development of benign but troubling tumours.

NOSE

Sneezing, with or without nasal discharge, is common in cats. While pollen and irritants in the air are the most common causes, flu viruses (affecting 10 to 20 per cent of all cats) also trigger sneezing. Although nasal tumours are rare, cats with white skin or white hair are much more likely to develop them.

Keep cat quiet and confined by placing hand gently round its neck

Apply cold compress before seeking veterinary attention

■ **IMPORTANT** Severe sneezing can lead to a nosebleed. Keep your cat quiet and apply a cold compress (frozen peas wrapped in clingfilm) to the top of the nose for five minutes. Don't tilt the head back – this only stimulates more sneezing. Recurring sneezing is always a sign of a medical condition. Consult your vet if your cat sneezes more than usual.

Cold compress
Nosebleeds in cats are rare, but when one does occur, ensure you keep your cat still. Applying a cold compress helps to shrink blood vessels, making it easier for blood clots to form.

LIPS

Chronic, salmon-pink, hard, non-itchy ulcers can develop on the upper lips, often near where the skin meets the mouth membrane. For some individuals, the problem is merely cosmetic, while for others, the ulcers cause pain, leading to a reluctance to eat. The condition is called eosinophilic granuloma complex.

MOUTH AND TEETH

Inflammation to the mouth (stomatitis) and ulceration to the tongue (glossitis) are painful conditions that interfere with eating. Inflammation to the gums (gingivitis) and associated dental disease has become the most common medical condition treated by vets. Unfortunately, mouth tumours are common in elderly cats.

■ **IMPORTANT** Contact your vet if your cat has ongoing bad breath. An accurate diagnosis of the mouth condition is vital. Infected tooth roots should be carefully removed and oral infection treated with an appropriate antibiotic. Some forms of severe stomatitis respond to cautious corticosteroid therapy.

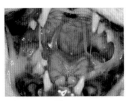

Feline stomatitis
Pus-producing infection is much more common than it need be. This cat is also suffering from ulcerated gums.

Cardiopulmonary conditions

It can be difficult to determine whether the heart or the lungs, or both, are involved in diseases of the chest. Many problems involve an accumulation of fluid that causes pressure and interferes with breathing. Airway disease is much more responsive to treatment than heart disease.

HIGH BLOOD PRESSURE

While hypertension (high blood pressure) without an underlying cause is a common problem in humans, hypertension in cats, although common, is almost always secondary to another medical condition.

■ **IMPORTANT** A cat's blood pressure can be measured using simple Doppler technology (*see* right). All cats over 12 years of age should have their blood pressure monitored routinely.

QUICK TIPS

CAUSES	SIGNS
■ Chronic kidney failure.	■ Sudden blindness.
■ Heart disease.	■ Sudden neurological signs.
■ Overactive thyroid.	■ Breathlessness and lethargy.

Monitoring blood pressure
High blood pressure, or hypertension, is a serious disorder associated with many conditions affecting older cats. Your vet can measure your cat's blood pressure using Doppler technology similar to the systems used in human medicine.

HEART DISEASE AND BLOOD CLOTS

Diseases of the heart muscle have different causes. Dilated cardiomyopathy (DCM) is caused by a deficiency in the nutrient taurine. Because this is routinely added to cat food, the condition is rare.

Hypertrophic cardiomyopathy (HCM), a thickening of the muscle that can virtually obliterate the chambers of the heart, has numerous causes. Sticky blood in the chambers forms clots that can have devastating consequences.

Checking pulse for blood clots
A cat's resting pulse rate is about 120 beats per minute, increasing to 200 when injured or frightened. Blood clots commonly prevent blood reaching the cat's hindlegs.

Check your cat has a pulse by feeling for the femoral artery on the inside of the hindleg

Handle the cat firmly but carefully to avoid being bitten

QUICK TIPS

SIGNS
■ Murmur or gallop rhythm picked up on routine veterinary examination.
■ Difficulty breathing or actual breathlessness.
■ Extreme pain in hindquarters (caused by blood clot).
■ Sudden paralysis of hindquarters.

WHAT TO DO
■ Vet can perform ECG, X-ray, and ultrasound heart examination.
■ Treat with anti-clotting drugs.

QUICK TIPS

SIGNS
- Coughing or wheezing.
- Difficulty breathing, or breathlessness.
- Hunched appearance.

WHAT TO DO
- Contact your vet immediately – even apparently minor breathing problems can be fatal.
- X-rays can show thickening of the airways.
- Airway washes (bronchial lavage) determine the exact cause.
- Anti-inflammatories and bronchodilators are given systemically or by inhalation.

LUNG DISEASE

Complications from cat flu may lead to lung disease, but the most common cause of airway disease is inflammation. An irritant causes the bronchial smooth muscle to contract, to prevent the irritant moving deeper. Mucus is produced to trap the irritant, and coughing expels the discharge. These changes narrow the air passages, leading to an asthma-like condition.

■ **IMPORTANT** Wheezing and asthma can be triggered by infection or inhaled irritants.

Pedigree breeds such as the Siamese may be particularly predisposed to asthma.

Treating feline asthma
Feline asthma can be treated using the technology behind inhalers used for treating human asthma. The cat's face is covered with a mask with an inhaler attached to it by a spacer chamber before steroid spray is released.

THYROID DISEASE

Hyperthyroidism, an increased production of thyroid hormone in the glands situated in the neck, is a common feline condition in cats over 10 years of age. It is often associated with a thickening of the heart muscle called hypertrophic cardiomyopathy. This condition usually improves once the underlying thyroid condition is controlled. For unknown reasons, thyroid disease is uncommon in the Burmese and even rarer in the Siamese.

■ **IMPORTANT** Kidney disease is not caused by hyperthyroidism, but the two conditions often occur together. Depending upon its stage and severity, overactive thyroid glands may help kidney perfusion. A vet will be able to determine the best treatment for a cat that has developed both of these age-related conditions.

QUICK TIPS

SIGNS
- Rapid heart rate.
- Hypertension.
- Increased appetite, but in actual fact cat loses weight.
- Increased activity/irritability.
- Diarrhoea and vomiting.
- Increased water consumption.

WHAT TO DO
- Blood testing will confirm the presence of the condition.
- Drugs can reduce blood pressure and heart rate.
- The need for medication often increases with time as thyroid overactivity increases.
- Surgical removal of the affected thyroid temporarily "cures" the immediate problem, although the other thyroid often eventually becomes overactive.

Checking the thyroid glands
The thyroids are located in the neck. Examine them by holding your cat's head firmly but gently in one hand and by feeling the throat with the other hand. A normal-sized thyroid is too small to feel, while an overactive thyroid feels like a pea.

Drinking and the urinary system

Conditions affecting the cat's urinary system are among the most common that vets treat. Changes in drinking habits almost always signal disease, while changes in either how and where a cat urinates have physical or psychological explanations.

DRINKING MORE

Increased thirst is a common and cardinal sign of disease in cats, especially middle-aged and elderly ones. It could be a sign of sugar diabetes, especially in overweight cats, while many Persians have an inherited predisposition to kidney failure (*see* opposite page).

■ **IMPORTANT** All cats drink more when they are hot, after physical exercise, and even after mental stimulation. Older cats should not drink more than when they were younger.

Increased drinking is often associated with increased urinating and is a sign of illness. Some of these illnesses, such as sugar diabetes, can be life-threatening.

Excessive drinking
If your cat is drinking more than usual, take it to see your vet. Excessive drinking may be a sign of serious illness, especially in cats over eight years old.

DRINKING LESS

Some cats are adept at finding sources of water to drink from – such as a running tap – rather than consuming the water you provide. Owners then wonder why their cats won't drink. Other cats drink less when their diet is switched to moisture-rich wet food. In all other circumstances, drinking less water is a serious clinical sign.

■ **IMPORTANT** If it is difficult to measure accurately how much your cat is drinking, then monitor its litter tray instead. If it appears to need changing more frequently than usual, then your cat is drinking more. If it is unnaturally drier than expected, your cat is drinking less, which could be a sign of dehydration. In either situation, consult your vet immediately for diagnosis and treatment.

Fill water jug to 250ml (8fl oz)

For good measure
The amount of water your cat drinks is a good indicator of its health. Measure 250ml (8fl oz) into a jug before pouring it into your cat's bowl. Compare how much your cat drinks on a daily basis.

SIGNS
- Squatting and straining longer or more frequently than usual.
- Digging more obsessively in the litter tray or outside.
- Licking the penis or vulva more.
- Wailing for no apparent reason.
- Cat resents being touched.
- Cat passes blood, sediment, or mucus.

DIFFICULT OR PAINFUL URINATING

The most common cause of non-obstructive urinary tract disease is called idiopathic cystitis. This painful inflammation usually spontaneously resolves itself in around five days. Unfortunately, it is extremely difficult to differentiate from much more serious obstructive urinary tract disease, requiring immediate veterinary intervention.

■ **IMPORTANT** Some cats associate the litter tray with the pain they experience when they urinate, so they go elsewhere: on carpets, vinyl flooring, even in sinks and bathtubs. This behaviour should not be confused with urine marking, a normal behaviour in which a cat uses urine to mark out its territory, even if its territory is entirely indoors.

Going pains
Your vet will want to test a urine sample to make an accurate diagnosis. Non-absorbent cat litter makes it easier to collect urine for inspection.

Special diets
Controlling the acidity of a cat's urine helps prevent or treat urinary crystals. Special diets are available to help do so.

CHRONIC KIDNEY FAILURE

All older cats are susceptible to chronic kidney failure. However, through early diagnosis and a change of diet to one that reduces the work of the kidneys, a healthy life can be considerably prolonged. Because chronic kidney failure occurs so suddenly, by the time symptoms have been recognized, a cat may have lost 80 per cent of its kidney function. Diagnoses can be made earlier through preventative blood testing.

■ **IMPORTANT** Polycystic kidney disease (PKD) is a condition that causes chronic kidney failure, often in relatively young cats. PKD is inherited by up to 40 per cent of Persians, and Exotics are also classified as high risk. The condition can be diagnosed by ultrasound examination.

A gene test is available and should be undertaken for all breeding stock.

SIGNS
- Increased drinking and urinating.
- A general slowing down.
- Weight loss.
- Poor coat.
- Gum disease and mouth ulcers.
- Eventual extreme lethargy and reduced drinking.

WHAT TO DO
- Feed a low-phosphorus diet.
- Vet can give intravenous fluids to flush the system.

Listlessness
Cats with kidney failure are sluggish because of the excess waste in their circulation. Contact your vet if your cat displays ongoing lethargic behaviour.

The gastrointestinal system

Your cat's size, weight, and appetite should all be constant. Any change, including an increase in appetite, signifies a potential medical concern. Gastrointestinal problems can cause vomiting, diarrhoea, or constipation, but these conditions can also be triggered by external events.

CHANGES IN APPETITE

Loss of appetite, especially if it is accompanied by loss of body weight, is always cause for serious concern. Routinely weigh your cat so you have a baseline to measure from. If weight is being lost, see your vet as soon as possible. An increase in appetite is not as immediately dangerous, but if it is not accompanied by an equivalent weight gain, it is a sign of significant illness. Again, seek veterinary advice for this condition.

■ **IMPORTANT** Increased appetite and thirst, accompanied by weight loss, could indicate the onset of sugar diabetes or a metabolic disorder. Increased appetite and activity, but no increase in thirst, accompanied by weight loss, is indicative of the development of an overactive thyroid gland.

QUICK TIPS

CAUSES OF INCREASED APPETITE
■ Boredom.
■ Overactive thyroid gland.
■ Sugar diabetes.
■ Inflammatory bowel disease.
■ Corticosteroid treatment.

CAUSES OF DECREASED APPETITE
■ Fever.
■ Tooth pain or mouth infection.
■ Nausea.
■ Serious internal problems.

WHAT TO DO
■ Measure daily food and water consumption.
■ Weigh your cat weekly.

VOMITING

Vomiting may be triggered by a condition within the gastrointestinal system, but it may also be caused by concerns elsewhere – in the bladder for example – that lead first to nausea and then to vomiting. The first signs of nausea are mouthing and salivating. Persistent vomiting requires veterinary treatment.

Nature's emetic
A cat may irritate its digestive system by eating grass, causing it to vomit. This behaviour is entirely natural, and it is believed that grass acts as a kind of emetic.

QUICK TIPS

CAUSES
■ Hairballs.
■ Eating grass or houseplants.
■ Food sensitivity.
■ Drug reaction.
■ Severe intestinal parasites.
■ Thyroid or adrenal conditions.
■ Liver, kidney, or other metabolic disease.
■ Ulcers, tumours, or foreign bodies.
■ Bacterial or viral infections.

WHAT TO DO
■ To treat mild vomiting, withhold food and reduce water intake.
■ After six to eight hours, give your cat small amounts of water frequently.
■ After six to eight hours, give your cat small, tasty portions of low-fat, low protein soft food.
■ Offer more food every two hours. Return to normal feeding the next day.

■ **IMPORTANT** Some cats are extremely noisy when they vomit, howling or even shrieking loudly. Generally speaking, this is a feline trait and is not necessarily associated with the severity of the problem. More seriously, vomiting associated with straining to urinate, severe diarrhoea, or swallowing thread, ribbon, or string is an emergency that requires same-day veterinary attention.

DIARRHOEA

Short episodes of simple diarrhoea are neither unusual nor dangerous. Persistent diarrhoea may be caused by food intolerance, parasites, infections, malabsorption problems, allergies, tumours, or metabolic disorders. Your vet will ask you detailed questions about your cat's faeces. The consistency gives clues about which part of the intestine is affected. Odour will explain whether there is bacterial action or blood in it, while the frequency of passing stools gives clues about irritation. Increased quantity may suggest a digestion or malabsorption condition. Colour indicates whether there has been bleeding and, if so, in which part of the intestines.

■ **IMPORTANT** Do not confuse the straining of diarrhoea with constipation; you can prevent constipation with cat laxatives. Simple diarrhoea can be treated successfully with a short fast. Persistent diarrhoea requires veterinary help. Any kitten with diarrhoea lasting more than 48 hours should be examined by a vet, even if the kitten seems generally healthy.

QUICK TIPS

WHAT TO DO
■ Prevent worms through routine worming.
■ Avoid sudden diet changes.
■ Prohibit scavenging.

■ Ensure a balance of soluble and insoluble fibre in the diet.
■ If diarrhoea occurs, feed easy-to-digest food, such as lean chicken.

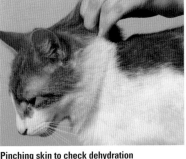

Pinching skin to check dehydration
Chronic diarrhoea can insidiously lead to dehydration. To check for dehydration, pinch the skin on your cat's neck. If it does not retract instantly your cat is probably dehydrated and needs fluid therapy administered by your vet.

DISTENDED ABDOMEN

Some cats, especially neutered cats, develop a pendulous flap of fat on their abdomens, giving the impression the abdomen is distended. The only other "normal" reason for a distended abdomen is pregnancy. While a potbelly may be due simply to being overweight, critical constipation can cause abdominal enlargement. All other reasons for distended abdomen are serious and call for veterinary intervention.

Abdominal gains
This heavily pregnant cat has a normally distended belly because she will shortly give birth.

■ **IMPORTANT** Feline infectious peritonitis (FIP) is a disease caused by a genetic mutation of the common feline coronavirus (FeCV). Fluid accumulates in the belly, causing a pot-bellied appearance. The condition is almost invariably fatal. There is a blood test for FeCV but not specifically for FIP. Diagnosis of FIP is based upon clinical signs.

QUICK TIPS

CAUSES
■ Pregnancy.
■ Constipation.
■ Obesity.
■ Heart disease.
■ Liver disease.
■ Tumours.
■ Feline infectious peritonitis (FIP).
■ Womb infection.

Caring for the sick cat

Some cats do not enjoy handling. Understand your cat's personality when caring for it when it is unwell. You may want to cuddle and nurture it, but it may be an individual who gets better faster when allowed to be on its own. Ensure the right environment for recovery.

REDUCING STRESS AND STRAIN

Provide a warm bed and give food and medicines according to your vet's instructions. After surgery, your cat will need to convalesce. Check wounds at least once daily for redness or discharge. Don't fuss over your cat. Respond if it asks for contact comfort, otherwise leave it in a quiet and comfortable location.

Rest and recuperate
Warmth is crucial for rapid recuperation. Either a well-insulated hot water bottle or a specially designed microwaveable heating pad placed in the cat's basket provide warmth during recovery.

Folded towel provides insulation between cat's coat and hot water bottle

QUICK TIPS

WHAT TO DO
- Keep other animals away from your cat.
- Warm food to body temperature.
- Offer small amounts of food frequently.
- Hand-feed your cat during the initial stages of recovery.
- Provide extra warmth with a wrapped hot water bottle or microwaveable heating pad.

GIVING TABLETS

If possible, hide medicines such as small tablets in a ball of meat or special treats shaped to hide pills. Ask your vet if it is practical to have the medicine formulated into a palatable form. Be firm but gentle when giving pills or liquids. It is sometimes crucial that cats receive their full course of medication. If your cat proves too resistant, arrange for it to be hospitalized for treatment or to have medications given on an outpatient basis by injection.

QUICK TIPS

WHAT TO DO
- Take care not to get bitten or scratched.
- If possible, have one person hold the cat's body while you give the medication.
- If giving tablets on your own, wrap your cat in a bath towel with only its head exposed.
- Reward your cat with a food treat so it associates accepting pills with something positive.

■ **IMPORTANT** An effective method of administering liquid medicine is by using a plastic syringe. Holding the cat's head at one side, squirt the measured dose into its mouth. Give the medicine as slowly as possible so that none is wasted.

1 Grasp the cat's head between forefinger and thumb and tip it back. Press the jaw to open the mouth.

2 Place the tablet as far back as possible on the back of the cat's tongue. Your cat may try to spit it out.

3 Close the cat's mouth and gently stroke the throat to encourage it to swallow the tablet.

GIVING EYE DROPS

Most eye drops are soothing, but cold drops can startle a cat. If eye drops must be kept refrigerated, warm them by rolling the dropper bottle in your hand for a minute before application. Warming ointment improves the flow. After giving drops or applying ointment, close the eye to help disperse the medication. Always praise your cat and give a food treat as a reward.

Administering eye drops
Gently hold your cat's head with one hand. Approach the eye from above and behind, and apply a drop or a line of ointment directly onto the cornea.

■ **IMPORTANT** Make sure the medicine container never comes into contact with the eye. This could not only damage the eye, but it can also potentially contaminate some medicines. Always ensure eye drops are within their use-by date.

GIVING EAR DROPS

Ear drops are usually needed to treat ear mites or ear infection. Dropper bottles often come with applicator nozzles large enough to fit the ear without causing damage. A cat will shake its head vigorously after ear drops are administered. Use a piece of tissue to prevent ear wax, ear mites, and debris from flying everywhere.

EAR DROPS

Administering ear drops
Wipe any dirt away from the ear, and then administer the required number of drops. Massage the ear afterwards.

QUICK TIPS

WHAT TO DO
■ Help clean the face after eating.
■ Ensure your cat's body is clean after it uses its litter tray.
■ Prevent any chance of violent encounters with other animals.
■ Take care that the collar does not cause your cat to get stuck under furniture or elsewhere.

PREVENTING SELF-INFLICTED DAMAGE

It may look faintly ridiculous, but a protective, cone-shaped, "Elizabethan" collar around the neck protects a cat's head from being scratched. Depending upon the depth of the collar, it also prevents the cat from licking or chewing its body. Made from toughened plastic, these collars are beneficial until healing is completed.

■ **IMPORTANT** Allergy to flea bites and a variety of immune-mediated conditions can lead to self-trauma in cats. It may take weeks before irritation diminishes. Your vet may use drugs to reduce self-inflicted damage. Bandages are sometimes used to prevent self-trauma to surgical sites.

Additional protection
A lightweight, flexible collar may not be enjoyable for a cat to wear, but it prevents the cat from inflicting further harm to itself.

Emergency first aid

There may be occasions when life-threatening problems arise so quickly there is not enough time to get to the nearest vet. Restarting breathing, inducing the heart to start contracting again, and treating clinical shock all follow the same principles as human first aid.

A–B–C CHECK

When serious accidents happen, remember your ABCs: A for airway, B for breathing, C for circulation. Clear any debris from the airway and pull the tongue forwards. Watch the chest and listen for breathing. If there is no breathing, give artificial respiration (*see* opposite, centre). If there is no heartbeat or pulse, give heart massage (*see* opposite, bottom).

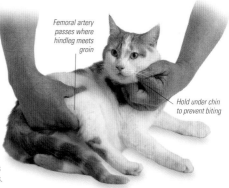

Femoral artery passes where hindleg meets groin

Hold under chin to prevent biting

Checking your cat's pulse
Familiarize yourself with locating the pulse in your cat's femoral arteries while it is healthy. This makes it easier for you to check when an emergency occurs.

SHOCK

Shock is a life-threatening medical condition that occurs when the body responds to changes in blood flow. These circulatory changes may happen for a variety of reasons, including internal or external blood loss. A cat may look fine after an accident but then die a few hours later of clinical shock. Always have a vet check your cat even after seemingly minor accidents or injuries.

QUICK TIPS

SIGNS
Early shock:
- Faster breathing.
- Pounding heartbeat.
- Pale gums.
- Anxiety or restlessness.
- Temperature remains normal.

Late shock:
- Shallower, irregular breathing.
- Irregular heartbeat.
- White or blue gums.
- Weakness or unconsciousness.
- Subnormal temperature.

WHAT TO DO
- Give neither food nor water.
- Give CPR as necessary (*see* heart massage, opposite).
- Place cat on one side with head extended.
- Elevate hindquarters to enable more blood to get to the brain.
- Take cat to vet for examination.

Shock tactics
Keeping warm is vital when suffering shock. Insulate your cat with a fleece blanket or other suitable material. Do not wrap so tightly that breathing is impaired.

BLEEDING

Even light bleeding (if it is prolonged) can lead to shock. Apply pressure with any clean, absorbent material, to control bleeding. If possible, keep the bleeding area above the heart, but don't elevate a fractured leg. Do not remove blood-soaked material. Leave that for the vet, who should be seen immediately.

Applying pressure to the wound
Use clean, absorbent material to help stop bleeding. Where possible, avoid materials (such as tissue) that will stick to the wound. Use bandages or cotton instead.

ARTIFICIAL RESPIRATION

Pink gums usually mean a cat is breathing and picking up oxygen in its lungs. If the gums are blue or white, artificial respiration may be necessary. The heart may still be beating.

1 Put a tissue in front of the nostrils to check for breathing. Place the cat on its side, clear debris, and extend the tongue. With the neck in a straight line, place your mouth around the cat's nose and mouth.

2 Blow in until you see the chest expand. Take your mouth away. The lungs will naturally deflate. Repeat the procedure 12–20 times a minute. Check the pulse every 15 seconds. If the heart stops, give heart massage (*see* below).

HEART MASSAGE

Give heart massage only if the heart is not beating. The eyes dilate when the heart stops. There is no pulse and the gums turn white or blue. Heart massage is always given in conjunction with artificial respiration. When combined, this is called cardiopulmonary resuscitation or CPR. Do not be timid. Press firmly. This is life-or-death first aid treatment.

IMPORTANT Use CPR after any of the following occur:
- Heart failure.
- Near drowning.
- Smoke inhalation.
- Deep shock.
- Electrocution.
- Concussion.
- Major blood loss.

Performing heart massage
Place the cat on its side. Grasp the chest behind the elbows with your fingers on one side and your thumb on the other. Squeeze firmly, compressing the ribcage, moving your fingers forward as you squeeze and compress, towards the neck. Repeat quick, firm pumps around 120 times per minute. Stop every 15 seconds and give artificial respiration for 10 seconds.

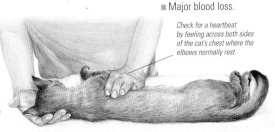

Check for a heartbeat by feeling across both sides of the cat's chest where the elbows normally rest.

Useful contacts

GENERAL VETERINARY ASSOCIATIONS

Australian Veterinary Association
www.ava.com.au
Unit 40, 2A Herbert Street, St Leonards,
NSW 2065, Australia
+61 2 9431 5000

British Small Animal Veterinary Association
www.bsava.com
Woodrow House, 1 Telford Way, Waterwells
Business Park, Quedgeley, Gloucestershire,
GL2 2AB, England
+44 1452 726700

Federation of European Companion Animal Veterinary Associations
www.fecava.com
40 rue de Berri, 75008, Paris, France
+33 1 5383 9160

Veterinary Ireland
www.veterinary-ireland.org
13 The Courtyard, Kilcarbery Park, Nangor
Road, Dublin, Ireland
+353 1 457 7976

Royal College of Veterinary Surgeons
www.rcvs.org.uk
Belgravia House, 62–64 Horseferry Road,
London, SW1P 2AF, England
+44 20 7222 2001

BREED REGISTRIES

Cat Fanciers' Association
www.cfainc.org

Governing Council of the Cat Fancy (GCCF)
www.gccfcats.org

The International Cat Association (TICA)
www.tica.org

Traditional Cat Association, Inc. (TCA)
www.traditionalcats.com

WELFARE, RESEARCH, AND SPECIAL INTEREST

Australian Cat Federation
www.acf.asn.au
PO Box 331, Port Adelaide, BC SA 5015,
Australia
+61 8 8449 5880

Cats Protection
www.cats.org.uk
National Cat Centre, Chelwood Gate,
Haywards Heath, Sussex, RH17 7TT, England
+44 8707 708 649

Feline Advisory Bureau
www.fabcats.org
Taeselbury, High Street, Salisbury, Wiltshire,
SP3 6LD, England
+44 1 747 871872

RSPCA – Royal Society for the Prevention of Cruelty to Animals
www.rspca.org.uk
Wilberforce Way, Southwater, Horsham,
West Sussex, RH13 9RS, England
+44 870 33 35 999

RSPCA Australia
www.rspca.org.au
PO Box 265, Deakin West ACT 2600,
Australia
+61 2 6282 8311

SSPCA – Scottish Society for the Prevention of Cruelty to Animals
www.scottishspca.org
Braehead Mains, 603 Queensferry Road,
Edinburgh, EH4 6EA, Scotland
+44 131 339 0222

USPCA – Ulster Society for the Prevention of Cruelty to Animals
www.uspca.co.uk
PO Box 103, Belfast, BT6 8US,
Northern Ireland
+44 28 9081 4242

ISPCA – Irish Society for the Prevention of Cruelty to Animals
www.ispca.ie
National Animal Centre, Derryglogher Lodge,
Keenagh, Co. Longford, Ireland
+353 43 250 35

Petlog – National Microchip Register
www.petlog.org.uk
4a Alton House Office Park, Gatehouse Way,
Aylesbury, Buckinghamshire, HP19 8XU,
England
+44 20 7518 1000

Glossary

ABSCESS A localized pocket of infection in body tissues.

AGOUTI The lighter areas of fur in the tabby coat; also a term for cats expressing any tabby pattern.

AILUROPHILE Someone who loves cats.

ANAEMIA Reduced red blood cells or a reduction in oxygen-carrying pigment (haemoglobin), associated with blood loss, bone marrow suppression, parasites, or immune-mediated disease that destroys red blood cells.

ANAPHYLACTIC SHOCK An exaggerated, life-threatening allergic response to foreign protein or other substances.

ANTIBODY Protein produced by specialized white blood cells in response to certain antigens. Antibody binds to antigen, a fundamental act of immunity.

ANTIGEN Any agent capable of inducing a specific immune response.

AUTO-IMMUNE DISEASE Any condition in which the body's immune system erroneously attacks healthy body parts.

AVERSION THERAPY Treatment of a behaviour problem involving the use of mild physical or mental discomfort.

AWN HAIR A bristly undercoat hair. *See also* Down hair, Guard hair.

BENIGN TUMOUR A local tumour that does not spread.

BICOLOUR Coats consisting of white hair combined with one other colour.

BREECHES Long fur covering the upper part of the hindlegs.

BREED An animal strain visibly different from other strains of the same species, particularly produced by human intervention. *See also* Family, Genus, Order, Species, Subspecies. Other individual interpretations apply within the cat fancy.

BREED CLUBS Organizations within a breed registry devoted to one or more particular breeds. Several clubs may exist within a registry for one breed. *See also* Registry.

BREED STANDARD A description of the ideal characteristics against which each cat in a breed is measured.

CAESAREAN SECTION The surgical opening of the uterus to deliver full-term kittens.

CASTRATION Usually refers to the surgical removal of the testicles in males (in law it may refer to the sterilization of both male and female). *See* Neuter.

CAT FANCY Umbrella term for registries and the people who breed and/or show cats worldwide.

CFA The Cat Fanciers' Association – the world's largest feline registry, founded in 1906, primarily based in North America.

CHINCHILLA Longhair with white coat ripped with black, or such a coat in any cat.

COLOSTRUM The first milk produced after birth, containing protection against a variety of infectious diseases.

COLOURPOINT A cat whose face, ears, feet, and tail are a different colour to its body. *See also* Pointed.

CONGENITAL Present at birth; congenital conditions may or may not be hereditary.

COOL Colours as far as possible from red.

CREPITUS Dry, grating sound when a joint extends or flexes.

CYANOSIS Purple-blue colour to mucous membranes, caused by lack of oxygen.

CYTOLOGY Examination of body cells under a microscope.

DEHYDRATION Loss of the natural level of liquid in body tissue.

DIABETES INSIPIDUS Deficiency in a pituitary hormone (anti-diuretic hormone or ADH) that controls urine concentration in the kidneys.

DIABETES MELLITUS, OR SUGAR DIABETES High blood sugar, either due to a lack of insulin production or because body tissue cannot absorb circulating insulin.

DISLOCATION The separation of a bone from its adjoining bone at a joint, often involving ligament tears; may be complete (luxation) or partial (subluxation).

DOMINANT GENE A gene that if carried is always expressed as a genetic trait. *See also* Recessive gene.

DOWN HAIR A soft, insulating hair in the undercoat.

ECHOCARDIOGRAPHY Imaging of the heart using sound waves bounced off the interior and exterior of the heart, then visualized on a monitor.

ELECTROCARDIOGRAM (ECG) Record of the electrical activity in the heart.

ELISA TESTING Enzyme-linked immunosorbent assay; a test used to detect or measure levels of an antigen or antibody.

EMPHYSEMA Pathological accumulation of air in tissues.

ENDOCRINE GLAND A gland that manufactures hormones and secretes them directly into the bloodstream.

ENDORPHIN Naturally occurring brain chemical that diminishes pain perception.

ENDOSCOPE An instrument inserted into hollow areas of the body to view the body's interior.

EOSINOPHILS White blood cells that increase in the presence of internal parasites and allergy.

EPILEPSY A disturbance in electrical activity in the brain that causes a seizure.

ESSENTIAL FATTY ACIDS Fatty acids that cannot be synthesized by the body and that must be acquired from the diet.

EUTHANASIA The painless termination of life; may be active (by giving a substance that causes death) or passive (by withdrawing medical support that sustains life).

EXCLUSION DIET A diet that excludes all components of any previous diet, usually consisting of novel sources of protein, fat, and carbohydrate.

EXUDATE Fluid that has escaped from blood vessels and deposited either in or on tissues.

FAMILY In biological classification, a group of animals within an order that share many defining characteristics and evolutionary descent. *See also* Breed, Genus, Order, Species, Subspecies.

FELINE IMMUNODEFICIENCY VIRUS (FIV) A relative of the HIV virus that weakens the immune system, causing death. Highly contagious to other cats, but not to humans or other animals.

FELINE INFECTIOUS PERITONITIS (FIP) A viral disease that is usually fatal. Symptoms include fluid accumulation in the abdomen, jaundice, and anaemia.

FELINE LEUKAEMIA VIRUS (FELV) A virus affecting the lymphatic system, suppressing immunity to disease.

FERAL An animal living wild but descended from domestically bred stock.

FIFÉ Fédération Internationale Féline – an umbrella organization for European cat clubs, founded in France in 1949.

FLEHMING Lifting the upper lip to bring a scent into contact with the vomeronasal organ. *See also* Vomeronasal organ.

FROWN LINES Dark lines forming a letter "M" on a cat's forehead.

GAUNTLETS White hindpaws in a coloured or bicoloured cat, ending above or below the hock. *See also* Mittens.

GCCF The Governing Council of the Cat Fancy, founded in 1910 – the governing body for most British cat clubs.

GENE POOL The genetic diversity available in any given species, race, or breed.

GENETIC DISEASE A medical condition known to be transmitted to an animal through a parent's genes.

GENUS A group of species within a family that share characteristics and ancestry not shared by other species. *See also* Breed, Family, Order, Species, Subspecies.

GHOST MARKINGS Faint tabby markings sometimes seen in the coat of non-agouti cats, usually in kittens.

GINGIVITIS Inflammation of the gums.

GLAUCOMA Increased fluid pressure inside the eye.

GUARD HAIR A long, course hair that protects the undercoat and provides a waterproof layer. *See also* Awn hair, Down hair.

HAEMATOMA A blood-filled swelling under the skin.

HAEMATURIA Blood in urine.

HOCK The middle joint in the back leg of an animal.

HOT Coat colours that resemble red.

HYPERSENSITIVITY An exaggerated immune response to a foreign agent.

HYPOGLYCAEMIA Reduction in blood sugar.

IDIOPATHIC DISEASE A condition of which the cause is unknown.

IMMUNE-MEDIATED DISEASE A condition caused by an overreaction of the immune system.

INCUBATION PERIOD The time between exposure to a disease-producing agent and the development of clinical signs of disease.

-ITIS An inflammation; for example, nephritis is an inflammation of the kidneys.

JAUNDICE A yellow pigmentation of the mucous membranes or skin, usually associated with liver disease.

KETOACIDOSIS Build-up of ketone bodies in the circulation as a result of kidney failure.

KITTEN In common understanding, a kitten below the age of separation from its mother at about 12 weeks. In shows, cats may still be called kittens for some months after this.

KITTEN CAP White cats carry the dominant gene *W*, which masks other colours. White kittens sometimes show a hint of their underlying colour in a "kitten cap" of hair on their heads, which disappears with age.

LAPAROTOMY The surgical opening of the abdominal cavity.

LIMBIC SYSTEM Part of the brain that is in control of basic emotions, hunger, and mating.

LIPOMA A benign tumour of fat, particularly common in older, overweight large breeds.

LOCKET Small area of white hair on the chest of a coloured cat – a fault in many breeds.

MACROPHAGES Large white blood cells that consume debris.

MAGNETIC RESONANCE IMAGING (MRI) Diagnostic imaging showing detailed cross-sections of the internal anatomy of structures such as joints or the brain; particularly useful for brain scans.

MALABSORPTION A condition in which insufficient amounts of nutrients are absorbed into the circulation from the small intestines.

MALIGNANT TUMOUR A tumour that has the capacity either to invade the tissue that surrounds it or to spread via the blood or lymphatic circulation to other parts of the body, such as the lungs or the liver.

MANX Tailless breed of cat. The taillessness is caused by a gene that can cause fatal problems if passed on by both parents.

MASCARA LINES Dark lines extending from the outer corners of the eyes.

MELAENA Black, tar-like diarrhoea containing old blood.

MENINGES Protective membranes surrounding the brain.

METASTASIS Spread of cancer cells from the area of origin to other parts of the body.

MINK A combination of Pointed and Sepia patterns, with coloured body and moderate pointing. The characteristic pattern of the Tonkinese breed (*see* pp.130–31).

MITTENS White forepaws in a coloured or bicoloured cat, typically stopping below the ankle. *See also* Gauntlets.

MOSAICING Random patching or mottling of coat colours, as in tortoiseshell colours.

MUCOSA Another name for the mucous membranes, which line the hollow body structures, such as the mouth and the small intestines.

MUCUS Clear lubricating secretion produced by cells in the mucous membranes.

MUTATION Change in a gene.

MYELOGRAM X-ray of the spinal cord after the injection of contrast material (a substance opaque to X-rays).

NECROSIS Cell death.

NEOPLASIA Cancerous cell growth that may be benign or malignant. *See also* Tumour.

NEPHRITIS Inflammation of the kidneys.

NEUTER To castrate males or spay females to prevent reproduction and unwanted sexual behaviour.

NICTITATING MEMBRANE *See also* Third eyelid.

NON-AGOUTI Any solid-coloured cat showing no tabby markings.

NOSE STOP A change in direction, slight or pronounced, seen in profile at the nose top.

NSAID Non-steroidal anti-inflammatory drug; this group of drugs includes carprofen and meloxicam.

ODD-EYED Cat with eyes of two different colours; in breed standards, one blue and one orange.

OESTROUS CYCLE The female reproductive cycle.

ORDER In biological classification, a large category of animals containing one or more families. The members share defining characteristics and ancestry. *See also* Breed, Family, Genus, Species, Subspecies.

OVARIOHYSTERECTOMY Removal of the ovaries and uterus – the normal spaying procedure.

PALLIATIVE TREATMENT Therapy that improves comfort but does not cure.

PARESIS An incomplete form of paralysis.

PEDIGREE A record of ancestry, showing a cat's parentage over several generations.

PERIANAL Meaning "around the anus".

PERINEAL Referring to the area between the anus and the genitals.

PERIODONTAL Around or near the tooth.

PERITONITIS Inflammation of the lining of the abdominal cavity.

PICA An appetite for unnatural and potentially dangerous substances.

PINNA The ear flap.

PITUITARY GLAND The "master gland" at the base of the brain, controlling all other hormone-producing glands and controlled by the hypothalamus (an area at the base of the brain).

PNEUMOTHORAX Loss of negative pressure in the chest cavity, causing the lungs to collapse.

POINTED Coat colour pattern in which colour is restricted to the extremities of the head, limbs, and tail, the body remaining pale, first known in the Siamese breed (*see* pp.124–27). Also a generic term to cover other less obvious pointing patterns. *See also* Mink, Sepia.

POLYDACTYLY Condition of possessing more than five toes on each paw.

POLYDYPSIA Excessive thirst.

POLYPHAGIA Excessive hunger.

POLYURIA Excessive urinating.

PYO- Pus-related, as in "pyometra" (a pus-filled womb) or "pyoderma" (purulent skin disease).

QUEEN Unspayed female cat.

RANDOM-BREEDING Process of animals choosing their own mates without human intervention. Also called free-breeding.

RECESSIVE GENE A gene that may be carried without being expressed as a trait.

REGISTRY An authority, national or international, that decides on breed recognition and standards, and maintains records of pedigree breeds. Made up of constituent breed clubs. *See also* CFA, FIFé, GCCF, TCA, TICA.

REX Term for any mutation causing a curly coat. Also referred to as rexing.

RUFF Longer fur that sometimes appears around the neck and on the chest.

RUFOUSING Red tones in the agouti parts of a coat, giving rich, warm tones. In silver coats, referred to as "tarnishing" and usually regarded as a fault.

SCENT-MARKING A cat marks its territory with urine, or with scent from glands on its face, lips, and ears.

SEBACEOUS GLAND Oil-producing skin gland that adds waterproofing to the coat.

SEBORRHOEA An increased activity of the skin's oil-producing sebaceous glands.

SEIZURE Abnormal electrical activity in the brain, causing unusual nervous responses; also known as a fit or convulsion.

SELECTIVE BREEDING Human intervention to determine the partners in any breeding.

SELF Coat of one colour. *See also* Non-agouti.

SEPIA Coat colour pattern in which the darkest colour is restricted to the extremities of the head, limbs, and tail, the body being a slightly paler shade of the same colour. *See also* Mink, Pointed.

SEPTICAEMIA Bacterial infection in the blood circulation.

SHADED A coat silvered for approximately half of its length. *See also* Silvering, Smoke, Tipped.

SHOCK A life-threatening emergency in which the cardiovascular system fails, causing physical collapse, rapid pulse, and pale mucous membranes.

SILVERING Inhibition of colour production in part of a hair, leaving it pale or white. *See also* Smoke, Shaded, Tipped.

SMOKE Coloured coat with white undercoat. *See also* Shaded, Silvering, Tipped.

SPAY Method of neutering female cats by removing ovaries and uterus. *See also* Neuter.

SPECIES A population of animals sharing a common gene pool through interbreeding. Members appear distinct from individuals of other species. *See also* Breed, Family, Genus, Order, Subspecies.

SPECTACLES Areas of lighter hair around, and particularly below, the eyes.

SPORT An animal that displays a naturally occurring genetic mutation.

SUBSPECIES Geographically separated population within a species that has differences from the rest of the species but will interbreed with other subspecies where ranges overlap. *See also* Breed, Family, Genus, Order, Species.

SYNOVIAL FLUID Lubricating joint fluid.

TABBY Pattern of stripes, blotches, or spots, used in the wild as camouflage. *See also* Agouti.

TCA The Traditional Cats' Association, a breed registry formed in 1987.

TESTOSTERONE Male sex hormone

THIRD EYELID A membrane concealed in the inner corner of a cat's eye, which draws across the eye in sickness or injury.

THROMBUS A blood clot.

THYROID GLAND The largest endocrine glands in the cat's body, producing hormones vital for growth and metabolism.

TICA The International Cat Association, a registry founded in 1979, based on genetics.

TICKING Banding of light and dark colours along a hair.

TIPPED A coat of white hairs with coloured tips. *See also* Shaded, Silvering, Smoke.

TOM CAT Unneutered male cat.

TOPCOAT The outer layer of protective hairs, carrying the pattern in tabbies. *See also* Guard hair.

TRANSUDATE Fluid passed through a tissue membrane or extruded from tissue.

TUMOUR Also called a neoplasm; a lump or bump, caused by multiplying cells, that can be benign or malignant. *See also* Neoplasia

TYPE The characteristic body build and/or head shape of a particular breed or group of breeds.

ULCER A lesion where surface tissue has been lost through damage or disease.

UNDERCOAT Layer of insulating fur under the topcoat. *See also* Awn hair, Down hair.

URAEMIA Build-up of waste in the blood as a consequence of kidney failure.

UROLITHS Stone in the bladder.

VOMERONASAL ORGAN A sensory organ in the nasal cavity that analyses smells and tastes. Also known as Jacobson's organ.

ZOONOSES Diseases transmissible between animals and humans.

Index

Author's acknowledgements

I confess. My name is on this book's masthead, but when it came to the nitty-gritty of breed specifics, I've relied, as I have in the past, on Candida Frith-Macdonald's unbeatable research abilities. Candida was the editor of *The New Encyclopedia of the Cat*, and when I needed help collecting new and relevant cat breed material, I knew there was no one better for updating and expanding that information for this book. Her contribution has been beyond simple research, which is why it is such a pleasure to acknowledge Candida as one of the authors of this book.

At Studio Cactus, a team of people converted picture requests and raw text into an attractive and sensible package. I worked primarily with Aaron Brown, and thank him both for his suggestions and willingness to listen.

At Dorling Kindersley, there's another group of people, most anonymous to me as they worked with Cactus, but Rob Houston in particular has been an excellent editor, always opting for lucidity and accuracy.

There's one person I've never met who has unknowingly made a major contribution to this book. Sarah Hartwell may have a website with an unusual name – www.messybeast.com – but her information is superb. This is an intelligent and reliable source of feline information; as good as any I have found.

Finally, thanks to everyone at the veterinary clinic, the vets Veronica Aksmanovic and Grant Petrie, and the nurses, Ashley McManus, Suzi Gray, Angela Bettinson, Hester Small, and Hilary Hayward, for arranging schedules so there was time to write.

Publisher's acknowledgements

Dorling Kindersley would like to thank Rebecca Warren for additional editing and Francis Wong and Lee Ellwood for jacket design.

Studio Cactus would like to thank Pets Corner and Park Farm Equestrian Centre for supplying props, and the following people for their contributions: **Indexer:** Eleanor Holme **Photography:** Damien Moore at Studio Cactus; Gary Ombler **Breeders and their cats:** Elizabeth James of Filandre Burmese and Tiffanies and her feline models Grand Champion Tahirah Silverfilandre, Champion Filandre Spirited Lady, Filandre Nutta, Champion Filandre Golden Promise, and a litter of kittens from Champion Filandre Aeneas; Lynne Studer of Mylynn Siamese & Orientals and her feline models Mylynn Matisse and Pippastro Sheer Indulgence; Fifi Schoenfeld, ConCarne Robertson, and Oscar and George Cohen.

Picture credits

The publisher would like to thank the following for their kind permission to reproduce their photographs:

Key: a = above, b = bottom/below; c = centre, l = left; r = right; rh = running header; t = top

Abbreviations: Al = Alamy; Co = Corbis; GI = Getty Images; SS = Shutterstock; CP = Chanan Photography/ Richard Katris; AP = Animal Photography/Sally Anne Thompson & RT Willbie; MEPL = Mary Evans Picture Library; BAL = Bridgeman Art Library

1t SS/Jean Schweitzer; 2 Al/Juniors Bildarchiv; 3 Al/Sébastien Baussais; 4–5 Al/Juniors Bildarchiv; 6 GI/Gordon Wiltsie; 7 Al/Juniors Bildarchiv; 9t SS/ Andre Klopper; 9br Photos.com; 10cr Photos.com; 10rh GI/Diane Macdonald; 11tr GI/John Livzey; 11b GI/Bill Truslow; 12–13 NHPA/Nigel J Dennis; 14 GI/Andy Rouse; 15rh Co/Royalty Free; 15cra Photos.com; 15bl SS/RJ Lerich; 16crb SS/J Norman Reid; 16br SS/Tina Rencelj; 17tl SS/Laurin Rinder; 17b Photos.com; 18cl Photos.com; 19tr SS/Alvaro Pantoja; 19cr Al/Blickwinkel; 20–21 GI/Michael S Quinton; 22cra SS/Koval; 22br Photos.com; 23bc Al/Terry Whittaker; 23crb Photos.com; 24bc NHPA/Vicente Garcia Conseco; 25tl SS/Vladimir Pomortzeff; 25cr Al/Manfred Danegger/Peter Arnold, Inc.; 25br NHPA/Daryl Balfour; 26b BAL/Ashmolean Museum, University of Oxford/Nina de Garis Davies; 27br Al/Diane Collins; 31b SS/Norman Chan; 32bl GI/China Photos; 33tr GI/Peter Parks; 34b SS/Alexander Tasevski; 35tr MEPL/Elenore Plaisted Abbott; 36cra SS/Vitaly Berkovych; 37tr SS/Dan Briski; 38cra SS/ ijamsempoi; 39tl SS/Sarah Cates; 40bl SS/Daniela Wolf; 41b SS/Tim Harman; 41cra reprinted with permission from Drs Foster and Smith, Inc.; 43t Al/David R Frazier Photolibrary, Inc.; 43br Co/Bettmann; 44 SS/Piotr Bieniecki; 45rh GI/Tim Hall; 45ca SS/Pierdelune; 45br SS/Victorian Traditions; 46cra MEPL; 46b BAL/Towneley Hall Art Gallery and Museum, Burnley, Lancashire; 47tr Co/Bettmann; 47b SS Maine Madness; 48–49 GI/James Strachan; 50ca SS/luminouslens; 50br Al/Mark Pearson; 51tl MEPL; 51br SS/Chris Sargent; 52bl Picture Desk/ Art Archive/University Library Istanbul/Dagli Orti; 53b BAL/School of Oriental & African Studies Library, University of London; 54bl Co/Historical Picture Archive; 55tc Co/Christie's Images; 55bl Co/Rick Maiman; 56bl BAL/Musee d'Orsay, Paris, France, Lauros/Giraudon; 57tr Co/Andy Warhol Foundation; 57b Co/Gerrit Greve; 58bl Co/Fine Art Photography Library; 58cra SS/tadija; 59br Co/Blue Lantern Studio; 60cra Al/Lebrecht Music and Arts Photo Library; 60–61 Co/Doane Gregory/Warner Bros./Bureau LA Collections; 61cra Co/Eric Robert; 62–63 Arena PAL/Carol Roseggi: Arena Images; 64cra Co/Sandro Vannini; 65cra SS; 65b Co/Bureau LA Collections/Rhythm & Hues; 66bc SS/Kenneth Sponsler; 68–69 Al/Juniors Bildarchiv; 70 NHPA/Yves Lanceau; 71rh Co/Royalty Free; 71ca SS/Suponev Vladimir Mihajlovich; 74–75 GI/American Images Inc.; 75cra SS/ Gary Nugent; 76br SS/Anne Gro Bergersen; 77t SS/Elisa Locci; 78cra SS/Linda Bucklin; 79cla SS/Justin Kim; 79ca SS/Marilyn Barbone; 79cra SS/Anne Gro Bergersen; 79bl Co/Brooks Craft; 81tr GI/Pat Powers & Cheryl Schafer; 81b SS/Aron Brand; 82cra Genetic Savings & Clone, Inc.; 82b Genetic Savings & Clone, Inc.; 83cra Photos. com; 84 Co/Henry Diltz; 85rh SS/Cindy Haggerty; 85b SS/Anne Gro Bergersen; 87br CP; 89cra SS/Anne Gro Bergersen; 89b AP; 90b AP; 90cr taken from An Historical and Statistical Account of the Isle of Man (1854) Joseph Train (out of copyright); 92b Al/Juniors Bildarchiv; 93br SS/Mathijs Ijsseldijk; 94cl CP; 94b AP; 95tr AP; 95cla CP; 96clb MEPL; 97cla CP; 97b CP; 98tr CP; 98b CP; 98crb CP; 99tr CP; 99b Edwina Sipos; 100tr CP; 100b CP; 101tr CP; 101b CP; 102–103 Co/Brooks Craft; 104tr CP; 104bl Patricia Peters; 105tr Gail Andersen; 105b Gail Andersen; 106tr CP; 106cla CP; 106b CP; 107tr Meryleen Greenwood; 107b Meryleen Greenwood; 108tr Naomi Taylor; 108cl Terry Goulden; 108b SS/Lee Torrens; 109tr Naomi Taylor; 110clb CP; 111tl CP; 112br Al/Juniors Bildarchiv; 114–15 AP; 116b CP; 117 GI/Mike Powell; 118b CP; 119tr CP; 119b CP; 120b SS/Marilyn Barbone; 121tr JIM; 121br CP; 122ca CP; 122b CP; 123br Anita H Engebakken; 125cra SS/Robert Adrian Hillman; 126–27 AP; 130tr CP; 132cla CP; 132b CP; 133t CP; 135tl Al/Chris Howes/Wild Places Photography; 137tr CP; 137b AP; 138cra Svetlana Ponomareva; 138bl Richard Horton; 142br Tourism Authority of Thailand; 143 Al/Juniors Bildarchiv; 144tr AP; 145br FLPA/Gerard Lacz; 147b Al/Arco Images; 148b Paul McSorley; 149tl Co/Alexander Natruskin; 149br CP; 151 SS/Shawn Hine; 152 Co/Julie Habel; 153rh SS/Peter Skjold Petersen; 153bl CP; 154tr SS/Alvaro Pantoja; 155b SS/Narcisa Florica Buzlea; 156–57 GI/Barros & Barros; 158tr SS/Paul-André Belle-Isle; 159cra SS/Sean MacLeay; 159b SS/Susan Mackenzie; 160b GI/Gary Buss; 161br June Mateer; 163b Co/Darrell Gulin; 164–65 Co/Darrell Gulin; 166tr CP; 166bl Al/Juniors Bildarchiv; 167b CP; 168b SS/Anne Gro Bergersen; 169br Co/Burstein Collection; 170–71 GI/Rosanne Olson; 173b NHPA/Yves Lanceau; 174–75 NHPA/Yves Lanceau; 176cl CP; 177crb Jo-Anne Simpson; 178cra CP; 178b CP; 179tr CP; 180tr Wanda Carroll; 180b CP; 181tr CP; 181b CP; 183b Al/Juniors Bildarchiv; 184–85 NHPA/Yves Lanceau; 186bl CP; 186crb Eileen Welsh; 190–91b Al/Juniors Bildarchiv; 192tr CP; 192cra Gavin Tasker; 193tr CP; 193b CP; 194cra Tracy Oraas; 194br CP; 195cl Colleen Walters; 196tc CP; 196b JIM; 197ca Patricia Peters; 197bl Gail Andersen; 197br CP; 198c Svetlana Ponomareva; 199tr CP; 199b CP; 200b SS/ Hannamaria; 201c SS/Dale A Stork; 202–203 GI/Johner; 204 Al/Nigel Wilkins; 205rh Brand X Pictures/Don Mason; 206b CP; 211t SS/Vladimir Odorcic; 214b SS/ Norman Chan; 216–17 AP; 223cla SS/Dmitrii N Birykov; 224b SS/Dainis Derics; 226b SS/Arlene Jean Gee; 227tl NHPA/Eric Soder; 228cra SS/Terrie L Zeller; 229fcla SS/Geary LeBell; 229cla SS/Kim Worrell; 229cra SS/Jean Schweitzer; 229ficra SS/Eline Spek; 230cra SS/Brian Steffen; 231tl SS/Ulrike Hammerich; 232b SS/Lee O'Dell; 232cr SS/ Karl R Martin; 233tl SS/Norman Chan; 233br SS/Julia; 234cr NHPA/Yves Lanceau; 234–35 NHPA/ Susanne Danegger; 237cra SS/Sheryl Koennecke; 238 Co/Jose Luis Pelaez, Inc.; 239rh GI/Andersen Ross; 240b SS/Suponev Vladimir Mihajlovich; 241cra SS/Vitaliy Berkovych; 242br SS/Jacqueline Shaw; 243br SS/Polosa; 245ca SS/Clara Natoli; 247br SS/Annalee Van Kleeck; 248cr SS/Tina Rencelj; 250bl SS/Suzanne Tucker; 251tl SS/ijamsempoi; 253–54 GI/Christian Michaels; 254cr SS/J Helgason; 255tr Al/Sami Sarkis; 256b Co/David T Grewcock/Frank Lane Picture Agency; 258b reprinted with permission from Drs Foster and Smith, Inc.; 260b SS/Daniel Gale; 264b Al/Konrad Zelazowski; 265tl GI/ Hulton Archive; 267br SS/Mrs Gill Martin; 268bl Al/John McCammon; 271bl Al/Nigel Cattlin; 273t SS/Yarik Chauvin; 273br SS/Neven Jurkovic; 274cra SS/Black Ink Designers, Corp.; 276bl SS/Jeff Oien; 277cr SS/Ryan Arnaudin; 277bl SS/Drilea Christian; 278b reprinted with permission from Drs Foster and Smith, Inc.; 279cr SS/Pam Burley; 282bl SS/Trevor Allen; 284bl SS/Lee O'Dell; 285tr SS/Melissa Ann Kilhenny; 285bl SS/Odelia Cohen; 287cra SS/Galina Barskaya; 288 SS/Marilyn Barbone; 289rh Al/Comstock Production Department; 289cra SS/pixshots; 291br Photos. com; 293b SS/Cre8tive Images; 303rh SS/Stuart Elflett

All other images © Dorling Kindersley.
For further information see **www.dkimages.com**